MOSAIC

TECHNIQUES

With gratitude and affection, this book is dedicated to my father, and to my husband and son

EARLY THAW. Pebbles, shells, melted glass, quartz, cracked windshield glass, and cullet, embedded in paste polyester resin. By Mary Lou Stribling.

Patio table of transparent Venetian tiles, melted glass chips, and melted bottle rings. By Bernice Brown.

MOSAIC
TECHNIQUES

new aspects of fragmented design

by **MARY LOU STRIBLING**

CROWN PUBLISHERS, INC. NEW YORK

LIBRARY OF CONGRESS CATALOG CARD NUMBER: 66-15121

ISBN: 0-517-025620

PRINTED IN THE UNITED STATES OF AMERICA

Fifth Printing, April, 1973

CONTENTS

Acknowledgments

A book of this nature is collected, as well as written, and represents the talents, advice, and inspiration of a great many persons.

My thanks go first to my husband, Robert Stribling, for his solutions to problems of mosaic installation, mounting, and framing, and for his invaluable help with working up some of the illustrative projects. Secondly, I thank my son, Brad, for contributing technical data and designing the fascinating device for slicing bottles which appears in Chapter 2.

The mosaic examples are works of dedicated amateurs, commercial designers, professional artists, teachers, and students, many of whom have attained an impressive status in the art world. I am deeply indebted to them for their time and generosity, and for the personal stimulation I received from our contacts.

Thanks to the M. H. De Young Memorial Museum (San Francisco) for providing illustrations of historical crafts; to the editors and staff of *Better Homes and Gardens Christmas Ideas, Ceramics Monthly, Craft Horizons, Popular Ceramics,* and *The Christian Home* for many favors, as well as permission to include material which originally appeared in their publications.

Thanks to the photographers listed in the Appendix, with special appreciation to Philip Planert for the cover photograph and significant additions to my files; to Ken Reichard and his associates for suggestions on photographic problems; to Lyman Emerson for photographing certain mosaics.

Thanks to Cummings Stained Glass Studios, Creative Merchandisers, Orco Glass, and to all the individuals whose interest, encouragement, and help with locating talented mosaicists sustained me during the months of my work.

M.L.S.

Contributing Artists

Foreword

The word "amateur" has fallen into disrepute and its original meaning become obscured by association with ineptness, plagiarism, and worse—lack of taste.

Actually, "amateur" is derived from the Latin *amator,* meaning "lover," and it is primarily toward the mosaicist who works from love that this book is directed.

This does not disallow possibilities that he may already be growing toward a place among the giants in the field, nor that he may gain financial returns for his investment in time and study. But for the lover, these compensations are simply welcome bonuses. His real reward is the joy of the work.

The amateur is never content with his store of knowledge, no matter how extensive it may be. He is a perpetual student, united by enthusiasm for his craft with an enormous class of individuals who have many different kinds of talents and ambitions.

This is challenging for the instructor, since not all mosaics are produced with either intention or hope of creating immortal works of art. Some persons are attracted by techniques which will enable them to make unique, functional accessories for their homes and offices, some by the satisfaction of building a unified pattern from bits of colorful materials. Others master the craft to use it as a means of communication—a tool for expression, rather than an end in itself.

To meet these diversified interests, the material presented here goes beyond traditional concepts of mosaics, and includes guidance for experimentation and design, ways of making unusual materials and original forms, as well as detailed directions for specific projects.

The demonstrated techniques may be applied to the ornamentation of objects for everyday use, or to ambitious works of great size and profundity. It is hoped that they will stimulate creative curiosity, rather than imitation, and will at least partly bridge the gap between overly simplified instruction for the hobbyist and formidable apprenticeship for the professional muralist.

Above all, it is hoped that the inspiring examples of other craftsmen will provide a glimpse of the tremendous potential of mosaics as a medium for personal expression.

There are many facets to the art and craft of mosaics, and each can be creative, regardless of the size of the project, the materials used, or the purpose for which it is intended.

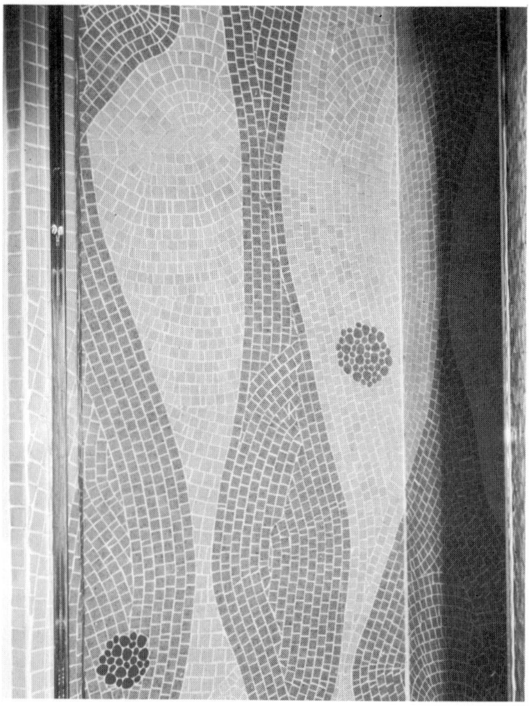

We can be creative with light and translucent color.

Fig. 1. Shower stall paved with vitreous clay tiles in earth colors. By Rosalis.

Fig. 2. Hanging lantern mosaicked with scrap aluminum and melted stained glass. By Robert Stribling.

We can be creative with functional surfaces— walls and floors and tables. . . .

Fig. 3. Detail of "The Law and the Prophets," a large panel in the Warren Wilson College Chapel, created by Charles and Rubynelle Counts from carved and glazed clay slabs.

Mosaic is a creative medium when art and craft are inseparable, and when the artist leaves the unique mark of his imagination and intellect on his arrangement of materials.

Fig. 5. "The Premonition" by Thomas Hunt. Smalti, Venetian glass, and stained glass chips in tinted mortar.

Fig. 4. Concrete garden sculpture with decorative pattern of smalti. By Ray Rice. *(Collection of Mr. and Mrs. Robert Howell.)*

Creative mosaics can tell an old story in a new way, and beautify great expanses . . .

. . . or tell a new story with three-dimensional forms.

Fig. 6. "Praying Mantis" by Helen Steinau Rich. Mixed media set directly into magnesite. *(Collection of Mr. and Mrs. Edgar Sinton.)*

The White Rabbit put on his spectacles. "Where shall I begin, please your Majesty?" he asked.

"Begin at the beginning," the King said, very gravely, "and go on till you come to the end: then stop."

—LEWIS CARROLL, *Alice in Wonderland*

chapter 1.

Introduction

WHERE DID IT START?

If the White Rabbit's subject had been mosaics, no doubt Wonderland's King of Hearts would have answered differently, unless he had been prepared to listen for quite a while.

All creative processes have many beginnings, some of which are not even recognized as such. Mosaics have been excavated from the debris of ancient civilizations which flourished more than five thousand years ago, but these are merely early examples, not necessarily beginnings. It is certain that primitive man arranged bright pebbles and shells into patterns long before his efforts intrigued him to the point of inventing ways of preserving them.

Mosaic art had become remarkably sophisticated hundreds of years before the birth of Christ, when Egyptian artisans ornamented the columns and walls of their temples with inlays of glass and precious stones. By the time the powerful tentacles of the Roman Empire had tightened around the Mediterranean, mosaic decoration had reached such heights of popularity that whole walls, floors, ceilings, and pavements were adorned with intricate designs.

A new industry was created as the brilliant light-refracting qualities of glass gained favor over stone. Increasing demand for materials stimulated glass manufacturers to produce tesserae (fragments) in hundreds of colors. Unable to resist the tempting variety, craftsmen vied with each other to produce works so perfectly blended they could scarcely be distinguished from paintings.

Preoccupied with craft and showmanship, they lost sight of art. The direct, forceful statements of the Byzantine period gradually weakened into trite and uninspired realism. For nearly five hundred years mosaic existed as a mechanical process, rather than a creative medium.

Its renaissance took place far from the valleys of the Tigris and Euphrates and the great empires of Greece and Rome. Where once mosaics were reserved for the palaces and mansions and temples of rulers and aristocrats, they were reborn in American homes, workshops, and studios.

Revitalized by artists with the vision and courage to use or reject tradition as it suits their needs, once again mosaic is assuming a place of importance in the art world.

2

WHAT IS A MOSAIC?

The most familiar historical examples of mosaics are made of small pieces of stone or glass set in mortar, and it is surprising to find many persons today convinced that only works of this nature should be called mosaics. It is reasonable to assume, however, that the early craftsmen were not deliberately trying to stay within a classical definition of the art, but rather were bound to the most readily available materials and the most practical process at their disposal for holding them together permanently.

Exceptions can be found in the functional crafts and in certain types of icons which could be classed as miniatures. In the latter examples, tiny tesserae were arranged to form religious emblems and were set into foundations of wax.[1]

As far back as the fifth century B.C., intricate mosaic patterns of glass and precious stones were set in gold to make jewelry and ceremonial vessels. (These effects were later imitated with enamels.)[2]

Fused glass mosaics, which are gaining popularity in our times, have an ancient heritage. The best examples are probably the Roman mosaic wares which were made by lining the bottoms and sides of molds with slices of patterned glass rods, and fusing them together in a kiln.[3]

But the Romans are not entitled to credit for discovering the process, since similar Egyptian wares have been excavated that were made between 2000 and 1780 B.C.

Modern innovations in adhesives and equipment and the development of the synthetic resins have opened up a whole new world of mosaic effects and techniques. The moment contemporary craftsmen discovered that grout often dimmed the brilliance of their arrangements of tesserae and that the weight and bulk of mortar was no longer structurally required, the old concepts of the art were ready to be updated.

According to a dictionary definition, a mosaic is something composed of small pieces of materials of various colors; or "anything resembling this."

Everything in the world might then be called a mosaic, including the atom. But for the purpose of classifying the art form, we could say that mosaic art is distinguished from other art forms by its *fragmentation*. Though its parts are organized into a unified composition, the parts themselves do not lose their separate identities, any more than do the words of which a poem is composed. When this fragmentation is not an essential factor in the design, or when it is concealed so that the mosaic imitates the appearance of painting, true mosaic quality no longer exists.

It is understandable that the broad field of mosaics is sometimes arbitarily subdivided into vaguely defined categories according to the physical nature of the materials or the particular process used for holding them together. Thus we find certain collages, inlays, intarsias, appliqués, constructions, and assemblages which might with equal accuracy be called mosaics.

These decisions are best left to the historians. It is possible that current interest in proper labels for art works has been generated by juried shows, where one is forced to fit one's entry into a specific slot. Unfortunately, the dividing lines are often obscure and subject to great controversy.

The time may come when electrical computers will solve the whole problem by reducing our creations to a series of holes punched in a small card. And that would really be too bad, for it would take all the fun out of arguing with the professional critics!

---

[1] René Huyghe (ed.), *Larousse Encyclopedia of Byzantine and Medieval Art* (New York, Prometheus Press, 1963), sec. II.

[2] *Ibid.,* "The Later Byzantine Empire," p. 137.

[3] Frederick Schuler presented an interesting study of Roman mosaic ware with instructions for duplicating the old processes in "Ancient Glassmaking Techniques," *Craft Horizons,* March–April, 1960. Copies may still be available.

Fig. 7. In 1958, Colonel Jack Saunders and his wife, Dorothy, uncovered a mosaic floor in a remote part of the desert east of Tripoli, Libya. Before excavation could be completed, the mosaic was mysteriously destroyed, evidently by natives looking for salable artifacts. Later, they accidently discovered a second floor a few inches below the first. Unlike the top floor, which had a geometric pattern of black, white, gray, and red marble cubes, it showed two Tritons with human bodies, horses' legs, and fish-like tails, surrounded by crabs, dolphins, and other sea creatures.

Fig. 8. One merman held a ship's rudder, the other a sheaf of wheat.

Fig. 9. The mosaic was lifted in sections by means of coating it with several layers of gummed tape. Although the exact date of construction has not been established, the coiffures are similar to those of the period of Alexander the Great (356–323 B.C.). The style is fluid and classical, as opposed to the more formal rigidity we find in works of the third century A.D. It is interesting to note that the tesserae are not set in at random, but arranged to delineate form. This technique is still used by many mosaicists today.

We can only speculate on the reasons why one floor was laid on top of another. Perhaps the house changed hands and a Christian owner found the pagan motifs offensive. The new floor could have been simply a remodeling project promoted by a third- or fourth-century housewife who complained to her husband, "But *nobody* uses *Tritons* on floors any more!"

Fig. 10. "The Young Christ" is one of Thomas Hunt's earlier pieces. Compare the arrangement of tiles with that in Figure 9. (*Collection of Mrs. R. O. Van Horn.*)

Fig. 11. Many ancient and now extinct cultures made mosaic designs from perishable materials, and few examples have been preserved. Thousands of brightly colored feathers make up the mosaic pattern of this poncho (Nazca) which is in the permanent collection of the Chicago Art Institute. *(Photo courtesy of the M. H. De Young Memorial Museum.)*

Fig. 12. An extinct Indian tribe from northern Napa County (California) used short tufts of feathers in green, yellow, red, and blue to mosaic a basket. *(Photo courtesy of the M. H. De Young Memorial Museum.)*

WHAT MUST WE LEARN?

The education of a mosaicist is no less demanding than that of a painter or sculptor. And unlike the weaver, potter, lapidary, or glass blower, whose attention has a central focus, you will find yourself involved with many skills.

You will experiment with cements and a bewildering variety of adhesives, each uniquely suited to a specific project. You will become a scavenger, and through the experience of re-evaluating the discards of your fellow man, rediscover the amazing bits and pieces of the intricately mosaicked world around us.

You will explore methods of working with clay, glass, woods, metals, and semiprecious stones in your search for beautiful, enduring materials and fresh effects. Fabrics will not escape your curiosity, nor will colorful papers, seeds, shells, buttons, nails, gravels, and broken bottles. Eventually, your perception will be as acute as that of the builder, enabling you to move beyond your first mental image of a completed structure, to the precise contribution required of each tiny fragment.

A certain amount of historical and technical background is necessary for the understanding of any art, though we shall administer it as painlessly as possible in small doses rather than in a single indigestible lump. The supplementary references listed in the Appendix will be invaluable for expanding the greatly condensed information presented here.

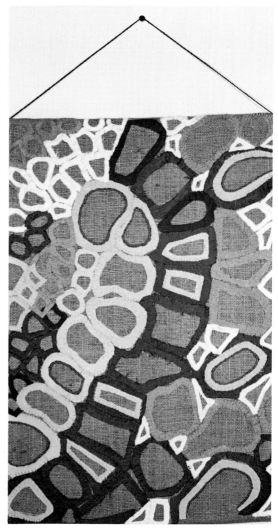

Fig. 13. "Iris Root" by Marlys Frey. The design for this appliqué was inspired by a microscopic section of iris root cells. Although created from bits of fabric rather than traditional stone or glass, the hanging has true mosaic quality.

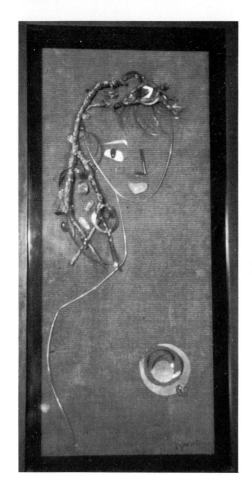

Fig. 14. Collage? Assemblage? Mosaic? "Autumn," by Stella Popowski, is an inventive arrangement of copper wire in various gauges, shapes cut from copper sheets, glass chunks, and gemstones, on a corduroy backing. Parts of the hair are lichened tree branches.

Fig. 15. Mosaic assemblage of carved wood, by Charles Clement.

chapter 2

Tools and Equipment

BASIC TOOLS

Initial investment in equipment for mosaics can be very modest, since it is possible to improvise many of the implements needed, and others are common to every household.

Such kitchen utensils as mixing bowls, measuring spoons, flexible plastic spatulas, and rolling pins are equally useful in the workshop. Add rubber gloves for working with colored mortars and grouts, and canvas garden gloves for leading or crushing glass.

Wooden toothpicks, tongue depressors, and sucker sticks make fine adhesive applicators, and divided aluminum pans in which frozen dinners are prepared are ideal containers for small amounts of decorative materials.

Long-handled tweezers are handy for lifting bits of misplaced material from wet cement, mastic, and synthetic resin. The self-locking type is indispensable for experiments with torch-shaped glass (see Chapter 8).

Tile Cutters

Nearly all basic equipment can be of the most inexpensive grades with the exception of nippers, and here it is poor economy to sacrifice quality.

Good nippers contribute to skill and professionalism, and minimize material waste from inaccuracy. And because demand has increased supply and stimulated competition among the manufacturers, nippers no longer fall into the luxury bracket.

Certain brands of imported nippers can hardly be distinguished from the more expensive tools manufactured in this country. Perhaps the workmanship is not as meticulous, and it is possible that they will not last quite as long. They are well worth their price, however. Several pairs in our workshop have had almost continuous use for a number of years.

There are many styles of nippers, and your choice is entirely personal, though those with carbiloid-tipped cutting edges are strongly recommended.

Fig. 16. Hold the tile firmly between thumb and forefinger and place between the jaws of the nipper at the exact angle at which a fracture is desired.

Fig. 17. Press handles together with a sharp snap, and the tile should break precisely.

Fig. 18. Textured materials are not as easy to control as those having smooth surfaces. Usually, shattering will be reduced if the nipper is handled like a "side-biter."

CUTTING TILES

The tool should feel right in your hand. The size and balance should be comfortable. The leverage should enable you to snap a tile precisely with the minimum of pressure. Crisp oblique breaks should be possible, as well as right angles. A spring return which automatically re-opens the jaws will save time and fatigue.

Some tools include plastic "handle-sleeves" to cushion the hands against callouses and blisters. Several layers of stretch bandage or masking tape will also help.

Cutting Tiles

Nippers do not actually *cut* tiles. They fracture them. With side-biters, a nip is taken about ⅛ inch from the edge and, with luck, the break will follow the angle of the jaws in a straight line. Newer and more efficient designs enable you to position the tile between the jaws exactly where you want the fracture, and results are more predictable.

It takes a little experimentation to determine how to control cuts in extremely irregular materials.

Unless you are going into large-scale murals, nippers are the only tools necessary for cutting tiles.

Glass Cutters

Good ball-end glass cutters can be purchased for less than a dollar from hardware stores, hobby shops, and jobbers who install windows and doors.

Square-jawed pliers are very useful for snapping away narrow margins or small protrusions that may remain on a ragged cut.

Cutting Glass

Like tile cutters, glass cutters do not really cut glass. They weaken it so that breaks can be controlled.

Fig. 19. TOOLS FOR CUTTING GLASS

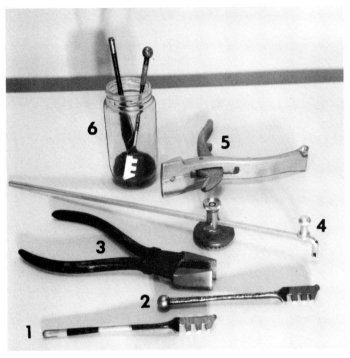

1. Straight-handled cutter.
2. Ball-end cutter.
3. Square-jawed pliers.
4. Circle cutter.
5. Tile cutter for cutting thin strips of glass.
6. Cutters stored wheel end down on a piece of sponge saturated with oil
   to prevent rusting.

The best way to hold a glass cutter is that which feels natural and comfortable. Some persons hold it like a pencil; others in a fist. Still others use both hands to steady it across an uneven surface or intricate pattern.

A straight edge is needed for absolutely straight cuts, and in this case, most workers draw the cutter downward from the top of the sheet. If a pattern with undulating lines is involved, it is best to start at the bottom so that the hands will not obscure the guide lines.

The cutting wheel must be held perpendicular to the glass, or a beveled edge will result. Guide it firmly across the glass to score a white line on the surface. Then turn the glass over and apply pressure with the thumbs to the scored line.

If the glass is thick or the pattern is complex, fracture the score by tapping the reverse side with the ball end of the cutter before applying pressure. Usually the break will not be as clean, and some polishing may be necessary. However, the danger of splitting the sheet or breaking off small corners of the form will be greatly reduced.

Glass has a tendency to take short cuts of its own choice around sharp curves. If the curves are extremely cupped, they will remain locked in the base glass, even though the outline is completely fractured. The solution is to

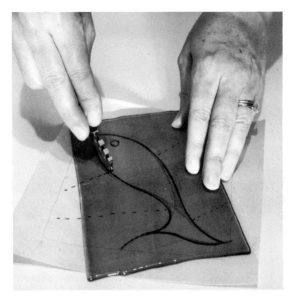

CUTTING CURVED SHAPES FROM GLASS

Fig. 20. Peninsular shapes are weakest at their narrowest point. Score the more complex outline first, as is being done here, then turn the glass over and fracture the line with the ball end of the cutter. Turn back to top side and score several radiating lines to the edge of the glass sheet.

Fig. 21. Turn glass over once more and apply gentle pressure to the radiating lines so that the margin may be removed in sections.

Fig. 22. Remove rough edges with a file, carborundum stone, or small electric grinder.

CUTTING GLASS CIRCLES

remove the margin in sections, rather than to attempt to break it away in a single piece.

A circle cutter is optional equipment. It costs some five times more than straight cutters, but is necessary for any project using accurate circles of glass.

The tool is constructed and operated in the manner of a compass. The cutting wheel is attached to a long bar marked with diameter measurements, which swings around a rubber-capped axis. Practice a few times to determine where to start the score. As indicated in Figure 23, you should be able to go entirely around the circle without lifting the cutter.

The rubber cap is inclined to slide against the glass unless it is held down firmly. A tip from our workshop—seat it with a coil of florists' clay or plasteline!

SUPPLEMENTARY EQUIPMENT

Certain pieces of supplementary equipment will enable you to expand your work beyond the range of commercial and "found" materials. Monetary investment in such equipment can soar into whatever price brackets your enthusiasm carries you, though some of it can be built in the home workshop.

Bottle Slicers

At the time of this writing, there is no commercial instrument available for accurately breaking bottles into sections which may be used for decorative materials or for mosaic forms. However, many individuals have devised intriguing methods and gadgets to turn ordinary "throw-aways" into elegant "keepers."

Bottle slicers operate on the principle of fracturing glass by thermal shock. In some models, a loop of Nichrome wire is heated by an electric current and the bottle positioned within it. When the wire is red hot, the bottle is turned several times so that it is heated all the way around. Cold water is then dripped directly on the point of contact, causing the glass to contract abruptly and break.

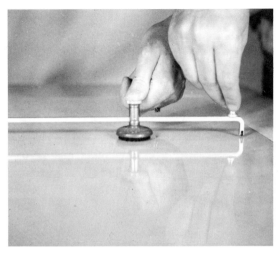

Fig. 23. Set the circle cutter for the required radius and press the rubber-capped axis firmly against the glass. Score the complete circle without lifting the cutter. Turn the glass over and apply pressure to the score until it fractures all the way around. Turn to the top side and using a straight cutter, score radiating lines from just outside the circle to the edge of the glass. As in Figure 21, remove the margin in sections.

Fig. 24. A SCORE PATTERN FOR CUTTING A GLASS CIRCLE

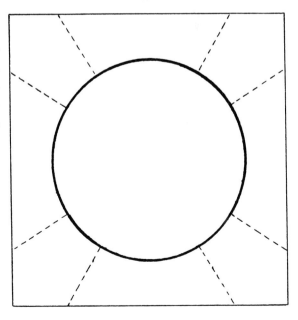

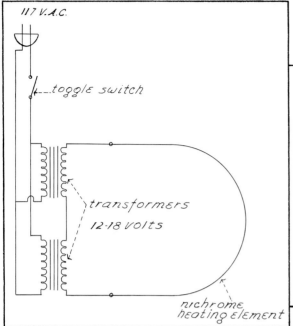

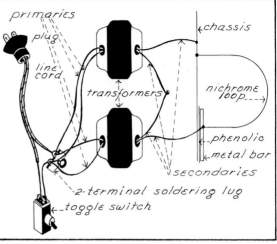

Fig. 25. SCHEMATIC DIAGRAM FOR BOT-
TLE SLICER.

Materials needed for construction:
  two transformers providing 6 to 10 volts each
    at 10 amperes. (One transformer providing
    15 to 20 volts at 10 amperes may be substi-
    tuted.)
  Box or chassis for mounting transformers and
    connections. (A small aluminum breadpan
    was used for the model illustrated.)
  Nichrome wire (19- or 20-gauge).
  Toggle switch.
  Line cord and plug.
  Two-terminal soldering lug.
  Miscellaneous wire and hardware.

Fig. 26. PICTORIAL DIAGRAM FOR BOTTLE
SLICER.

If two transformers are used, their primaries
should be connected in parallel across the line
voltage, the line voltage being provided by the
cord and plug after passing through the on–off
switch. The secondaries should be connected in
series and then attached to the Nichrome heating
element. Note that where the Nichrome wire is
attached to the transformer secondaries, a heat
sink of some sort is required. In this model, one
side was connected to the chassis (or breadpan)
and the other was attached to a thick aluminum
strip which was insulated from the chassis by a
strip of sheet phenolic. One secondary wire from
each transformer should be connected to an end
of the Nichrome loop. The other two wires are
cleaned on the ends, crimped tightly together with
pliers, and securely soldered.

In a few seconds the fracture will encircle
the bottle and the top section can be lifted off.

This principle is simple enough, but a
combination of water and electricity should be
treated with great respect. Some bottle slicers
which have been tested in our workshop are
capable of delivering a severe electric shock if
accidental contact is made across the heating
element. The degree of danger is increased if
the operator's hands are wet.

The original model presented here is easy
to construct for anyone experienced with electricity. (It should not, of course, be attempted
by anyone who is not.) Its apparent complexity

is caused by the measures taken to ensure its
complete safety. This is accomplished by using
transformers to step down the *voltage* to a
harmless level, while at the same time stepping
up the *current* to the level required for heating
the wire.

This little instrument was built at a cost
of a little more than $3.00. If new trans-
formers had been used instead of the mis-
matched (but functional) pair which was purchased from an electrical surplus store, it
would have been considerably higher.

Later in the book we shall show some
fascinating things that can be done with it.

Fig. 27. A DEVICE FOR CUTTING GLASS BOTTLES.

1. Metal tool for manipulating hot wire.
2. On–off switch.
3. Nichrome loop.
4. Transformers.
5. Breadpan chassis.
6. Decorating wheel for rotating bottles.

CUTTING GLASS BOTTLES INTO RANDOM SLICES

Fig. 28. Place the bottle within the Nichrome loop and flip switch to "on" position. When the wire is red hot, turn the bottle so that it is heated all the way around. Turn heat off and immediately drip cold water on the glass at the point of contact with the wire. If fracture is not complete, turn bottle and repeat.

Fig. 29. A decorating wheel will facilitate smooth rotation of the bottle. The slicer can be elevated on wooden blocks or bricks for segments of various widths. Instruction for more accurate cuts, such as required for the forms in Chapters 16 and 22, are given later in the book.

Tumblers

Small tumblers, such as those used by lapidaries for polishing gemstones, are now on the market at reasonable prices. With a little inventiveness, similar machines can be built using continuous-duty motors for power.

Low-powered motors are preferable, since the grinding action is accomplished by grit or sand and water kept in constant motion. Motors can be salvaged from record players, electric fans, and even some kinds of toy trains. Porcelain ball mill jars used by ceramists for grinding clay and glazes are excellent drums for tumbling mosaic materials. A quart glass jar bound with several layers of masking tape is useful for small amounts.

Fig. 30. Large door push, by Charles Clement. Smalti, glass nuggets, and polished pebbles, cast by the reverse method in epoxy with aggregate. Screw attachments are countersunk on the back.

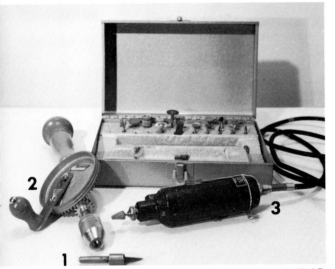

Fig. 31. TOOLS FOR GRINDING, POLISHING, AND DRILLING.
1. Bit for drilling holes in glass.
2. Eggbeater hand drill.
3. Kit including small electric drill and interchangeable bits for drilling and polishing various materials.

Drills and Grinders

Lightweight electric drills with interchangeable bits have many uses aside from those pertaining to mosaics. Several types of kits are marketed which include a number of accessories for cutting, polishing, and drilling.

Although emery bits will refine glass shapes and remove sharp, dangerous edges which might remain after fracturing, a special tool will be needed for drilling holes in glass.

If production justifies the investment, a drill press will perform this operation quickly and efficiently. However, the average craftsman can get along nicely with a glass bit mounted in an ordinary "eggbeater" hand drill.

The hand method has the added advantage of enabling you to control the speed, drill holes in convex surfaces, and bevel the edges of holes where necessary for countersinking bolt heads.

Used glass bits can often be purchased from glass jobbers.

Drilling Holes in Glass

Mark the spot to be drilled and place the glass over a pad of carpet or foam rubber. Hold the eggbeater drill so that the spade bit is perpendicular to the glass, and, turning the handle slowly, grind out a small indentation. Dip the bit in turpentine and keep it well lubricated from here on. If you feel it drag or see white powder forming around the edges, it is time to remoisten.

Do not apply heavy pressure. Let the bit do the work. Once the hole is started, you can turn faster, slowing again at the final point of penetration.

To bevel the edges for certain installations (see Chapter 21), lean the bit slightly outward and keep it moving slowly around the perforation until the desired slant is obtained.

Torches and Soldering Irons

Small inexpensive torches using compressed gas as fuel will reach temperatures up to 2100° F. The flame is adjustable, and a special tip for soldering can be attached to the nozzle.

A crude but serviceable cradle for holding the propane torch in position for glass work can be made by bending a metal towel rack into an M shape and stapling it to a strip of plywood. An asbestos pad or sheet of heavy-duty aluminum foil should be placed beneath the torch to protect the working surface from fragments of hot glass.

Metal strips and edgings may be shaped and glued to a backing when their function is purely decorative. If the piece is self-supporting, however, it must have a strong framework and the joints must be soldered or welded.

Tiny "hobby" irons will solder wire, thin lead, and copper foil. More professional equipment is needed for welding rod, coat-hanger wire, and heavy copper.

Soldering Metal Joints

A flux serves the same basic purpose in soldering as it does in glass and clay formulas. (It is not, of course, the same material.) It

Fig. 32. PORTABLE PROPANE TORCH FOR SOLDERING METALS OR SHAPING SCRAPS OF GLASS.

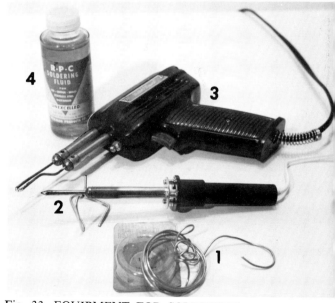

Fig. 33. EQUIPMENT FOR SOLDERING.
1. Solder.
2. Small hobby iron.
3. Trigger-type all-purpose soldering iron.
4. Soldering flux.

Fig. 34. A ceramic kiln is an essential piece of equipment for melting glass and firing clay. Bob Lawrence's whimsical sea creatures were assembled from random fragments of bottle glass which were melted to the point where they fused without losing separate identity. Supporting framework and chains are of soldered copper.

Fig. 35. The basic form for "Roundelay" was made in a mold. The tray was then textured, bisque-fired, and stained black. The inside was mosaicked with Venetian glass tiles and melted glass nuggets in shades of green, cobalt, and turquoise.

promotes fusion by lowering the melting point of the solder, causing it to flow more freely.

Briefly, to solder a metal joint, coat it with flux, then hold the hot iron on the seam until it is well heated. Hold the solder to the iron at the junction of the two pieces of metal and melt away a small droplet. Direct the molten solder into the joint and add more if necessary. Run the iron lightly over the seam to smooth it.

Be sure that the metal is hot before adding solder or you may get a "cold joint." This is a seam which has the appearance of permanency, but actually is not fused and will come apart easily.

In Chapters 23 and 24 we shall show variations of soldering in specific projects, especially a type of open-flame soldering that is decorative, as well as functional.

Fig. 36. SMALL ELECTRIC KILN FOR CLAY AND GLASS. *(Photo courtesy of J. J. Cress Company, Inc.)*

Kilns

Glass and clay are silicate compounds and therefore both classified as ceramic materials. Although firing procedures vary somewhat, the same kiln can be used for both kinds of work.

To mature clay to a durable state, it is heated to a temperature specifically related to the ingredients of which it is composed. Ideally, this is high enough to fuse the clay into a hard substance, yet not so high that it is warped, distorted, or discolored. Clays of different formulas will have different maturing temperatures, which are established by experimentation or supplied by the distributor of the material.

Following are descriptions of three basic types of electric kilns which are most popular and practical for mosaic work.

1. A *high-fire* kiln, which reaches temperatures up to 2300° F., can be used to fire porcelain and stoneware, as well as glass and earthenware bodies. They are available in a wide range of sizes, and most of them require a 220 electrical outlet.

2. *Low-fire* kilns usually have a maximum firing temperature of 1950° F. and are used for glass and non-vitreous pottery bodies. The smaller sizes (up to 11 × 11 × 11 inches) can be plugged into an ordinary electrical outlet.

In this second category we should mention the miniatures designed for tests and for jewelry, and small clay or glass objects. They fire and cool quickly, use little current, and with the addition of shelves can produce a quantity of interesting materials in a short time.

Fig. 36A. If firing is critical, two cones should be used, one which registers the temperature desired, and one of a lower temperature to serve as a warning. Here, the warning cone (019) has matured. When the upright cone (018) has bent half over, the kiln should be turned off.

Many ceramists use three consecutive cones arranged from right to left in this order: 1. warning cone; 2. cone of desired temperature; 3. higher cone to indicate whether or not the kiln has overfired.

Fig. 37. Marble cubes, smalti, chunks of melted bottles, and hand-made clay shapes were used in this panel by Rosalis.

Several types of miniature kilns are on the market. Economy models are top-loading with a simple firebrick lid and an off-on switch. More deluxe designs have neat metal casings and controls for regulating heat.

3. A third type of electric kiln is designed for copper enameling. Since the brilliance of the layer of glass on metal is achieved by rapid heating and cooling, they are not actually recommended for firing clay or glass. However, small pieces of clay which are thoroughly dry can be fired in an enameling kiln successfully, and some workers use them for small pieces of glass. Their greatest value to the mosaicist is for making enameled materials.

Pyrometers can be installed on kilns so that the interior temperature can be ascertained at all times. Pyrometric cones will indicate when specific temperatures have been reached.

Cones are bits of specially formulated minerals shaped like elongated pyramids and manufactured in standard sizes for larger kilns, and in smaller sizes, "juniors," which can more easily be observed through small peepholes.

They are set at a slight angle in a pat of clay which must be dried before firing. The cone will soften and bend over at an established temperature designated by a number pressed into the side of the cone.

Standard and junior cones of the same number will deform at the same time, but some variation will occur according to the size of the kiln, the rate of temperature rise, and the manner in which the kiln is stacked. A chart of temperature equivalents is given in the Appendix.

Forms and Backings

Almost any rigid, substantial surface can be mosaicked if it is properly pretreated and has the durability for its intended function. The suggestions which follow are general in nature. We shall discuss others in connection with particular techniques and applications.

Aside from the familiar backings of natural and pressed woods, many craftsmen use discarded items of furniture, lumber rejects, and odd forms collected from beaches, city dumps, and salvage stores.

PANELS AND TABLES

Small semipermanent mosaics from such lightweight materials as paper, fabric, seeds, beads, etc., can be attached to heavy cardboard which has been sealed with several coats of shellac or spray acrylic. The panel should be framed before being decorated, and another layer of cardboard should be glued or taped firmly to the back to prevent warpage.

Plywood seconds make excellent table tops and panels. Exterior grades, treated with a waterproofing compound, are required for projects subjected to weather. The finished mosaic should be rewaterproofed once or twice a year.

With cross-bracing on the back of the frame to ensure rigidity, panels up to 2 feet square may be made on ¼-inch to ⅜-inch plywood or pressed hardboard. Three-quarter-inch plywood is recommended for large panels and tables, and 1-inch thickness is safer for benches designed to hold more than one person.

Quarter-inch chipboard is adequate for table tops not more than 1 foot square if the legs are a part of the framework and not merely attached to the backing itself.

Mill rejects of unfinished furniture and doors can often be purchased at a fraction of the cost of top-quality products. Since their imperfections usually consist of surface flaws rather than structural weaknesses, they are entirely suitable for mosaic decoration.

REFLECTIVE COATINGS

Opaque backings must have reflective coatings to bounce light back through transparent materials. Flat white paint is generally satisfactory and will not influence colors. Interesting effects may also be obtained with metallic paints and papers, but they should be pretested for resistance to adhesives.

Certain precautions should be observed with reflective coatings for panels to be embedded in plastic. Some paints affect the curing or hardening capacity of polyester resins. For best results, frame the panel first, then pour a thin layer of white plastic over the backing. Extra luminosity is obtained with white pearlized pigments in a mix of clear casting resin.

EXPOSED BACKINGS

Many mosaicists use the backing as a part of the design. In this case, thought might be given to the interesting textures of canvas, linen, and burlap, which can be glued to the backing in the manner of wallpaper. Grass cloth, rice paper, and metallic wrapping papers are other possibilities.

Some of these materials have rough, uneven surfaces, which can be a problem unless the entire panel is embedded in plastic. The protrusion of even a small thread can prevent decorative materials from making adequate contact with the foundation, and special measures should be taken to ensure permanency.

Large sections of glass or clay can be bolted to the retaining structure. This is, of course, impractical where small tesserae are employed, and adhesives of extra strength or and cushioning capacity should be used.

TRANSLUCENT BACKINGS

Translucent mosaics can be made on Plexiglas, Lucite, and glass. Double-strength window glass is strong enough for lanterns and small panels, but crystal or plate glass is required for large pieces.

If decorative materials are extremely transparent and the piece is to be lighted from within, some diffusion may be necessary to eliminate distracting glare from the light source. You might experiment with obscure glass, such as that used for windows and shower doors. (Decoration is applied to the smooth side.) The textured surface will bend and break up the light rays so that they do not pass through in a straight line.

Transparent glass can be made translucent by attaching a sheet of fiberglas or frosted acetate to the underside. Various brands of frostlike paints which are manufactured for

Fig. 38. "Blue Star" by Stella Popowski is in many shades of sapphire glass. The rays are large Mexican puddlers arranged around a central three-dimensional form of thick glass fragments. Mounted on grey velvet, the glass pieces are attached to the backing both with glue and with invisibly tied nylon monofilament line. (*Photo courtesy of the El Presidente Hotel, Mexico City.*)

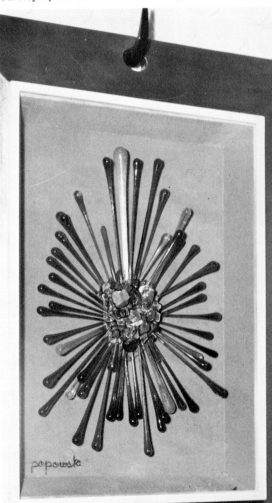

Fig. 39. SIMPLE POTTERY SHAPES SUITABLE FOR MOSAICS.

Fig. 40. Pottery jars intended to hold food should be glazed on the inside. Exposed surfaces can be textured before firing and stained afterward in colors which complement the mosaic. The foreground canister has a random pattern of Venetian glass tiles and melted taillights. The canister in back has a "woven" pattern of blue tiles.

windows and aquariums might also be satisfactory. You can test their resistance to discoloration by applying them to a low-wattage light bulb and observing the effects of light and heat over a period of time.

FORMS

Pottery forms for mosaics should be uncomplicated in shape and preferably unglazed on the surface to be decorated. Several coats of shellac or spray acrylic will reduce the absorbency of low-fire bisque. Porcelain bisque is already waterproof.

Glaze the insides of clay flowerpots and planters, or moisture seeping through the walls may weaken the mosaic adhesive. Wooden planters should have metal liners for the same reason.

For better adhesion of decorative materials, roughen the surface of metal forms with sandpaper or a wire brush, and remove wax finishes from wooden trays and bowls.

Rugs are sometimes rolled around heavy cardboard cylinders which with a little processing can be turned into handsome lamp bases. Cut wooden disks to fit the ends and drill holes in the centers to accommodate the line cord. The cylinders should be weighted with sand or plaster before the final assembly. Lengths of clay drainage pipes can be similarly equipped, and need no weighting.

If a bottle slicer is available, a variety of mosaic forms can be made from glass jugs and bottles. For hanging light fixtures, remove the necks and bottoms from gallon or half-gallon jugs. For vases, canisters, and candy jars, only the necks or top sections need be cut away. Later, in Chapter 16, we shall show ways of making lids for such pieces.

Damaged edges of chipped stemware can be trimmed away and the remaining form mosaicked. Delicate hand-blown pieces are more difficult to handle, but if your attempts at salvage are futile, the rest of the glass can still be used for decorative materials (see Chapter 8).

24

FORMS AND BACKINGS

Fig. 41. The oversized bottle on the left is used for advertising. On the right, the paint and bottom have been removed to convert it into a form for a hanging light.

TRIMMING CHIPPED STEMWARE

Fig. 43. Use a glass pencil to mark a trim line at least ½ inch below the broken area. Attach a circle of masking tape on the mark, and cushion the glass on a towel or sheet of sponge rubber.

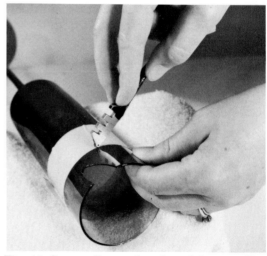

Fig. 44. Score a line at the edge of the tape. Tap inside the score with the ball end of the cutter until the glass is fractured and the margin can be removed. Polish rough edges with an emery grinder, or finish with lead or plastic metal.

Fig. 42. A bottle slicer was used to cut these forms for flower containers. The sharp edges can be bound with self-adhering lead tape, or plated with plastic metal after the decoration is finished.

chapter 4

Structural Materials

ADHESIVES

The decorative fragments of a mosaic have traditionally been secured by glues or cements, but in contemporary works they may also be held together by wire, solder, thread, rope, nails, plastic, molten glass—and sometimes, by what appears to be sheer optimism.

With a remarkable variety of adhesives on the market, it is often difficult to decide which will best serve a particular purpose. Three aspects of the project will provide clues: 1. the decorative materials; 2. the intended function; 3. the area where it will be displayed.

To simplify the picture, we shall classify the major types of adhesives according to their chemical make-up and their resistance to weather. The group into which each falls affords a basic reference for its most appropriate use.

Water-soluble Adhesives

Pastes

A water-soluble paste should be used on mosaics constructed by the indirect method.[1] In this process, the decorative materials are glued face down on heavy paper, then flipped over into a bed of mastic or cement. When the mosaic has been leveled and the setting bed

[1] See Chapter 19.

has partly set, the paper is dampened to dissolve the glue and peeled away.

Ordinary library paste might be suitable here, though a little experimentation may be necessary to choose a brand which is not too brittle when dry to keep the tiles from dropping off before they can be embedded.

Wheat paste (wallpaper paste) is used for attaching fabric or paper coverings to backings which will be partly exposed around the mosaic design. It also makes an excellent binder for papier-mâché.

Water Resistant Adhesives

Casein-based Glues

Casein-based glues (often called simply white glues) are manufactured by several companies and are recommended for seeds, gravels, and small pieces of glass. Even tiles and rocks can be permanently secured with white glue if it is applied liberally and the piece is protected from weather. These adhesives are handy, also, for securing tesserae to net for embedding directly in mortar. In this instance, the glue actually unites with the mortar, which is the real adhering agent. The piece is then safe for exterior installation.

White glues have no objectionable fumes and are transparent when dry.

FORMS FROM PAPIER-MACHÉ

Fig. 45. This large free-form core for a bird bath was built upon shaped wire mesh, which was bound with several layers of cloth dipped in diluted white glue. When the shell was dry, prepared papier-mâché pulp was molded on one side at the time for a total thickness of about 1½ inches. Paper was trimmed and shaped to fit the inside and a pattern sketched on it.

Fig. 46. A sheet of Mylar and then one of coarse cotton net were placed on the pattern and the decorative materials set in place with white glue. Notice the vacant wedges for adapting it to the concave surface. The mosaic can now be peeled away from the Mylar and installed (net and all) face up in a bed of mortar. Another layer of mortar will be troweled on the outside of the form. By Rosalis.

Waterproof Adhesives

Rubber Cements

Rubber cements are not permanent enough for most mosaics, but are useful for holding materials in place temporarily. This has special application for fused-glass projects, since the rubber will burn completely away without leaving a scum or residue.

Mastics

Rubber-based mastics are thick and putty-like and permanently plasticized. White mastic should be used where transparent materials are involved, unless they have a reflective backing. The more common yellow-brown mastics are suitable for any opaque materials except fine sand, seeds, gravels, etc., where their appearance might be objectionable.

Mastic is appropriate for both exterior and interior mosaics. It can be spread directly on the backing and the decorative materials pressed into it, or each separate fragment can be liberally buttered on the back and arranged in place.

Use mastic only in a well-ventilated room, and avoid breathing the fumes for extended periods of time.

The consistency and resiliency of this adhesive make it an excellent choice for irregular materials, as well as counter tops and walls. Its stickiness is highly advantageous when working on curved or vertical surfaces.

All-Purpose Cements

This popular classification for transparent household cements and model-airplane glues is somewhat misleading, since it is evident that an adhesive equally suited to all purposes does not exist.

Some brands in this group are fairly permanent when used for interior mosaics and, being perfectly colorless, they have certain advantages for glass work. Some are inclined to become brittle with age, however, and unless the mosaic is grouted, it may in time separate from the backing. The most efficient all-purpose cements are newer products which contain epoxy.

Fig. 47. "St. Michael" by Thomas Hunt. Glass tiles in tinted mortar. *(Collection of Colonel and Mrs. J. Y. Adams.)*

Reactive Adhesives

Epoxy resin adhesives are packaged in two components which must be mixed together. In comparison to other adhesives, they are expensive, but for versatility and strength are indispensable.

Some epoxies are opaque and primarily formulated for metals. Most transparent epoxies have a faint honey tint which is hardly noticeable when the material is dry. They bond well to glass (and other materials) and may be used outdoors and indoors.

CEMENTS

Ready-Mixes

Much has happened to cements in the past few years, and the ready-mixes are of special interest to the amateur craftsman. They can be purchased in small quantities, contain sand and cement in accurate proportions, and need only the addition of water. Retarding agents can be added to slow the setting time, and if weight is a consideration, certain cellular aggregates will displace some of the cement without overweakening the structure.

Fig. 48. "World Travelers" is made of concrete cast in a mold containing mosaic embedments of Byzantine glass and polished pebbles. This sculpture group was created by Charles Clement for the Portland Cement Association's display at the New York World's Fair, 1964–65.

Magnesite

Magnesite is probably the most versatile cement for mosaics since it sets up slowly and can be spread as thinly as ½ inch without cracking. Panels should be reinforced with hardware cloth or screening to ensure a good bond with the backing.

Magnesite first appeared as an interior material only, but waterproof magnesite is now available, making it practical for projects in any location.[2]

The dry cement is mixed with a solution of magnesium chloride crystals instead of water. Since the crystals are difficult to store for any period of time and the solution must be of a prescribed density, it is best to purchase the prepared liquid if possible.

Sculptured magnesite forms may be built over armatures of wire, galvanized mesh, or papier-mâché. If the cement becomes dry before the modeling is finished, it should be thoroughly soaked with water before a fresh layer is added.

Grout

Grout is a cement of such fine texture that it resembles flour. It is blended with water to a creamy consistency, spread over the surface of the mosaic, and rubbed into the crevices between tesserae. When the grout has set but not completely hardened, the mosaic is cleaned with rags, sponges, and fine steel wool.

Special additives (such as Grout-Tite) will decrease shrinkage and porosity, but diluted white glue is also useful. A final coat of silicone polish, liquid wax, or waterproofing compound will seal the surface and make it stain resistant.

All cements, including grout, may be tinted with mineral pigments, which are added either to the dry mix or to the wetting solution. By volume measurement, not more than 1 part of dry pigment to 10 parts of cement should be used, or the strength of the mortar will be affected.

Where deeper colors are desired, the finished surface can be stained with a strong solu-

[2] See Chapter 19.

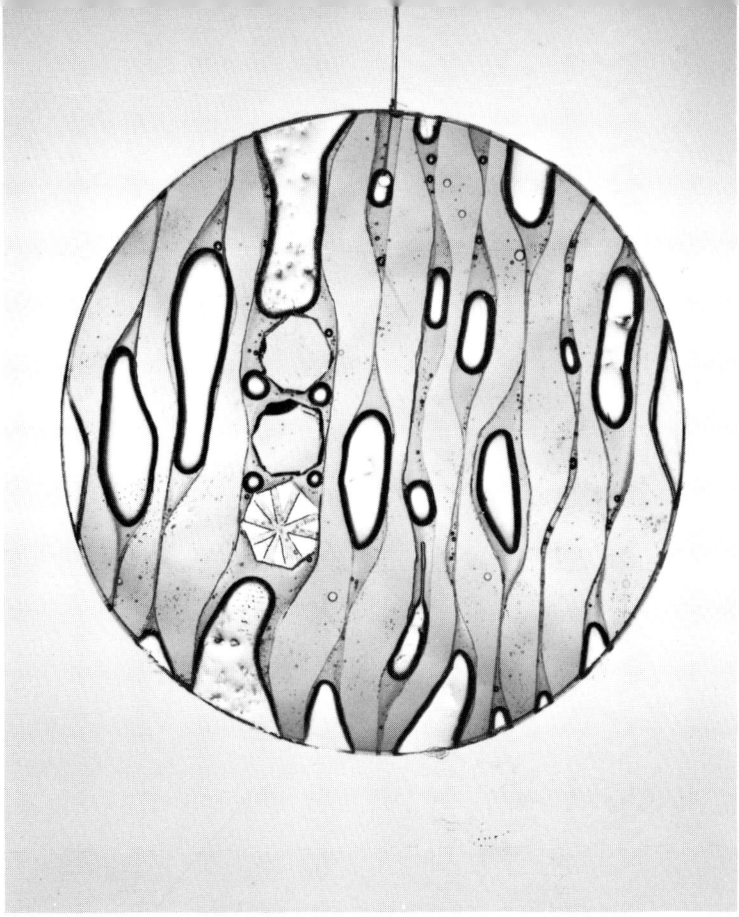

Fig. 49. Dick Seeger uses plastic blocks and sheets for his decorative pieces, sculpture, and architectural panels. Disks of this kind are designed for coasters and trivets, or for suspending as mobiles. They are made by laminating colored forms cut from sheets.

tion of dye and water before waterproofing. Since the colors are considerably lighter when dry, preliminary tests should be made to determine suitable proportions.

All functional surfaces, such as counter tops, tables, ash trays, dishes, etc., should be grouted. On purely decorative pieces this is optional.

PLASTICS

Synthetic resins are a development of our time and probably the only mosaic materials that can really be called new. In spite of the fact that there are many different types of resins, they are commonly all lumped together as "plastics."

When plastics first appeared, serious craftsmen were inclined to disfavor them, regarding them as imitative materials which at best were ne'er-do-well relatives of glass, china, wood, and metal.

More recently, they have discovered that certain things can be done with plastics which cannot be done with anything else. Through the unprejudiced and creative work of a relatively small group of artists they have finally earned their own special niche.

A great deal of research would be necessary to investigate fully the tremendous scope of this field. Although simple projects with the more workable resins require little study or equipment,[3] some basic understanding of their physical and chemical natures is essential to give them a fair trial.

To this end we will separate the resins most useful for our purposes into two major categories: the *thermosetting* resins, which include the polyesters and epoxies, and the *thermoplastic* resins, which include the acrylics, acetates, and vinyls.

Resins are changed from a liquid to a solid state by a chemical process called *poly-*

[3] See Chapter 13.

merization. We can explain how this works by comparing the molecules that make up a batch of liquid resin to a bowl of tiny beads, each separate and unattached to the other and able to roll about freely. If we strung these beads on lengths of wire and interwove them tightly together, they would form a rigid mass.

This is precisely what happens when resin is hardened, or polymerized. The individual molecules join together in long chains which entangle until no further movement is possible.

This reaction is most often activated by physical or chemical heat. Although liquid plastics will in time spontaneously congeal from sunlight or atmospheric conditions, a more controllable method is to add a catalyst which will promote polymerization immediately.

Catalysts are supplied with polyester resins at the time of purchase. Acrylic and acetate resins, for reasons we shall explain later, are usually purchased already catalyzed, in solid form.

Once polymerized, the thermosetting resins will not change viscosity with further applications of heat. While they may be burned, scorched, or charred, they will not again return to a liquid state.

On the other hand, the little "bead" molecules of thermoplastic resins become slippery and unattached again with heat. This means that they can be repeatedly softened, regaining rigidity as they cool.

These opposing reactions to heat make a great deal of difference in our choice of a plastic most appropriate for a particular work.

Thermoplastic Resins

The average craftsman is not concerned with handling the thermoplastics in liquid form. Special equipment is required for casting them under pressure, and the fumes are highly inflammable and toxic. They are, therefore, generally used in granulated, block, or sheet form.

Lucite and Plexiglas (acrylics) are familiar trade names in the last two categories, and as already mentioned in Chapter 3, make excellent backings for translucent panels or windows. If we fully understand their classification as thermoplastic, however, we will not make the mistake of using them where they will be subjected to excessive heat. They may soften to a degree where the mosaic is warped or loosened.

Rather than considering this characteristic a fault, we can use it to our advantage. For example, sheet Lucite and Plexiglas may be softened in hot water or the kitchen stove until it is malleable enough to be shaped into original mosaic forms.[4]

Thermoplastic Crystals

Polystyrene pellets (sometimes called cooking crystals or beads) are newcomers to the craft world, and can be melted to a completely liquid state in a kitchen oven. They are inclined to bubble, but some control can be exercised by raising the heat slowly and maintaining it for an extended period of time.

Mosaics designed for mobiles, paperweights, and wall decorations can be embedded in the melted granules up to the size that an oven will accommodate. Larger panels can be made in sections and joined together on a backing. The crevices between sections can be filled with grout, liquid casting plastic, or plastic metal, or left untreated if the effect is pleasing.

Anything that is ovenproof will serve as a mold. The plastic will contract as it cools, and will pull away from the container. The mold must not, of course, have any undercuts, or the hardened form will be locked in it.

Acetate and Vinyl

Sheet acetate, which may be purchased in art stores and hobby shops, is of greater value decoratively than structurally.[5] It is available in thin, flexible sheets which are easily cut with scissors. Reds and yellows are more subject to fading than greens and blues, but will hold up satisfactorily for some time.

---

[4] See Chapter 22.
[5] See Chapter 17.

Fig. 50. "The Emblem of the Stained Glass Association of America" by Ruth Dunn. Faceted glass in epoxy resin. *(Collection of Orco Glass, Inc.)*

Fig. 51. Linoleum and abalone shell, glued to uncoated sheets of Formica with contact cement. By Emmy Lou Packard for the S.S. *Mariposa*.

Vinyl is also primarily used as a decorative material. It can be softened in a warm oven, then cut with heavy scissors.

Thermosetting Resins

Phenolics, such as Bakelite and Formica, are sometimes used as backings for special projects where bulk and weight are considerations,[6] but the polyesters are the most versatile products in the category of thermosetting resins.

Liquid Polyester Resin

Various liquid polyesters are formulated for specific purposes, and one cannot always be substituted for another. For example, the resin manufactured for boat building is not entirely suitable for embedding thick chunks of glass. Resins designed for preserving biological specimens will not be the perfect answer for thin laminated windows or screens. With such a wide choice in this group, there is no reason for the craftsman to "make do" with second best.

Almost any dry material can be embedded in polyester resin. It scratches easily, however, and will become discolored from lighted cigarettes and extremely hot dishes. Unless the resin is used purely as a setting bed, not as a surface material, there are more practical solutions for table tops, work counters, and ash trays.

Liquid resin should be bought only in quantities for which there is an immediate need. It keeps longer if stored in a cool, dark place, but even there, it will gel in time and become unusable.

Some of the difficulties beginners experience with liquid resins may be attributed to carelessness in following manufacturers' directions, though working conditions play a part in them. Dust or lint in the air, excessive humidity, extremes of heat or cold, can affect both the curing and the quality of the finished product. Other factors will be discussed in Chapter 13.

Fig. 52. Paste polyester resin may be spread on a backing and decorative materials pressed into it, or separate fragments may be buttered and attached one at a time.

Some persons suffer an allergic reaction to plastic fumes, but in any case the working area should be well ventilated.

Paste Polyester Resin

Semiliquid resins are about the consistency of petroleum jelly and are especially useful for cushioning chunky, irregular materials.[7]

They can be colored with transparent dyes and opaque pigments, and have the advantage of setting up very slowly, giving you several hours of working time.

MISCELLANEOUS EMBEDDING MATERIALS

Plastic steel and aluminum may be used for embedding opaque materials, as well as for plating forms to give them the appearance of metal.[8] Squeezed in a thick ribbon between sections of stained glass and burnished after hardening, they simulate lead or wrought iron.

Many other products which are designed for home repairs have a place in the mosaic workshop. Dry wood putty, mixed with water to the consistency of soft dough, will bond to wood and pressed hardboard backings. It can be tinted with dry pigments and used as a type of grout. It is very hard when dry, and there is little shrinkage.[9]

[6] See Chapter 15.

[7] See frontispiece, "Early Thaw."

[8] See projects in Chapters 15, 21, and 23.

[9] See Chapter 17.

Decorative Materials to Buy

"Tessera" (plural, tesserae) is of Latin origin and means "cube," or a little square of mosaic material. In common usage, however, this original definition has been expanded to include not only small angular materials, but also all of the decorative fragments which might make up a mosaic design.

A glance around an exhibition of contemporary mosaics would seem to indicate that almost any decorative material is permissable if it will not evaporate, spoil, or disintegrate within a reasonable period of time. Nearly all professional mosaicists, however, rely heavily on commercial products for large commissions. The advantages are their availability in quantity, and their uniformity in size and color.

It would be useless, even deceiving, to quote prices of commercial mosaic materials. Costs vary according to distance from original sources, and according to the profit markups among wholesalers and retailers. Japanese tiles, for example, may be cheaper in San Francisco than New York, while Italian tiles are usually cheaper on the East Coast. But even these generalities do not apply where competition is keen.

The prices of domestic products are more stable, but freight costs must still be included.

TILES

Commercial Clay Tiles

Each type of clay tile has distinct characteristics which stem both from basic ingredients and from processes of manufacturing. Some kinds can be purchased in art and hobby shops; others from companies which sell building materials.

Commercial clay tiles, whether of low- or high-fire bodies, are cast in molds for uniformity of size and thickness. Level surfaces can usually be obtained by gluing them directly onto a backing.

33

Figs. 53, 54. Two of the fourteen Stations of the Cross designed and executed by the Cavallini Company for St. Francis of Sales, Houston. The mosaic patterns are Venetian glass tiles, and the panels are ready for installation.

Porcelain Tiles

Unglazed porcelain tiles have a soft, velvety finish and are excellent for functional surfaces, such as floors and counter tops. One-inch squares are most common. Hexagons, rectangles, and triangles are harder to find but are useful for keeping cutting to a minimum on large patterns.

Glazed porcelain tiles have a thin skin of glass on a white clay body, and are manufactured in a wide range of colors, including brilliant red, orange, yellow, and gold, as well as delicate tints.

In the past few years, Japanese manufacturers have added an intriguing selection of bars, circles, free forms, and leaf shapes to the traditional squares. They are pasted face up on paper or webbing and arranged into patterns of several colors.

For certain functional purposes, these "instant mosaics" are both appropriate and convenient. However, their completeness and rigidity can greatly discourage original design. If they are chosen for a creative project, the sheets should be soaked in warm water until the tiles can be removed from the backing and re-sorted by size and color. The designer can then study them objectively from a fresh viewpoint without being influenced by their former arrangements.

All porcelain tiles are vitrified and therefore waterproof.

AN INTRODUCTORY PROJECT FOR CLAY TILES

Forms for square or diamond-shaped cutting boards can be made from framed sections of ¼-inch Masonite or plywood. More interesting shapes can be cut from ⅝-inch "glue-edge" wood stock, and a frame provided for the mosaicked area by a large wooden embroidery hoop, flexible plastic edging, or copper stripping.

Glazed porcelain Japanese tiles as shown in Figure 55 are a practical choice for the decorative cutting surface. (Leaf shapes and squares were used for the illustrated project which follows.) Remove tiles from the backing and sort by sizes and colors.

Prepare the dry grout mix in a jar and set it aside. Fifteen tablespoons of grout, 1 tablespoon of brown pigment, and 1 teaspoon of green pigment will make a medium-brown filler which will not show stains. Mix separately 1

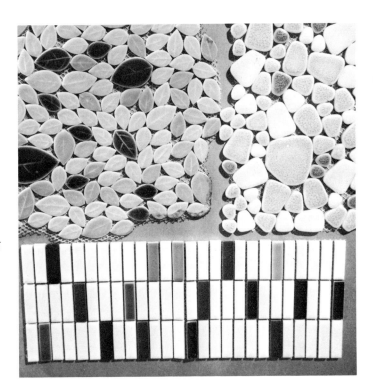

Fig. 55. GLAZED PORCELAIN TILES FROM JAPAN.

part white glue with 2 parts water to use as a wetting agent.

Before you begin, experiment with different ways in which the tiles can be arranged. A simple pattern involving as little cutting as possible will be more appropriate than one of overcomplexity.

MAKING A CUTTING BOARD

Fig. 56. Strips nailed to the back of the cut-out board will prevent warpage and make it easier to handle. Buff the wood with fine steel wool and finish with stains and low-gloss varnish.

Fig. 57. Quarter-inch copper stripping is easy to shape to a pattern and makes an attractive frame for the mosaic. Small brads nailed on alternate sides of the metal will hold it in place until the ends can be soldered together. Attach the copper outline to the cutting board with epoxy and weight with bricks for twenty-four hours.

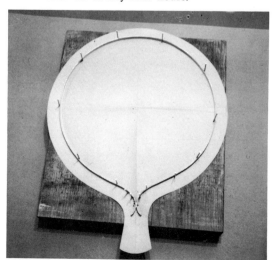

Fig. 58. Arrange tile motif on a paper pattern. Draw radiating lines from the center of the board as guides for keeping the pattern balanced. Use a foil-lined jar lid to hold small amounts of mastic at a time. Each tile can be "buttered" separately and set in place, or the mastic can be spread on the board and the tesserae pressed into it.

Fig. 59. From time to time, lightly hammer a wooden block against the tiles to seat them evenly. Finish the central motif first, then a border (if one is needed). Fill the remaining space with tiles cut into random shapes. Tesserae should be spaced so that crevices between them are fairly consistent in width.

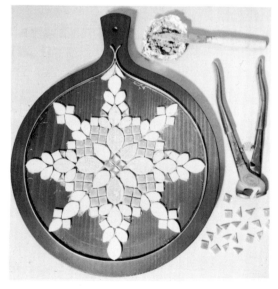

Fig. 60. Let the mastic harden twenty-four hours, then blend about half the dry grout mix with the solution of glue and water to form a soft, creamy paste. Spread it over the mosaic with a flexible spatula, forcing it into the crevices.

Fig. 61. Wipe lightly with paper towels, and wait until the cement is firm (but not dry) before cleaning with damp rags and sponges. Go over the mosaic again with a fresh thin mix of grout and rub it into hairline cracks and pinholes. Polish the tiles with steel wool and paper towels.

Fig. 62. When the grout is dry, apply a coat of liquid wax to both board and mosaic.

Low-Fire Clay Tiles

Earthenware bodies are porous and must be glazed to obtain a waterproof surface. Glaze effects have become increasingly varied, ranging from crystalline textures to marbleized spatters to interesting grayed tones. Standard 4-inch squares used for tiling bathrooms and kitchens can often be purchased quite cheaply in odd lots left over from building contracts. They are quite thick and difficult to cut with any accuracy. This is a blessing of a sort, since the simplest method of reducing them to tesserae of usable size is to break them with a hammer. The resulting random shapes are conducive to freedom of design.

Because of the porosity, mosaics made of low-fire tiles should be thoroughly soaked in water before grouting, or the cement mix will be desiccated.

Commercial Glass Tiles

Glass is one of the oldest materials for mosaics, yet the availability of commercial glass tesserae in this country is a fairly recent development. Most of these products are imported from Italy, though Mexican imports are becoming more widely distributed.

"Pressed" glass tiles are made in molds, but the process is not as precise as the casting of clay. As a consequence, they have a certain irregularity of shape, texture, and thickness. The better grades of Venetian glass tiles are moderately uniform by the sheet, but different sheets, even of the same color, may vary considerably. The indirect method should be used where an absolutely flat surface is required.

Earlier Italian imports were generally opaque, though lighter colors were translucent to a limited degree. Newer offerings include transparent tiles, some of which are dusted with gold or copper flakes.

Mexican glass tiles are less dense than the Italian products and many colors have a frosted, pearly iridescence. Sizes range from ¾-inch squares to bars and miniature ¼-inch squares. Because of the graininess and surface striations, they are often inclined to shatter,

Fig. 63. Variations in the thickness of Venetian glass tiles give a three-dimensional quality to "Sea Weed" by Jean Burton.

Fig. 64. A cricket is not a usual subject for mosaic, yet treated with sensitivity and imagination, it becomes a brilliant composition which is closely related to the quality of Byzantine art. Notice how the encircling lines in the background convey the feeling of a small, close hiding-place. By Helen Steinau Rich.

rather than to fracture in a straight line, and it is difficult to clean grout from the tiny pits and folds.

Smalti (also called Byzantine glass or enamels) are irregular opaque glass cubes which are considered by many mosaicists to be the aristocrats of all decorative materials. They may also cost from three to five times more than other glass tiles.

Smalti are chipped by hand from larger slabs or "pancakes," and the resulting faceted surface is highly reflective. They have a strength distinctly their own which is not appropriate for small fussy designs.

Fig. 65. "Madonna and Child" by Thomas Hunt. Smalti, Venetian tiles, and stained-glass chips pressed deeply into a bed of colored cement. *(Photo courtesy of the M. H. De Young Memorial Museum.)*

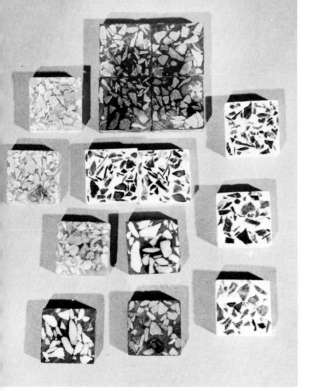

Fig. 66. Mozo tiles are made of crushed shells and gravels embedded in plastic. They have a terrazzo-like appearance and may be cut with nippers in the manner of clay and glass tiles.

Commercial Plastic Tiles

Plastic tiles have been manufactured for some time for walls, floors, and counter tops, but those designed specifically for mosaics are relatively new. Since the field has great potential, production will undoubtedly grow in scale and distribution.

STAINED GLASS

When we speak of stained or cathedral glass, we are referring to a type of glass which was originally manufactured primarily for church windows. It is being increasingly used today in homes and public buildings.

Cathedral glass can be molded, blown, seeded, rippled, smooth, transparent, translucent, multicolored, and even completely color-less. An attempt to distinguish it accurately from other types of glass could involve us in many technicalities, and it is sufficient to say here that cathedral glass is especially designed as a *decorative* material.

A decorative window must meet the same structural requirements as any other window, of course, but its essential function is beauty. For this reason, absolute clarity is neither nec-essary nor desirable. It would, in fact, give a harsh, glaring quality to the design. Distortions and irregularities which would be unacceptable in ordinary window glass are deliberately in-troduced into cathedral glass to soften and diffuse the light.

The old cathedral glass was made by blowing a gather of molten glass into a cylindri-cal bubble, then scoring it vertically and firing it to the point where the cylinder opened up and flattened onto the kiln shelf.[1]

Sheets made in this manner have beautiful gradations of color intensity and sometimes swirling ripples and tiny bubbles.

Some contemporary manufacturers, such as Blenko Glass Company, have clung to the ancient methods of producing hand-crafted art objects and sheet glass, and their products are greatly in demand by glass craftsmen and mosaicists all over the country.

MISCELLANEOUS COMMERCIAL MATERIALS

Thin hand-drawn ribbons of opaque glass are imported from Italy and useful for sharp, linear accents. They average from $\frac{1}{8}$- to $\frac{1}{4}$-inch wide and may be broken into suitable lengths with tweezers or pliers.

Mosaic canes are made by melting to-gether a bundle of glass threads and drawing them out into long rods.[2] When sliced cross-wise, they reveal intricate patterns. They may be melted into copper glazes or glass for bursts of variegated color or nipped into segments for miniatures.

Most mosaic shops now carry colored cul-

[1] Note method of obtaining small bottle panes in Chapter 8.

[2] Tiny canes are called pattern chips and may be purchased in shops which carry supplies for copper enameling.

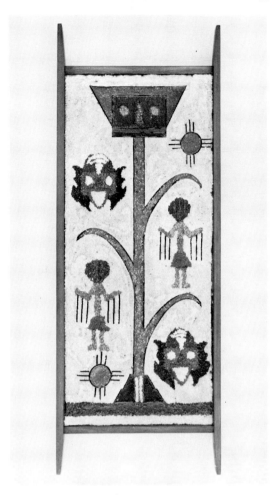

Fig. 67. "Corn Dancer" by Harold Hickson, a gravel mosaic set in polyester resin. The figures are authentic as far as symbolism is concerned, and were derived from a sand painting. The composition and the interesting mahogany frame are original.

Fig. 68. "Navajo Rug" is an original design by Harold Hickson, created from the symbols used by the Navajos in their rugs and blankets. The panel has the traditional black border. The gray represents rain, the white zigzag the lightning; the light brown is the dry earth, the dark brown the wet earth, the light blue is the clear sky, and the coral is the sunset after the rain has passed. Colored areas are dyed gravel. Black lines are rubber strips and shoe laces.

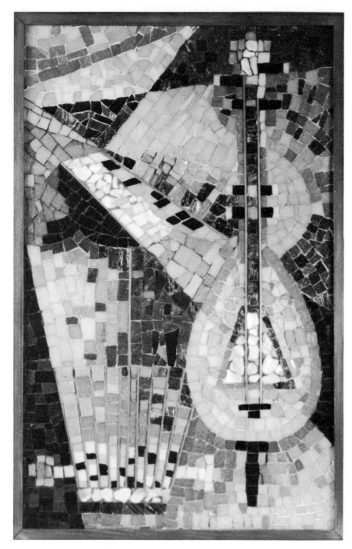

Fig. 69. A variety of commercial materials were used by the author in "Trio." Thin brass strips are linear accents for the decorative pattern of smalti, Venetian tiles, salvaged glass, and mother-of-pearl chips.

let (crushed glass) in grades from fine powder to large chunks. It can be pressed into beds of white glue, resin, or cement.

Dyed gravel, which was received with great joy a few years ago, has lost favor with many craftsmen. This is probably because materials, like people, are often judged by the company they keep, and gravel has been closely associated with kits.

For certain purposes, dyed gravel is extremely useful. It comes in many beautiful and brilliant colors and is inexpensive enough for large wall panels and seasonal decorations which might be brought out only once a year.

Gravel is an excellent medium for children's craft groups and occupational therapy where, for reasons of safety, cutting instruments are prohibited.

Small cubes of marble called marmi are not standard stock with smaller mosaic shops but may occasionally be found in studios which produce large architectural commissions.

Aquarium pearl chips, sheet cork, wood veneers, fabrics, enameled papers, self-adhering sheet vinyl, and even oilcloth are among the hundreds of other commercial products which will stimulate the imagination of the alert craftsman.

chapter 6

Decorative Materials to Collect

In *Folk Art of Rural Pennsylvania,* Frances Lichten says that it is possible to divide the world into two kinds of people: the savers and the throwers-away. Without question, the mosaicist is a saver, and he is indebted to the throwers-away for some of his most cherished materials.

It requires a certain discipline to resist the temptation to use a little bit of everything in a single composition, purely for the sake of novelty. Yet, there is no more merit in a carelessly organized assemblage of nails, bottles, and cogwheels than in a carelessly organized assemblage of commercial tiles.

It is not our intention to shock or astound an audience by displaying the contents of a trash bin on our walls, but rather to search for beauty in the humble things around us.

SALVAGE MATERIALS

Roadsides and refuse heaps are likely sites for broken automobile taillights, signal lanterns, crockery, mirrors, old keys, weathered wood, and odd bits of metals which have acquired colorful patinas from the oxidizing action of rain and sun.

Ordinary window glass and bottles which have been burned or buried sometimes reflect the iridescence of an oil slick on a pool of rainwater. Sometimes they acquire a shriveled encrustation, like the skin of an old orange. Ultraviolet rays and heat from the sun often react on the chemicals in old glass to produce tints of pinkish-mauve and purple.

Scrap metals from the floors of foundries, machine shops, and small factories can be treated in various ways to relieve the monotony of polished surfaces. Intense heat alone from a blowtorch or propane torch will be effective in some cases. Exposure to weather for a period of time will do interesting things to all metals.

Liver of sulphur, which can be purchased in craft shops and drug stores, will antique copper, silver, and lead. For a colorful patina on copper, dissolve a small, pea-sized lump of sulphur in about a quart of hot water. Burnish the copper with fine steel wool (polish lightly areas you wish to remain bright) and brush on the sulphur solution until you attain the desired depth of color.

Weaker solutions will produce tints of iridescent blue, purple, and red. Stronger solu-

Fig. 70. By Ira Jacobson.

Fig. 71.
By Marilyn Morales.

Fig. 72.
By Diane Lovassen.

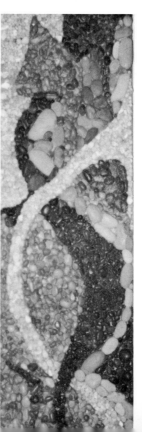

Fig. 73.
By Janice Chieso.

Fig. 74.
By Sylvia Ludins.

Figs. 70, 71, 72, 73. These mosaics were made by eighth- and ninth-grade students in James Denman Junior High School, San Francisco. Pebbles, seeds, gravel, broken rocks, and odds and ends of tiles were collected and sorted by colors and values. Then, under the supervision of instructor Jean Thompson, each student made a number of charcoal sketches, working for interesting value patterns and variation of lines and shapes. Sometimes the best parts of several drawings were combined for the final design.

Decorative materials were arranged to carry out the feeling of the sketch, and attached directly to a backing with white glue.

Fig. 74. An interesting composition of values and textures has been obtained with chipped rock, water-washed pebbles, and wood fragments which were carved by a woodpecker. By Sylvia Ludens.

tions will produce deep gunmetal tones. Mix only the quantities for which there is an immediate need, for the solution will deteriorate within twenty-four hours.

Lead and certain other soft metals can also be darkened with solutions of lye or household-drain cleaners. (These are caustic materials and should be handled with care.)

To antique brass, apply butter of antimony to the surface and let it dry. Rub here and there with soap pads or silver polish to expose lighter colors of the metal.

Lacquer finishes must always be removed before coloring metals. Recoat them after processing to preserve the finish.

Buttons, beads, rusted fishing lures, old keys, small wheels and works from broken clocks, and parts of discarded toys have mosaic possibilities. Bottle corks can be sliced and rubbed with shoe polish or wood stains to accentuate the cellular structure. Marbles can be cracked by heating them in the oven, then dropping them into a pan of cold water. Concentrated dyes or stains added to the water will make the veining more prominent. If crystal-like tesserae are better suited to your needs, a light tap with a hammer will break the crackled marbles into glittering fragments.

NATURAL MATERIALS

Beaches are nature's savers of what the ocean throws away. Wash weathered bark and bits of driftwood to remove sand and salt, then dry them in the sun before using for mosaic. Scrape away spongy parts and apply several thin coats of low-gloss acrylic or varnish as a protection against decay.

Small shells can be used just as they are. Large shells can be cracked with a hammer and positioned with either convex or concave sides up. If equipment is available, shells with substantial walls can be sawed into slices which reveal the translucent whorls of their inner chambers.

The stony outside casings of oyster and

Fig. 75. Aluminum scraps, made by machines which stamp out openings for locks and other hardware at Hollywood Window Company (Meridian, Mississippi), are combined with green and blue melted glass into a geometric pattern. By Robert Stribling.

abalone shells are surprisingly beautiful after tumbling for about twenty-four hours in lapidary grit (or fine sand) and water. As soft, chalky deposits are removed, an interesting pitted texture and unexpected color will be exposed.

A coat of clear acrylic intensifies the color of beach pebbles. For an unblemished surface and high gloss, polish them in a tumbler, starting with coarse cutting grit and ending with fine buffing grit. Several consecutive polishing sessions will be necessary.

The permanence of seed mosaics depends to some extent upon geographical location. In dry climates, they will last indefinitely. They are more subject to decay and loss of color in warm, humid areas. An hour in a 250–300° F. oven will prevent germination and destroy insect eggs and bacteria.

Seeds can be collected from field and garden, though the pantry shelf is an excellent place to start. You might try whole allspice and coriander, dried beans and peas, Indian corn, whole coffee beans, and even barley.

Many flowers, such as dogwood, magnolia, four o'clocks, sweet peas, and nasturtiums have interesting seeds, and some pits are useful. Chinaberries have a durable pit which may be tinted with Easter-egg or dress dyes.

It is best to collect such fruits before they drop to the ground. Cook them until they are soft, then press through a sieve to remove the pulp, and dry them in the sun.

Cones of various species may be used whole, sliced, or separated into petals. Like seeds, all cones and pods should be sterilized.

Properly cured, the rinds of limes, grapefruit, lemons, and oranges, have a leathery texture which combines agreeably with seeds, sheet cork, and wood veneers. It takes patience to process a useful amount, but there is some satisfaction in redeeming a material which would ordinarily be destined for disposal as garbage.

Left to dry naturally, citrus skins will curl. To keep them flat, remove as much of the white inner membrane as possible, spread out on a pad of paper towels, cover with screening, and weight lightly.

Replace the paper daily until most of the moisture is gone, turning the skins so that they will dry evenly. Leave them in a pilot-lighted oven for twenty-four to forty-eight hours for final curing.

To preserve the color, keep the skins away from strong sunlight and leave them exposed to air for several weeks before using. Then spray with several coats of acrylic.

Egg shells are durable and handsome when glued to a substantial backing and thin grout (or a mixture of pigment and lacquer) is rubbed into the crevices.

Exquisite inlays for small chests and jewelry have been created by Oriental artists from these delicate, porcelain-like fragments. We have in our collection of unusual materials colorful shells of eggs laid by Araucana chickens (sometimes called Easter Egg Fowls).[1] They are in muted tones of olive green, peach, and sienna, and have been earmarked for the top of a walnut cigarette box.

These are rare finds for the craftsman interested in nature's oddities, but lacking such accommodating chickens, you can dye ordinary shells with any penetrating pigment.

[1] Supplied by the Ike Davises of Virginia Court, Meridian, Mississippi.

Fig. 76. "The Three Ambassadors" by Florence Ludins Katz. Shells, rocks, metallic sand, chenille rope, and parts of cast-off jewelry create a setting of decaying opulence in this amusing and satirical panel. The figures are made of papier-mâché, figured wallpaper, raveled hemp, feathers, shells, pipe cleaners, and beads.

Fig. 77. "Running Horses" by Henry Imm. Water-frosted scraps of bottle glass. *(Collection of James Sloan.)*

Fig. 78. Whole allspice, brown peas, yellow popcorn, barley, and coriander seeds.

Fig. 79. This decorative panel by Dorothy Saunders is made of eggshells tinted in shades of blue, charcoal, antique gold, and iridescent gold. Strips of heavy black cord were used to define the color areas.

chapter 7

Decorative Materials
to Make from Clay

Creative curiosity is the capacity to *wonder,* the unique spark of energy behind every discovery and invention of man. In the preceding chapter, we investigated this quality in relation to seeing beauty in ordinary things. It becomes more physically active here as we work for the creation of new substances; or perhaps we should say, the reconstitution of old substances so that they may be used in new ways.

The craftsman who is attracted to this area must have both curiosity and imagination for original research, and the patience to be undaunted by failures. Failures, in fact, are extremely important, for often we discover what *will* work, only by first eliminating everything which *won't.*

THE NATURE OF CLAY

Clay is malleable when it is wet and unfired. Once heat has permanently fused it into a rigid structure, it cannot be resoftened. This means that, like certain resins discussed in Chapter 4, clay can be considered a thermosetting material.

There are many different kinds of clay, and usually several are combined in a formula to produce a body with certain characteristics. We shall, however, confine our experiments to clay bodies which are formulated to fit the limitations of small kilns and may be obtained ready-to-use from ceramic supply houses and hobby shops.

Pyrometric cones and pyrometers were described in Chapter 2, and a cone temperature chart is in the Appendix. The most commonly used earthenware (or low-fire) bodies mature at cones 06–04 (1859–1940° F.). All the experiments at the end of this chapter are made with clays in this category, though others may be similarly treated.

49

Popular high-fire bodies of porcelain or stoneware mature at cones 4–6 (2174–2246° F.). Professional potters may use materials with a much higher firing range, but they are not necessary for mosaic materials.

Detailed instruction about clay processes must of necessity be kept brief and limited to those which are applicable to mosaics. The basic information in this chapter will prepare you for the projects in Chapter 12. But it is assumed that readers who have had no experience at all with clay will supplement these sections with classes or books which treat the subject in depth.

Clay may be purchased dry and mixed with water to the consistency which fits your needs. It will be more responsive and less inclined to crumble if it is set aside in a warm place to age for several weeks before being used. When it has acquired the full, ripe odor of an oyster bed at low tide, it will be very good indeed!

Where only small amounts of clay are needed, it is simpler to buy it already prepared in a plastic or liquid state. Plastic clay is used for modeling and can be kept in working condition by wrapping it in damp towels and storing it in a covered crock, old refrigerator, or plastic bag.

Liquid clay (called slip) is used for casting in molds and can be stored in any rustproof container with a tight lid. Mosaic materials can be made from both kinds.

FIRING

Clay must be thoroughly dry before firing. Even then, a certain amount of moisture will remain. At the beginning of both bisque and glaze firings, the lid of the kiln should be propped open about an inch to allow fumes and steam to escape. The heat should be built up slowly until the interior temperature is about 1000° F.[1] The lid may then be closed

and the kiln fired rapidly until the maturing temperature is reached. It should not be opened again until it is completely cold.

GLAZING

A glaze is a thin skin of glass on a clay form. It may be applied with a soft brush or sponge, or by dipping or spraying. Prepared glazes will include instructions for thickness of application. Three thin brushed coats are usually recommended, except for crackles and clear glazes. These should be thinner.

For certain mosaic materials, glaze can also be mixed with clay for interesting, and sometimes unpredictable effects.

EXPERIMENTING WITH CLAY

For an investment of a few dollars in clay, one or two glazes, and a variety of underglaze colors or body stains, you can produce many, many square feet of fascinating materials. A sharp knife and a rolling pin are your essential tools. Plaster bats are handy. The fabric side of a sheet of oilcloth is a practical working surface from which clay slabs can be easily removed.

Some of the following processes have been used by potters for so long that we could call them classics. With adaptations, however, they have special application for making mosaic tesserae, and even the most ancient craft techniques reveal new dimensions when they are agitated by an inquisitive mind.

We shall start with the usual way of making tiles, and move into the unusual. Once you have begun, hundreds of other possibilities will occur to you.

---

[1] You can estimate this temperature without a pyrometer by the color of the interior of the kiln. At 1000° F. it will have a dark-red glow. Place your hand near the vent and if the heat feels dry, it is usually safe to close the lid.

Simple Glazed Clay Tiles

EXPERIMENT 1

Fig. 80. Knead and pound a lump of clay on oil-cloth to remove bubbles, then roll it into an even sheet between two boards or rulers. One-eighth-inch to ¼-inch thickness is most practical, unless you have some special requirement. Remember that clay shrinks as it dries, then further when it is fired. The thinner the sheet, the greater the chance of warping.

Place the slab between sheets of newspaper or paper towels with a light weight on top, and let it dry for several hours. Then use a large, soft brush to puddle on a layer of glaze. Make sure the clay is well coated, but do not attempt to brush it out smoothly. An irregularity of thickness will be interesting.

When the slab has completely lost its shine and is firm to the touch, it may be sliced into small pieces or strips. The latter are generally more useful, though the slab can also be left intact and broken into random shapes after firing.

Arrange the glazed pieces close together (but not touching) on a kiln shelf when dry, and fire to the maturity of the clay.

If you are not familiar with the different types of glazes which may be purchased, you will be astonished at the many effects which are possible from this one simple process. Several kinds of glazes can be spattered on one slab and allowed to drift into spills of variegated colors. (Try opaques over transparents.) Art glazes are especially beautiful. Some form starlike crystalline bursts, others pits and craters. Crackles, which are deliberately formulated to have a different coefficient of contraction from clay, form a network of fine lines as they cool. The pattern can be emphasized with a wash of India ink or other concentrated pigments.

Textured Clay

EXPERIMENT 2

While it is still soft, clay can be textured with a comb, hack-saw blade, grater, or other objects around the kitchen or workshop. Experiment with impressions from a fountain pen cap, a piece of screening, seed pod, or sharply veined leaf. When the sheet is leather hard, break it into random shapes.

We can leave red or brown clay unglazed and treat the finished mosaic with clear mat varnish or wax.

Fig. 81. A length of braided picture-hanging wire has been unraveled on the ends to make a stiff, fan-shaped brush. Drag it over the clay, scratching deeply. Slice the slab into strips and brush away loose crumbs before firing.

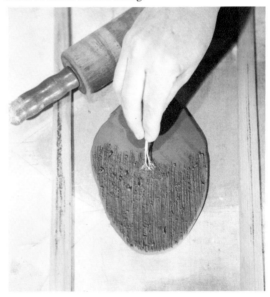

EXPERIMENT 3

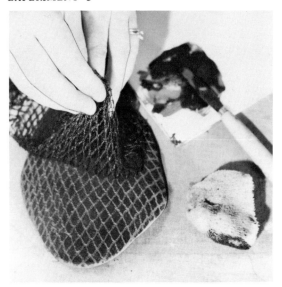

Fig. 82. Nets, laces, and open-weave fabrics can be used as stencils. Here we have rolled a coarse hairnet firmly into the clay. Dark underglaze color, diluted with water to a thin, creamy consistency, was dabbed over the net with a fine slightly moistened sponge, and the net peeled away.

EXPERIMENT 5

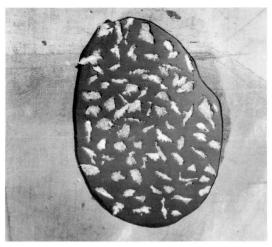

Fig. 84. Burnable materials pressed into clay will leave pits and craters after they are consumed by heat. Try a few hard cereals, rice, and sawdust. These are crumbs of Styrofoam. (Clay rolled on a sheet of Styrofoam is interesting, too.) Flood the fired slab with wood stains or oil paints diluted with turpentine. Buffing the surface with a soft cloth before it is dry ensures that a darker color will remain in the impressions.

EXPERIMENT 4

Fig. 83. The texture of these tiles came from an imprint of a plastic doily. Two coats of clear mat glaze were brushed on when the slab was leather hard. It was sliced into small irregular pieces to break up the rigid pattern.

EXPERIMENT 6

Fig. 85. Save used coffee grounds and dry them on paper towels. Sprinkle liberally over the clay and roll with enough pressure to create ripples around the embedments.

Fig. 86. Slice into strips when the slab is firm, shake off loose crumbs, and fire.

EXPERIMENT 7

If we glazed the fired pitted strips described in Experiments 5 and 6, the glaze would flow into the impressions and form deeper pools of color than would remain on the rest of the surface. This is interesting in its own way, but a different effect can be obtained by mixing glaze with the texturing material.

As a start, try moistening 2 measures of coffee grounds with 1 measure of prepared glaze and rolling the mixture into the clay. Increase or decrease the proportion of glaze as preferred.

Fig. 87. The fired fragments at the bottom were made by Experiment 6. The upper dark, glossy fragments were made by Experiment 7.

EXPERIMENT 8

Make a plaster bat, using a large cake pan as a mold (see Chapter 15). As soon as it has set, inscribe the surface deeply with a sharp tool. Work for free all-over "doodle" patterns—scrolls, pinwheels, cross-hatches, etc. When the bat is dry, clean away loose flakes of plaster and roll a clay slab into the carving. The imprint will be transferred in reverse to the clay, which can then be sliced into strips or cut into individual tesserae.

Surface Additives

EXPERIMENT 9

Some non-flammable materials, such as metallic sands, fine gravel, and crushed glass, are effective when pressed into clay. Make sample slabs before attempting to produce large quantities, because if aggregates are quite large, the clay may crack as it shrinks around them.

On dark clay, opaque glass is more striking than transparent. Both will show up well on a white body.

EXPERIMENT 10

Sift bronzing powder (which is mixed with varnish to make gold paint) *very* lightly over a coat of wet glaze, and fire. The powder will form bright green speckles.

EXPERIMENT 11

Try iron filings on light-colored opaque glaze by the same method as used for bronzing powder, described in Experiment 10. Then for exterior mosaics, make some tesserae with iron filings rolled into the surface of a clay slab. They will continue to oxidize with exposure to weather.

EXPERIMENT 12

Make a clay slab and trim the edges, then peel it away from the oilcloth. Sprinkle a fairly heavy layer of mica (used for Christmas decorations) on the oilcloth and replace the clay slab over it. Roll firmly until the flecks of mica are embedded.

Glaze will spoil the effect. Instead, after bisque-firing, rub a colored stain into the clay and buff the mica clean with a soft cloth. This will produce rich, terrazzo-like tesserae that are handsome for functional surfaces as well as decorations.

EXPERIMENT 13

Fig. 88. Roll pellets of clay between the fingers to make balls ranging in size from a large pea to a small marble. Spread thin slip on a tile or saucer, and sprinkle a layer of mica beside it. Flatten the clay slightly, dip into slip, then into mica.

Fig. 89. Press lightly against a plaster bat to remove excess slip, then turn right side up to dry. Loose mica can be brushed away after firing. Try white clay tinted with turquoise, blue, or green body stains, and spray the finished tesserae with wax or satin-finish varnish.

EXPERIMENT 14

Other materials can be formed from clay pellets. Prepare a good number and keep them moist under a damp cloth. Then, one at the time, cup them in your palm with the forefinger, and release them on a kiln shelf with a flick of your thumb.

The fragment will be shaped like a tiny clam shell. Either the convex or concave side can be used face up. Try setting them into mastic or cement at an angle so that one overlaps another like the scales of a fish.

Slip-trailed Tesserae

EXPERIMENT 15

So far, we have been working with moist clay. Now let us see what we can do with slip. We must use a plaster bat instead of oilcloth for these experiments, so that excess water will be absorbed.

Fig. 90. On a dry bat, trickle thick slip in a circular "doodle" pattern. Wait a few minutes until the slip has lost its shine, and repeat. After another short wait, build up the slip to between ⅛- and ¼-inch thick. When it is dry enough to slip easily from the bat, turn it over. The slab will have a delicate tracery of indented lines, which may be accentuated by a wash of underglaze color.

EXPERIMENT 16

Fig. 91. The preceding experiment can be altered slightly for other effects. This time, trickle the slip in about four layers, criss-crossing them from side to side without allowing the trails to flow into a solid slab. Leave a few interesting apertures. Both sides can be used. The top resembles melting snow, or eroded rock.

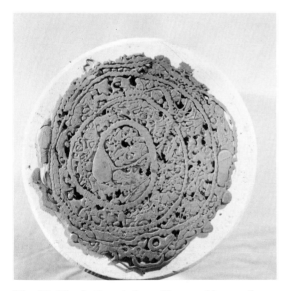

Fig. 92. The bottom is lacy. Try crackles on these, or pale transparent colors. You might like to add body stains to part of the slip, and weave contrasting threads of color into the pattern. Slice before firing or break into random shapes.

Marbleized Tesserae

EXPERIMENT 17

Mix body stains with white slip to make two different colors. (Dry stains will blend more evenly if they are first moistened with water.) One tablespoon of stain to 1 cup of slip can be used for a test slab, and more color added if this is not deep enough.

Fig. 93. Moisten a bat so that the slip will remain liquid for a longer period of time, and pour the colors in alternating stripes. Drag a pointed stick or the tines of a fork across the stripes to marbleize them. Try zigzag trails or circular swirls . . .

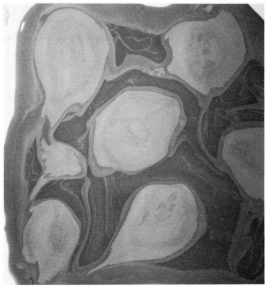

Fig. 94. . . . then pour one color into little puddles and surround them with another. These sheets will probably be fairly thin, and are best dried overnight between two bats. Finish with a clear glaze.

EXPERIMENTAL MOSAIC MATERIALS.

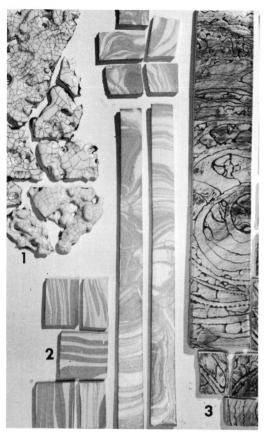

Fig. 95

1. Experiment 16. The slab was glazed with white crackle and broken into fragments before firing. India ink brought out the network of lines.
2. Experiment 17. Marbleized slabs were sliced before firing, then cut into tiles with nippers.
3. Experiment 15. Rust underglaze color was brushed over the slab, then wiped lightly with a sponge. It was finished with clear mat glaze and sliced before firing.

Poor Man's Porcelain

EXPERIMENT 18

A porcelain substitute can be made in a low-fire kiln with mixtures of glaze and slip. It is impossible to provide an accurate recipe, since results will depend on the amount of water in each material.

Use teaspoon measurements to make small test patties, starting with 1 teaspoon each of prepared slip and clear glaze and progressing to 1 teaspoon of glaze to 4 of slip. Pour the tests on a plaster bat to dry, and scratch a number on each as a reference for your notes.

The best mix will be that which produces a hard, vitreous material with a satiny finish. It will be waterproof without glazing.

Try adding body stains for pastel colors, and texture the surface by some of the methods already described.

Cellular Fragments

EXPERIMENT 19

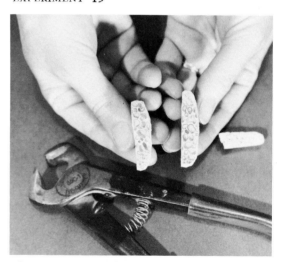

Fig. 96. FOAMED CLAY. At 2000° F., a thin patty of low-fire clay and opaque chartreuse glaze mixed in equal volumes puffed up to a thickness of ½ inch. It resembles a kind of cookie, and will float in water. The honeycomb structure is caused by expanding gases in the glaze. These make fascinating tesserae when they are nipped into small pieces and set on edge to expose the cellular formations.

EXPERIMENT 20

Tear a natural sponge into small fragments and soak them in the clay and glaze mixture. Squeeze lightly, leaving the cells saturated, and place on a plaster bat to dry. Spray *very* thinly with clear gloss or mat glaze before firing on a shelf that is well protected with kiln wash.

The sponge will burn away, leaving odd, coral-like formations which may be combined with pebbles, shells, bits of bone, or other found materials.

If you have a high-fire kiln, use real porcelain or stoneware for this experiment.

Lustered Tiles

EXPERIMENT 21

We can obtain many beautiful effects with overglazes. As the term implies, they are applied on top of fired glaze, and the piece is fired again to a much lower temperature.

China paints, lusters, and metallics are in this category. Let us try lusters first, applied over gloss glazes. Although they can also be used on mats for a subdued effect, it is generally too subtle for mosaic materials.

Moisture and dust are enemies of good luster work, as are brushes which are contaminated with other materials. A special brush should be reserved and labeled for each color. Keep them clean by washing in turpentine or alcohol, then soap and water. Make sure they are dry before using again.

Mother-of-pearl is the most popular luster. Apply a thin coat to the glazed clay and let it get tacky. Then, with a freshly moistened brush, go back over the surface with a light swirling motion. Do not apply enough pressure to drag the luster into thick ridges, or it may flake after firing.

When the luster is dry, fire it to 1000° F. with the kiln lid propped open about an inch to allow the fumes to escape. Close the lid and continue firing to cone 020–019. The tiles will have the iridescent gleam of the inside of a seashell.

EXPERIMENT 22

Deep luminous platings can be obtained with overlays of different colors of luster. Each must be fired before applying the next. A white background is best, such as a glossy transparent glaze over a white body.

Fire as described in Experiment 21.[2]

[2] Lacking a pyrometer, watch the luster during the early period of firing. The burning oils will turn black. When they have burned away and the luster shows true color, you can close the lid.

Metallic Overglazes

EXPERIMENT 23

Liquid silver, copper, or gold overglazes will be bright on glossy glazes, dull on mats. Apply them evenly with a soft brush and fire as lusters. For spectacular effects, try colored lusters over fired gold. Mother-of-pearl will produce tints of rose, purple, and blue. Applied over fired copper, it will pick up deep green and bronzy sparks.

EXPERIMENT 24

Over a glossy colored glaze, paint a coat of liquid bright gold and deliberately overfire it to cone 012–014. At this temperature, the glaze will begin to flow slightly, carrying flakes of gold along with it. The surface will be broken up' into a webbed pattern of dulled gold, with little rivulets of colored glaze running through it. Brown, orange, red, and black glazes are stunning under gold. Try liquid platinum on cool greens, blues, and turquoise.

EXPERIMENT 25

Marbleizing liquid is applied over *unfired* metallic overglazes to cause them to separate into delicate veins not unlike the texture of leaf skeletons. The pattern will vary with the thickness of application. The gold should be dry, and the marbleizing liquid brushed on quickly without disturbing the undercoat. Let it dry overnight before firing to cone 020–019.

Egyptian Paste

Mention must be made here of a material which falls somewhere between clay and glass. It has the same deep, brilliant blue color characteristic of the paste used by ancient Egyptian craftsmen for beads and trinkets, and can be shaped into pellets, or pressed against textured plaster slabs for mosaic tesserae.[3, 4]

We have had but a small glimpse into the fascinating world of clay, but we must move on now into another.

[3] Charles F. Binns, Myrtle Klem, and Hazel Mott, "An Experiment in Egyptian Blue Glaze," BULLETIN OF THE AMERICAN CERAMIC SOCIETY (4055 North High Street, Columbus, Ohio), May, 1932.
[4] Helen Young, "Egyptian Paste Jewelry," CERAMICS MONTHLY (4175 North High Street, Columbus, Ohio), January, 1962.

chapter 8.

Decorative Materials to Make from Glass

Chemically speaking, glass is a liquid, though we usually think of it in the form of a hard, brittle substance. As opposed to clay, which loses malleability when it is subjected to heat, glass becomes pliable when it is fired to a temperature high enough to lower its viscosity, or density.

This characteristic greatly expands our scope in the area of glass mosaics. It means that such finished products as smalti, stained glass, bottles, etc., can also be considered thermoplastic materials to be changed and re-shaped for special functions and effects.

It is hard to decide which aspects of mosaic glass can be adequately presented in a limited space. The area of making materials is not difficult, however, once you accept the unreasonableness of trying to force glass to do something contrary to its nature.

COMPATIBILITY OF GLASS

It is natural to assume that "glass is glass" and that all kinds can be treated and fired alike. Actually, glass families have as many distinctive qualities as people families. But technical differences concern us here in only one respect: *reaction to heat.*

There are dozens of kinds of glass around every home—beverage and food containers, windows, medicine bottles, cosmetic jars, dishes, vases, art objects, planters, shelves, canisters, cooking utensils, light bulbs—and each has been formulated to serve a particular purpose. The ability of two different kinds of glass to fuse smoothly together without cracking is called compatibility. It has the same connotation as when applied to human personalities. In other words, a type of glass is like an individual who behaves agreeably with others of similar nature, but becomes an element of disharmony with those he does not "fit." The disagreement of two kinds of unlike glass can be quite violent when they are subjected to heat.

Glass expands as it heats and contracts as it cools. The rate of contraction and expansion will vary with different glasses, and if we attempt to fuse them into a single unit, inner strains may be set up which can cause fracturing.

These strains can exist regardless of the

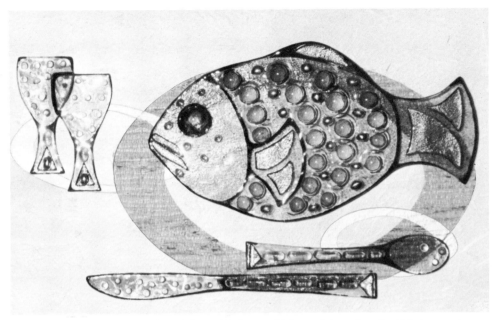

Fig. 97. This panel is designed for a kitchen, which explains why the fish has such an unhappy expression. The background is a collage of rice paper and grass cloth. Cathedral glass motifs are patterned with melted glass chips, marbles, and cut-outs backed with metallic overglaze. Some fragments are fused to the subsurface of the glass, some to the top. The fish is mounted out on ½-inch pegs. Other elements are attached with epoxy.

size of the pieces of glass, though naturally, size will have a bearing on the degree of damage. A small incompatible attachment on a large sheet may exert only enough tension to create a thin, hairline craze around the point of contact. Large laminations of the same materials may split completely apart.

If we reduced these two glasses to granules, mixed them together, and melted them, each tiny particle would retain its chemically established nature. As the molten batch cooled, it would craze, shatter, or crawl into puddles. This reaction would be disastrous if we were trying to make textured panes, but sometimes it produces odd shapes we can use in other ways.

According to its reaction to heat, we can classify glass as soft, medium, and hard, soft glass having the lowest melting point on the scale. Nearly all glass which melts at the same temperature will be compatible, but there is only one way to be absolutely sure. Obviously, this is to fire several scraps together and evaluate the results.

FIRING GLASS

In the last chapter we applied the term maturity to the temperature at which clay reaches its ideal state of *hardness* and glaze becomes completely fused. If the term were appropriate for fused glass, it would mean the temperature at which the material reached its ideal state of *softness*.

But we cannot actually establish a single perfect firing temperature for any glass, because it will change according to the *degree* of softness which produces a particular *effect*.

If we were sagging glass into a mold to create a form, the ideal temperature would be that at which the glass assumed the shape of the mold, had smoothly rounded edges, was clear and sparkling, and had picked up no encrustation of the separator.

But if we were rounding scrap fragments into jewel-like tesserae, a greater softness would be required; therefore, more heat. It would take an even higher temperature to melt several layers of broken pieces into a solid slab.

Fig. 98. Compatibility tests not only indicate whether or not two kinds of glass can be successfully fused together, but often have design possibilities also. These resemble Oriental calligraphy, flying birds, and leaves.

For these reasons, with every new kind of glass or project, we must depend on eyesight, rather than mechanical devices, to tell us when to terminate the firing.

Cones are of little value in glass firing, except as a warning that a certain temperature has been reached. A pyrometer is very useful and well worth its cost. By keeping careful records of the physical appearance of the glass at different temperatures, we can eventually draw up a firing scale as it relates to special needs.

When glass begins to soften, it becomes sticky, much as a batch of rock candy. We must, therefore, protect the surface on which it is fired or the two will be permanently attached.

Several materials may be used as glass separators. Ordinary kiln wash will be suitable if a white encrustation on the subsurface is not objectionable. For example, where glass is embedded in dark mortar, it reflects, rather than transmits, light, and a bright backing is necessary. In such situations, the kiln wash which sticks to the bottoms of melted transparent tesserae will save having to undercoat them with white paint or a metallic plating.

The glass for transparent mosaics (windows, screens, mobiles, etc.) must remain clear

Fig. 99. Odds and ends of leftover glass should be saved in separate, labeled containers. The chips can be fired into rounded nuggets, and the large pieces into domed, irregular shapes.

"Duck," by Roger Gadow, was assembled from such materials and attached to a backing of tinted Masonite. Spaces between sections of glass were packed with cullet.

and unobscured. The classic separator for such purposes is whiting,[1] though some craftsmen prefer alumina hydrate or feldspar. Use a fine tea-strainer to distribute the separator evenly over kiln shelves or shallow molds.

Sloping surfaces, such as the sides of deep bowl molds, make sifting impractical, and separators should be used in wet solutions.

A good brush-on separator for medium to hard glass can be made by increasing the flint content of kiln wash to 4 or 5 parts flint to 1 part EPK china clay. There are, also, excellent commercial products which harden to a smooth, dustless film and do not have to be replaced after each firing.

Glass will pick up a film of any separator if it is fired to a completely molten state.

There is no great mystery to the technique of firing glass, though basic instructions may have to be altered for special situations. We shall review a few variations later in relation to certain projects and experiments, but the simple steps outlined below will suffice in most cases.

These directions apply specifically to an average ceramic kiln with a firing chamber approximately 11 × 11 × 11 inches, and a control mechanism for regulating the heat. (Adjustments may be necessary for kilns of other dimensions.) They differ very little from those for firing clay. With both materials, the larger and thicker the ware, the slower the firing and cooling must be.

1. Prepare kiln shelves or molds with a coat of glass separator. Only a thin layer is needed. (If wet separators are used, allow shelves or molds to become completely dry before firing.)

2. Arrange glass fragments, cut-outs, or blanks. Large pieces should not be closer than 1½ inches to kiln elements. Unless fusion is desired, fragments should not be touching.

3. Prop kiln lid open about an inch and remove plug. Turn on low heat for about an hour.

4. Turn heat to medium for an hour.

5. Turn heat on high. When temperature has reached 1000° F., or interior chamber is dull red, replace plug and close lid.

6. From time to time, peek inside to observe the progress of the glass. When it has reached the desired state of viscosity, turn heat off and immediately prop the lid open again for fifteen minutes. This will permit the escape of latent heat which would cause the melting process to continue past the ideal stage.

7. Close lid and do not open until kiln is cold.

These steps are adequate when the firing temperature is not critical or when only small fragments are being melted. For thick slabs, laminations, or sagged shapes, an additional heat-soaking step will lessen the chance of fractures.

After step 6, close the lid and turn on low or medium heat for fifteen to twenty minutes. Then turn heat off and cool.

This is a way of tempering or annealing glass to reduce the shock of too rapid contraction.

Fig. 100. The large ceramic ash tray form was heavily textured with a piece of hack-saw blade before firing. It was finished with ebony wood-stain, and the inside mosaicked with Venetian glass and melted nuggets of colored bottles.

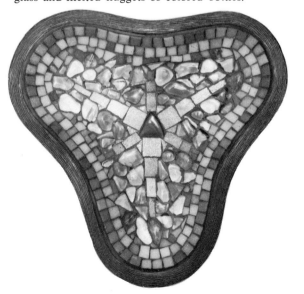

[1] Calcium carbonate, available in hardware stores and ceramic supply houses.

EXPERIMENTING WITH GLASS

Complete instructions for cutting and firing glass will not be repeated for the experiments which follow.[2] Remember that a separator must always be used between glass and the support on which it is fired.

Sliced Bottles

Containers for food and beverages are made of some of the best commercial glass being produced in the United States. This is a readily available and expendable material and therefore excellent for experiments. While the color range is limited, there are a number of greens, browns, and ambers in the most common bottles, as well as the beautiful deep cobalt which is used primarily for cosmetic jars and medicine bottles.

Remove labels from bottles and thoroughly clean away any residue of adhesive before using them for mosaic materials.

EXPERIMENT 1

We can salvage small panes from bottles by removing the necks and bottoms, slicing the cylinders in half, and firing the sections to the point where they flatten on the kiln shelf. These little panes may then be cut into strips or special shapes as needed.

As described in Chapter 2, glass is cut by scoring (or weakening) it with a glass cutter, and applying pressure to the line from the opposite side. A gauge cutter or bottle slicer will simplify the problem of removing bottle necks, but we can improvise another method.

Place a strip of masking tape around the top of the bottle just above its widest curvature. Brace it on a towel or cushion of foam rubber, and, using the edge of the tape as a guide to keep the cutter from slipping, score a line completely around the bottle.

Now, we need a way to apply pressure to the inside of this line to fracture it.

Score and break away the bottom in the same way. It will be much easier to reach and can often be reached with the ball end of the regular cutting tool. (Set aside the trimmings for other materials.) Score vertically up each side of the cylinder and tap from the inside to break it in half.

[2] Instructions for cutting glass are in Chapter 2.

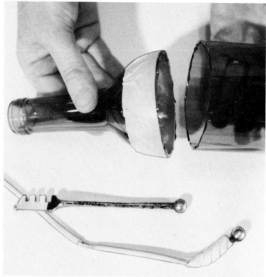

Fig. 101. Cut off the ball end of a worn-out cutter, leaving a stem about 1½ inches long. Bend a length of rigid wire or welding rod into a shape such as that shown at the bottom of the picture, then bind the ball end firmly to it with masking tape. Insert it inside the neck of the bottle and tap lightly along the scored line.

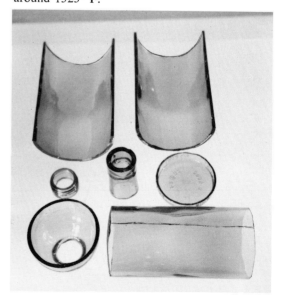

Fig. 102. These pieces are ready to be fired. Leave enough space around them on the kiln shelf so that they will not overlap when they flatten. The panes can be fired quite low—usually around 1400° F., since it is not necessary to round the edges. Necks and bottoms should be fired higher—around 1525° F.

There should be at least ½-inch margin around any shape to be cut from a glass sheet, or it will be difficult to remove. So, to cut flattened bottles (or other sheet glass) into narrow strips less than ½-inch wide, we must alter the usual procedure.

CUTTING THIN STRIPS OF GLASS.

Fig. 105. Use your regular cutter to score the glass, guiding it forward so that the pattern remains clearly visible.

Fig. 103. For strips no more than 4 or 5 inches long, score the line, then snap it away with square-jawed pliers.

Fig. 104. Long, thin strips with either straight or undulating edges can be cut with a tool designed for breaking ceramic tiles.

Fig. 106. Place the glass between the jaws of the tool so that the scored mark is exactly aligned with the small hole on top of the cutter and the wedge-shaped bottom plunger. Squeeze handles together . . .

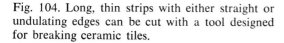

Fig. 107. . . . and the strip will fracture cleanly.

EXPERIMENT 3

Rings can be cut from bottles by the method described in Experiment 1. They will seldom be exactly even, but irregular widths make interesting conformations when they melt. With a bottle slicer, you can cut fairly uniform rings. It takes a little practice, for this is a delightful gadget, not a precision instrument.

Refer to the description in Chapter 2 for cutting bottles into random slices. The best method for obtaining even rings involves a few extra steps.

Sometimes round bottles will break clean the first time. Square and bulbous shapes are harder to control. Remove residue of masking tape with a razor blade and then acetone (or cleaning fluid), before it sets up.

Once the bottom is off you can continue slicing the bottle up to the point where it narrows into the neck. Turn it upside down then, and remove as many small rings as you can. The sharply curved areas are best saved for other purposes.

CUTTING EVEN RINGS

Fig. 108. Mark a cutline around the bottle about an inch from the bottom, and place a strip of masking tape just below it. Use the masking tape as a guide and score around the bottle. Place squares of wood, metal, or asbestos under the Nichrome loop as needed to bring the scored line up to the same level. Set the bottle inside the loop and pull it taut.

Fig. 109. Turn on the heat and draw the bottle outward to keep the wire on the score as it stretches. (The masking tape may smoke or sizzle, but it will not cause a conflagration.) Turn off the heat and wait a few moments until the glass fractures from the abrupt change of temperature. Turn the bottle so that its point of contact with the wire is slightly past the fracture. Repeat the heating and cooling treatment until it breaks all around.

Fig. 110. Bottles are thicker in some parts than in others, so rings will have varying degrees of sag at the same temperature. Thicker segments can be fired in the hottest areas of the kiln to equalize the difference in part, though in most cases they should be fired separately. These were fired to 1525° F. Chapters 15 and 20 have ideas for using them in mosaics.

Fig. 111. Unfired bottle rings are useful, too. Sharp edges can be polished with an emery-tipped electric grinder or carborundum stone, or they can be bound with lead (see Chapter 24). This is a test block for the perforated insert for a garden wall outlined in Chapter 20. The insert will be made of colored rings 1½ inches thick, ranging in diameter from 1 inch to 3½ inches. The encircling mosaic patterns will include melted bottle nuggets as well as pebbles.

Stretched Rings

EXPERIMENT 4

Bottle rings can be hung from a support so that as they soften with heat, they will stretch and droop downward into ovals and teardrops. Several kinds of supports can be devised, and you will think of a number of possibilities as you work. The terra cotta "bookends" explained below can be made for practically no cost, from materials you probably have on hand from the experiments in the preceding chapter.

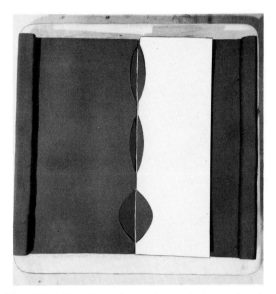

Fig. 113. Trim the slabs meticulously by a triangle and ruler so that they exactly match. Make a cardboard template for scallops or grooves to hold the horizontal rods. Cut the top (thin) edges by the template.

Fig. 112. Wedge a large lump of heavily grogged clay and roll it into a tapered slab between two boards, one of which is 1 inch thick, the other ¼ inch thick. Trim the thick side by a straight edge, and replace it against the guideboard. Roll again before trimming the other three sides into a rectangle which will fit your kiln shelf. 7½ × 4½ inches will accommodate small and medium-sized rings.

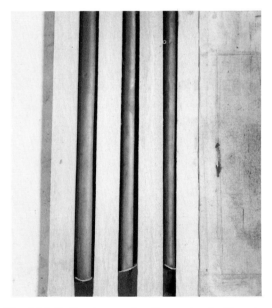

Fig. 114. Roll out several coils ranging in diameter from ¼ to 1 inch thick and not more than 10 inches long. (Longer coils may break under the weight of the glass.) Make them as smooth and even as possible, then arrange them between strips of wood to dry straight.

Sand the bottoms of the slabs so that they stand level, and polish the coils with a damp sponge. Bisque slowly to the maturity of the clay.

Wait until the clay has stiffened a bit before transferring it to a plaster bat. Then roughen a narrow margin along the thick edge, paint it with slip, and attach a coil about ½ inch in diameter. This will provide a footing to keep the slab from tilting.

Press a wood block or board firmly against the bottom to make sure it is straight.

Prepare two of these slabs and let them get almost leather hard.

Fig. 115. Coat rods and inside walls of the slabs with separator, and string bottle rings about ½ inch apart. Experiment with rings of different sizes, some of which may be large enough to touch the kiln shelf.

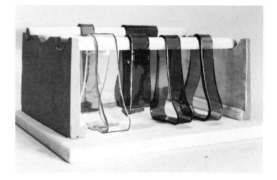

Fig. 116. The rings will begin to stretch by 1200° F. and must be watched closely from that point. You may like them just slightly sagged into ovals. These were fired at 1325° F. Notice that the bottom areas have flattened on the shelf. With prolonged heat, they would eventually pull away from the support and drape beneath it. (Some of these accidental forms are interesting.) Try placing straight glass strips across three rods for scalloped ribbons.

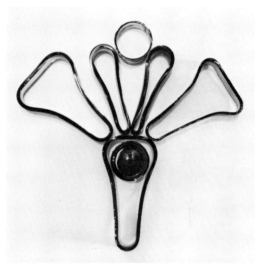

Fig. 117. When you have a number of "drooped loops," experiment with arrangements. Perhaps they will suggest a transparent grill to place behind a favorite stoneware pot, perhaps an arabesque to hang at an entryway. Lead the edges and solder them together if you like. You can combine them with rings and bottoms and mosaic the cells, or fill them with resin and colored cullet.

Fig. 118. Stretched loops of the same thickness can break the monotony of round eyelets in a screen or perforated wall.

Faceted Eyelets

EXPERIMENT 5

Heat several thick bottle bottoms in a kitchen oven set at 450° F., then drop them into a pan of ice water. Wrap the fractured pieces in a heavy cloth, lay them on a concrete floor, and tap them with a hammer.

The glass chunks can be used just as they are, or fired to any degree of roundness.[3]

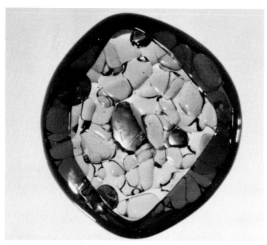

Fig. 119. On a kiln shelf, arrange overlapping pieces of coarse cullet (fired or unfired) inside a bottle ring. Fire to about 1525° F., until the cullet has rounded and the ring edges have folded over to form a fused binding. Several rings can be placed close together and fired into units for filigree wall decorations or room dividers.

This is a brown ring enclosing chartreuse, pale amber, and antique gold nuggets.

EXPERIMENT 6

For thick faceted eyelets, fill a bottle bottom with cullet of all sizes. Fire to 1525–1550° F., and temper. Bottles with flaring sides are not suitable. They will usually sag outward, leaving the mass of cullet in the middle. Look for forms which cup or slant inward.

EXPERIMENT 7

Unfired faceted eyelets can be made by using a bottle ring as a mold for embedding glass chunks in resin (see Chapter 13). Coat the inside of the glass with mold release, place it on a sheet of mylar or acetate, and seal the bottom edge with a coil of plasteline. Fill with coarse cullet, then pour in catalyzed resin to a depth which leaves the top surfaces slightly elevated.

[3] As already mentioned, marbles and melted nuggets can be crackled in this manner.

Peel away the mylar when the resin is hard and trim any excess from the bottom. Let it cure for several days before removing from the mold.

Pebbled Panes

EXPERIMENT 8

Fig. 120. Saw soft firebrick into strips an inch thick (or make them from clay) to serve as a frame. Coat the inside and bottom edges of the strips with separator and arrange on a kiln shelf. Fill with fine cullet to a level of ¼ to ½ inch. Tamp down firmly and fire until it becomes nearly molten, but texture remains.

Narrow strips and rectangles can be made as easily as squares, and crushed sheet or bottle glass used instead of the commercial cullet shown here. It is best to nip the fused panes into random shapes rather than to try to cut them into tesserae of equal size.

EXPERIMENT 9

Test window glass for compatibility with either commercial crushed glass or bottles. Coat the top side lightly with a gum solution, and sprinkle on a thin even layer of the cullet.[4] Fire just to the point where the cullet has rounded into small droplets on the surface.

[4] Mix liquid gum tragacanth with equal parts of water. A solution of CMC (a gum used in glazes) is prepared by mixing 1 tablespoon with a pint of water. A few drops of oil of cloves or formaldehyde will retard spoilage.

Coloring Glass

Unfired Color

EXPERIMENT 10

Clear scrap glass can be colored in many ways. A simple treatment which requires no special equipment is to spray one side with paint, then cut the glass into random shapes. (Always score glass on the uncoated surface.) When the pieces are set paint side down into glue or a bed of mortar, the color will be completely permanent.

Unfired glass lacquers may be used the same way, as well as glass "frost" paints.[5] But some shades are fugitive and will fade from prolonged exposure to sunlight.

Thick, textured glass, such as that used for shower doors, will refract the light and keep the undercoating from appearing flat and monotonous.

Fired Color

EXPERIMENT 11

Low-fire glazes which are completely liquid at 1400° F. (or lower) can be used to tint colorless glass. Unless you have experience with glaze formulation, commercial glass glazes are more practical than investing in bulk materials to make your own.

The student who already has a stock of ceramic supplies will enjoy experimenting with frits and colorants.[6] Although most glass craftsmen prefer transparent glazes, beautiful mosaic materials can be made with those which are semitranslucent.

Standard low-temperature colorless frits can be obtained from ceramic supply companies. Test the frit first to see if it is compatible with window glass. If it fuses smoothly, you can then try adding small proportions of the same oxides, carbonates, and glaze stains used for clay glazes. (In fact, these low-temperature glazes can also be used on matured clay.)

Start with 7 to 10 parts of frit to 1 part of colorant, reducing or increasing the proportions according to the shade desired. They can be mixed for intermediate colors, but do not mix the basic frits.

Grind the materials in a mortar and pestle, and screen through a very fine strainer. Pour the mixture into a jar and shake thoroughly.

To apply the glaze, paint a coat of gum on the surface of the glass, then sift on the dry mix. (The small sifter-containers in which copper enamels are packaged are just right for good distribution.) Use enough glaze to cover the surface evenly, but do not pile it up.

Glue a fired sample to the lid of the storage jar as a reference. If the color is good but the glaze crazes, reserve it for laminating.

Lustered Glass

EXPERIMENT 12

Lustered glass fragments have such a high degree of surface brilliance that they can dominate a composition. Used with discretion, they can be striking.

Either ceramic lusters or special glass lusters are suitable. Pale ceramic lusters, such as mother-of-pearl, opal, light yellow, ivory, etc., are usually too delicate to show up on clear glass.

Apply and fire lusters on glass fragments following the directions for clay in the last chapter.

Bubbled Tesserae

EXPERIMENT 13

Smooth a sheet of thin aluminum foil on a prepared shelf and arrange scraps of clear glass on it. Fire until the edges have rounded. The foil will melt and oxidize, forming on the subsurface a rind of tiny bubbles which range from pale silvery gray to dark gunmetal. Peel away the excess margins of foil.

EXPERIMENT 14

Bubbles can be formed by trapping air or other gases between fused layers of glass. Although we cannot completely control the size and spacing of these bubbles, they are always interesting.

It is best to fuse strips or large sheets together first, then cut them into small pieces. They can be fired again for rounded lumps without losing the bubbles.

For an experiment with lamination, fuse together two sheets of heavily textured glass with rough sides facing. Bubbles will form where air is locked in the crevices. Sheets with a pattern of parallel ridges should be arranged so that the grooves face and cross each other. A regular formation of bubbles will be created in the depressed square between the raised lines.

---

[5] See Chapter 3.

[6] A few test recipes are given in the Appendix.

Fig. 121. Sections of the butterflies were cut from flattened bottle panes and "patches" laminated over the joints for reinforcement. Decorative elements are bubbled tesserae and melted scraps, some with reflective backings.

EXPERIMENT 15

Paint or sift a coat of glass glaze on the top side of a sheet of window glass and cover it with a plain sheet. As the glaze expands with heat, it will form colored bubbles of different sizes.

EXPERIMENT 16

Sprinkle flakes of Christmas mica (such as that used for clay experiments in Chapter 7) between sheets of glass. Most of the flakes will form bubbles as they swell with heat. Others will remain as silvery flecks.

EXPERIMENT 17

Transparent copper enamels will usually craze, even flake, when fired to the surface of glass, but they can be laminated for delicately seeded colors. Apply a coat of gum to the glass and sift on enough enamel for a good coverage. Cover with another piece of glass and fire.

Textured Tesserae

EXPERIMENT 18

When glass is fired until it becomes soft, it will retain the imprint of the surface on which it rests. This enables us to texture the underside of mosaic materials for a livelier refraction of light.

Sift a layer of whiting on a kiln shelf, then pattern it by combing, finger-printing, or pressing it with a coarse screen. Arrange bits of double-strength window glass on the whiting and fire until they have completely rounded.

They will have the quality of fine crystal, and will pick up colored reflections when attached to a tinted or metallic background.

Try a similar experiment with wet separator. This time, brush one thin coat on the shelf, then spatter, trickle, or stipple a thicker application on top of it.

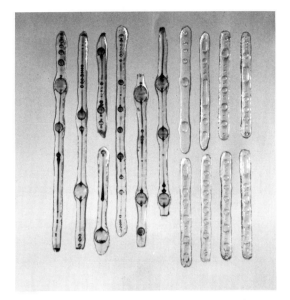

Fig. 122. Drip glass glaze into lengths of glass tubing with an eyedropper. Dry for forty-eight hours, then use a pipe cleaner to clean out about an inch at each end. Protect the kiln shelf with a very heavy coating of separator, for the expanding glaze may spit. Bubbled rods at the left are turquoise. The shorter lengths at the right are yellow. Both were fired to 1475° F., though the bubbled patterns are different. The deformity of the casings is partly due to the bubbles, and partly to coarsely sifted whiting on the kiln shelf.

EXPERIMENT 19

Special shelves can be made for more controlled textural patterns. Roll out slabs of grogged clay about ½ inch thick and cut to fit your kiln. Try some of the suggestions for clay textures described in Chapter 7, but avoid deep gouges, which may form undercuts and crack the glass. Cross-hatches, dots, scribbled lines, and parallel dashes made with a blunt tool are best.

Fire the clay to maturity. Unless the slab is quite large and must support considerable weight, it can be used in place of the regular kiln shelf. Apply glass separator carefully so it does not fill up the indentations.

EXPERIMENT 20

Certain kinds of inexpensive mirrors will become satiny with a silvery iridescence when they are fired coated side up to about 1000° F. At this low temperature, the metallic backing burns to a fine ash which can be brushed off. Since manufacturers use different materials for the reflective layer, test a few small pieces before firing a quantity. You may prefer the mirror just as it is. Some copper-backed mirrors, for example, merely turn an uninteresting yellow-green.

EXPERIMENT 21

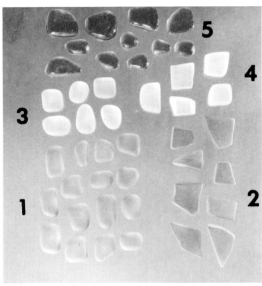

Fig. 123. Glass scraps can be satinized by rotating them in a lapidary tumbler for about twenty-four hours in medium grit and water. (Fine sand and water will take longer.) For tesserae with flat backs and completely rounded edges, kiln-fire the scraps first.

Flashed glass is unsuitable, since the thin layer of color would be ground off.
1. Frosted, fired green bottle glass.
2. Frosted, unfired green bottle glass.
3. Frosted, fired clear window glass.
4. Frosted, unfired clear window glass.
5. Fired green bottle glass, unfrosted.

Nuggets and Rounded Chips

EXPERIMENT 22

Cathedral glass of the type made by Blenko and Kokomo soften at a much lower temperature than bottle glass, though some of the imported stained glass is surprisingly hard. Small nuggets of different kinds of cathedral glass will have varying degrees of roundness when fired in the same kiln. The soft glass may become domed by the time the edges on the harder glass have barely blunted.

Generally, melted chips are more useful if some irregularity of shape remains. (No annealing is necessary for these materials.)

Some soft glass has a tendency to acquire a scummy skin when it is fired. (This can be determined only by tests.) A thin film of low-fire flux or colorless glass glaze will usually eliminate the problem. It is tedious where a large number of small pieces are involved, but the clarity it ensures is worth the trouble.

Fig. 124. Scraps of cathedral glass (or other sheet glass) can be quickly cut into small tesserae by scoring criss-crossing lines about ½ inch apart. Turn the glass over and tap along the scores to separate the chips.

Fig. 125. At 1450–1475° F., bottle chips will have rounded edges, but retain angular shapes which are easy to fit closely together. These were attached to a cork backing for a distinctive texture behind the lighter colors.

EXPERIMENT 23

Save leftover crumbs of smalti to make tiny cabochons for miniatures, jewelry, or small patterns. They are very soft and will be round at 1350–1375° F. Many colors of smalti are compatible with soft cathedral glass and form brilliant notes of contrast against a transparent base.

Taillight Jewels

Automobile taillights deserve special and separate experimentation from other scrap glass, for their reaction to heat can be unique. Although plastic has replaced glass on the newer cars, the old light covers can still be found in automobile "graveyards" and outlets for junked parts.

Most taillights are soft. To appreciate fully the range of materials which can be made from them, we shall run three tests on small batches, with the understanding that the products you find may differ from those tested in our workshop.

EXPERIMENT 24

Crack the lights as described in Experiment 5, and arrange the broken fragments on a kiln shelf. Fire only until the edges are blunted. Generally, the faceted chunks will be clear, deep, transparent red.

EXPERIMENT 25

Fire another batch about 50° higher, or until the sharp edges have rounded. Interesting variations will now begin to appear, depending on the particular glass formula and the position of the bits in the kiln.

Some pieces will be opaque, and some transparent. We have obtained beautiful examples which are semitranslucent with inner sparks as vivid as a fire opal. Colors will range from a brilliant vermilion to bright orange.

We can speculate on the reasons for these differences. Study a broken fragment against the light and you will notice layers of yellow as well as red. When the scraps are fractured, some chunks will have more of one color than another. In addition, the glass is extremely sensitive to heat, and no kiln maintains precisely the same temperature all over. Areas in front of the peep hole, for instance, will be cooler than those in a back corner. Shelves on different levels will be hotter or cooler according to the circulation of heat and the location of the elements.

These are logical causes for variety in the fired materials.

EXPERIMENT 26

Now fire the taillight fragments until they melt into half-spheres. According to our tests, all the tesserae will be opaque. Colors will range from a warm canary yellow to lemony shades to an incredible avocado green. The green tones are less common and we have been unable to determine whether they result from a particular glass, or a particular kiln atmosphere.

Antique Metallic Effects

Many better-quality mirrors have a protective coppery coating over the plating of quicksilver. By removing thin layers of these two materials to expose different metallic colors, we can make tesserae with the rich patina of old brocades.

EXPERIMENT 27

Fig. 126. Pour a small amount of water-soluble paint remover into a paper cup and pinch a spout in the rim. Trail a thin trickle of solvent over the back of the mirror and, when the plating begins to soften, immediately run water over it. Scrub with a stiff brush, and bright runnels of copper will appear.

Repeat the process several times. Where the trails go over pretreated areas, the copper will be removed and silver exposed. If the pattern is too sharp, dab it with a solvent-saturated sponge.

The slab on the left is mostly antique silver. On the right, less solvent was used to retain more copper.

EXPERIMENT 28

Coat the top sides of small bottle scraps with liquid gold or silver overglaze. Fire high, until they are domed. The plating will be dulled and slightly webbed, much as the glaze effect in Experiment 24, Chapter 7. Try silver on greens and blues, gold on browns and ambers.

EXPERIMENT 29

Glass gold can be marbleized in the same manner as in clay Experiment 25. For something different, drip a few drops of gold on the surface of a shallow pan filled with water. Shake the pan slightly to set the gold in motion. Lower a piece of glass flat against the water and lift straight up. The swirled deposit will be almost invisible before it is fired, but do not be tempted to recoat it. The effect should be delicate—bright in heavy streaks and iridescent violet where it is thin. Air-dry the pieces and fire to 1250–1350° F.

EXPERIMENT 30

Over certain dark bottle colors, over-fired copper luster will have the subtle, satin sheen of hand-crafted metal. Apply a thin, even coat and let it dry before firing to 1500–1525° F.

EXPERIMENT 31

Fig. 127. Salvaged glass dishes often fire in an unexpected manner. The nuggets at the lower left came from a transparent brown plate with a lacy indented pattern on the back. The textured side was painted with a type of self-contracting gold, which withdrew from the raised areas into the crevices. At 1450° F., the fragments rounded and turned a surprising opaque ivory with flat gold prints where the texture had been.

Upper tesserae and those on the right were made by Experiment 28.

EXPERIMENT 32

Interesting things happen to raw chunk vermiculite when it is fired.[7] As it is mined, it
resembles a soapy rock, rather claylike. Roast
several chunks on a kiln shelf at cone 07–06
and they will swell like flaky pastry to many
times their size and turn a gold-bronzy color.

Press the flakes through a sifter until they
are pulverized. Sprinkle the dust sparsely between layers of glass, and fire. The tesserae will
have floating gold flecks similar to those in
Venetian glass.

Reflective Metallics

Colored glass tesserae with gold leaf backings may be purchased in mosaic shops, but
they are very expensive. The traditional method
of undercoating these materials is to brush on
a sizing or varnish; when it is tacky, the delicate
leaf is lifted from its protective sheath of tissue
and pressed gently against the varnish with a
soft brush. Excess leaf is then trimmed away.

EXPERIMENT 33

Japanese tea paper and thin florists' foil (gold,
copper, or silver) will have almost as much
sparkle for but a fraction of the cost of gold
leaf. Press the foil out flat, shiny side up, and
paint it with a film of transparent adhesive.[8]
Arrange small pieces of glass close together on
the coated sheet and weight them down with
books. When the glue is dry, cut around the
glass with a razor blade.

Thin aluminum foil may be used the same
way and is more reflective if it is first crumpled,
then smoothed out flat.

EXPERIMENT 34

Bright glass gold or platinum make brilliant
reflective backings. Coat large scraps of glass
evenly and fire them plated side up to about
1200° F., or until all the black smoke has
burned away. Cut or nip the scraps into small
pieces, arrange on a kiln shelf metallic side
down, and fire until rounded.

Torch-shaped Fragments

Blowing and casting are the usual methods
of manipulating glass in a molten state, but
both require equipment and training which
may be beyond the reach of the craftsmen liv-
ing in small or isolated communities. Although
understandably more limited, a portable propane torch will soften small scraps so that they
can be stretched, bent, or twisted into decorative fragments.[9]

These inexpensive torches are sold for
soldering and general repairs and have replace-
able fuel tanks. The flame is adjustable and
will reach temperatures up to 2100° F., yet
the heat is so localized that fingers may be
held two or three inches to the side of it without becoming uncomfortably warm.

Aside from the uses we might find for
torch-shaped glass materials, the work will expand your understanding of the nature of
glass far beyond that gained from observing its
reaction to heat through a crack in the kiln.

Organize your work area with the torch in
proper position. Place several self-locking
tweezers close by for handling the glass. Flint
rods can be fused to scraps for "holders," but
long strips of double-strength window glass
(about ¼ inch wide) can be substituted.

Sun glasses will protect your eyes from
the glare of the flame and the flying fragments
which might bounce away from glass which
has been heated too rapidly.

[7] Vermiculite is also used in plant mixes and as a
concrete aggregate. This may be a clue to supply
sources.

[8] See Chapter 4.

[9] See Chapter 2.

Fig. 128. "Seeds" and ribbons pulled from scraps of cathedral glass were arranged on a cathedral-glass blank and sagged into a shallow bowl mold. Colors are dark brown and green on an amber base.

Fig. 129. Turned on full force, the torch has a cone of intense heat extending about 15 inches beyond the tip of the flame. At half-force (more commonly used), the cone will range from 8 to 12 inches. This cone is the warming or annealing area. The melting area is the hottest point at the tip of the bright blue flame.

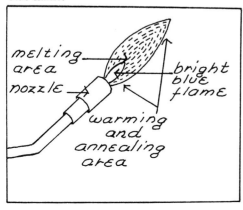

EXPERIMENT 35

Locate the heat cones before you start to work, then try a simple exercise to observe how they affect the glass.

Turn the heat to about half-force and place the end of a glass strip about 12 inches from the nozzle—just inside the large cone of faint blue light. Twirl the glass between the fingers so that it warms evenly on all sides. Gradually move it closer to the flame tip until you see it enveloped in a yellow glare.

Almost immediately the edges of the glass will glow red, then become transparent scarlet. Within a short time, it will begin to droop and round. At this stage, it can be drawn into ribbons and threads.

Time can be saved if the glass is pre-warmed in a small kiln or on the grill of a little hibachi, one of those sold for roasting hors d'oeuvres. Four or 5 lumps of charcoal will keep the glass hot for some time. The hibachi is also handy for annealing the drawn fragments.

PULLED GLASS THREADS

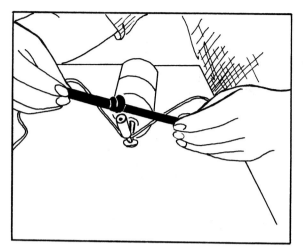

EXPERIMENT 36

Cut two narrow strips of glass 6 to 8 inches long, and grind off sharp edges or round them in the kiln. (Commercial glass rods are easier to handle, but are expensive for experimental work.)

Adjust the flame to half-force and warm the tip of one strip. Twirling it constantly, move it into the melting area and at the same time warm the tip of the other strip. (If the glass fractures, you have heated it too suddenly.)

Fig. 130. As the ends of the strips become molten, bring them together and press firmly. With several twists, they will adhere. Continue pressing, and a soft ball will form at the junction.

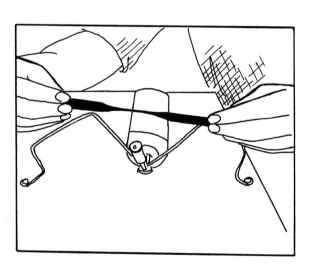

Fig. 131. Move the glass upward out of the flame and wait a second before pulling the molten ball into a thread. The diameter of the thread will depend on the softness of the ball of glass and the amount of tension you impose. If you pull too fast, too hard, the thread will be too thin to be useful. If the glass does not give, it has become too cool. Pull only until the glass loses elasticity, then snap it away with tweezers or pliers. Make other threads while the rods are still hot.

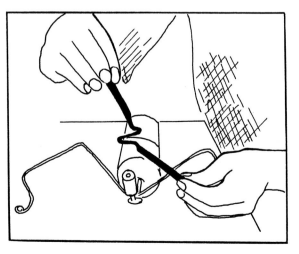

Fig. 132. For small loops, pull out a fairly heavy thread and immediately flip the tip of both rods toward each other, inscribing a circle in the air. Place the loop in the warming area for a few moments and nip away when it is rigid. S curves are made by reversing the direction of one rod.

EXPERIMENT 37

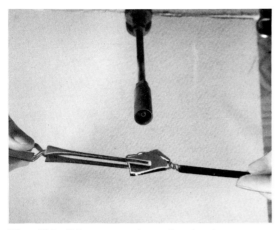

Fig. 133. Select a number of soft glass scraps. Grasp one edge with self-locking tweezers and twirl it in the warming zone. Move it slowly into the melting zone and, at the same time, warm the tip of a holder. Attach the holder to the scrap and move it back into the warming area until the joint is rigid.

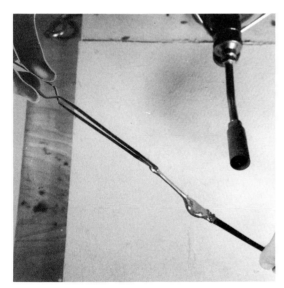

Fig. 134. Now, handling by the holder alone, bring the tip of the scrap into the melting area and twirl until it becomes molten. Move it toward you out of the flame and with the tweezers pinch up a small lump about the size of a pea. Pull gently until the stem is about 2 inches long. Melt the base of the thread in the flame and pull it free. Drop the fragment to the asbestos pad and continue.

This will make short tapering rods about the diameter of a wooden match. The stems may be nipped off and used as shown in the paperweights in Chapter 13. The "seed" on the tips of the rods were arranged as petals in the glass pendant in Chapter 15.

Try this experiment with smalti, too. Being thicker and denser than thin scraps, they must be warmed for a longer period of time or they will shatter.

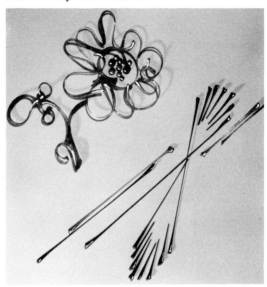

Fig. 135. Drawn threads and loops can be arranged for linear elements in a miniature, or they can be fused to the surface of compatible sheets for texture.

EXPERIMENT 38

Glass plated with gold overglaze is usually opaque or spotty against strong back lighting, thereby losing its effectiveness in many types of transparent mosaics. By stretching a plated strip of colored glass, however, we can make a glass which both *reflects* and *transmits* light.

We call it "disappearing gold." It has special application for decorations which can be attached to plate-glass doors as safety measures.

Prepare a number of narrow, gold-backed strips as described in Experiment 34, but do not round them. Join the tip of a gold bar to a holder, then grasp the free end with tweezers and bring the glass back into the melting area just past the point where the two strips are attached.

Be careful not to melt the bar away from the holder, and keep the gold side upward to protect it from the intense heat. Move the bar back and forth until you feel it relax and become elastic.

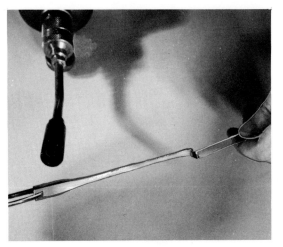

Fig. 136. Stretch the bar, holding it taut to keep it from sagging. Immediately move the stretched area to the left of the flame and feed the adjoining unstretched portion into it.

The glass is already hot and you must work quickly. It takes very little heat from here on to manipulate the entire bar. Practice to acquire a smooth, rhythmic motion—heat, melt, stretch, move—until you draw out a thin, glistening ribbon about ¼ inch wide. A 6-inch rod can be stretched to nearly double its length.

Now notice what has happened to the gold. It has broken into a feathery, iridescent veil which floats on the surface of the glass. Hold it against the light and the gold disappears.

This phenomenon comes partly from the layer of metal being greatly thinned. It is partly caused by changing a solid plating to a finely stippled pattern of dots which permits light to pass through in the interstices.

The ribbons can be snapped into lengths with pliers.

Fig. 137. Thinned ribbons, gold or otherwise, can be shaped into curves or zigzags by simply reheating and bending the minute they soften. The glass will melt quickly and should be cooled slowly in the annealing area after shaping.

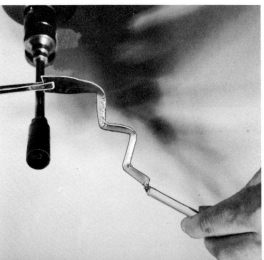

EXPERIMENT 39

Large Tile Inserts

Large tiles and bars for inserts in functional surfaces can be made by variations of the preceding experiments. The 4-inch squares in Figure 138 were designed by Dorothy Saunders for combining with ceramic tesserae on bathroom counters and walls. (The camera angle makes the lower tiles appear distorted.)

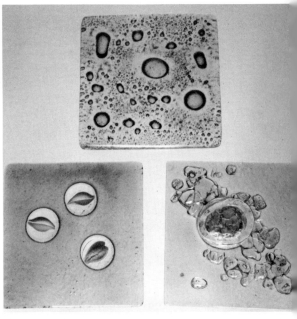

Fig. 138. The upper square was bubbled by laminating glass glaze between two pieces of window glass. The circlets in the lower left example are marbles fused on top of a layer of sifted glaze. On the right, a small bottle ring and sprinklings of crushed bottles have fused into a striking, fluid pattern.

chapter 9

Planning a Mosaic

A mosaic design is popularly conceived as a prepared pattern to be copied in tiles or other decorative materials. Actually, it includes everything that goes into the work, even the original motivation.

To avoid implications that design means simply a diagram and that this chapter will provide a foolproof formula for drawing one, we have substituted the less formidable word *plan*.

There are no *rules* for planning a mosaic, but there are certain *tools* which have been used by artists since art began. These are not laws set forth by a school of learned scholars. They are elements relating to the forces of gravity, the composition and order of the universe, and the very rhythm of life itself.

Entire books could be written about any one of them, but we must be content to point out some of the ways they will be useful.

TOOLS OF DESIGN

Contrast

Color Value and Intensity

The value of a color has nothing to do with its worth, but signifies its relationship to light and darkness. It becomes lower in value as it approaches black and higher as it contains increasing proportions of white.

Value contrasts are important tools. They can be used to create form and give an illusion of size and distance. They can hold our attention within the confines of the decorated space or cause it to wander out of the picture.

Sometimes, we must manipulate values to offset optical illusions which result from certain combinations.

The same illusion in Figure 139 can cause black opaque lines in a translucent mosaic to be swallowed by the "spread" of brilliant light

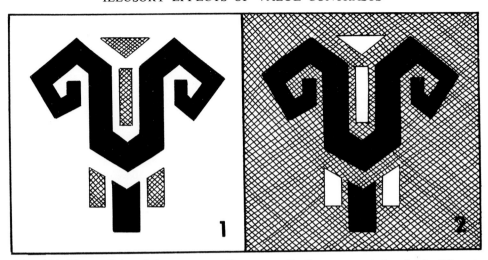

Fig. 139. The outlines of these two motifs are exactly the same, yet they look different because of the placement of values. Move back and notice that in number 1, the black elements appear to diminish. As you move back still further, the white background seems to flow slightly into the black, narrowing it even more. In number 2, the black areas appear heavier and closer because the contrast is reduced.

Fig. 140. "The Shepherd," designed by Cecil Casebier and executed by Jo Wood, is essentially a value pattern in random cuts of glazed ceramic tiles. The range is from white through many shades of brown, the deepest of which is almost black. A few bits of gold add sparkle. Contrasts, rather than outlines, establish the form and create an effect of light.

around them. This means that we must make such lines considerably wider than would be necessary in a drawing, or the composition will lack strength.

The intensity of a color is its degree of purity or brilliance. Red, for example, is most intense if it is not diluted with white, darkened with black, nor dulled by its complementary color, green.

An intense color usually attracts more attention than one which is neutralized, but situations govern its degree of prominence in a composition. Warmth or coolness of a hue may determine whether it appears to recede or move forward. But there are thousands upon thousands of possible combinations in which the opposite effect might be made, according to the size of certain areas, juxtaposition of one hue against another, and the textural attractiveness of specific materials.

We might keep in mind, however, that if all colors in a mosaic were of equal intensity, they would negate each other in the same manner as a composition of drab colors. Where there is no variation of intensity, the design is dreary, dull, or tiring.

Texture

The texture of a mosaic results from the surface character of the decorative materials, as well as the manner of fragmentation. A pattern made of a single material, such as commercial tiles, would have one texture if the pieces were used intact and quite another if they were cut into triangles and oblique shapes.

The geometric precision of an arrangement of square tiles is functionally appropriate for a checkerboard or the floor of a public building, but it can hardly be called stimulating.

This book is filled with examples of imaginative use of textures. Thomas Hunt emphasizes fragmentation by forcing mortar up into thin, raised lines between the tesserae. In Figure 441, Aleksandra Kasuba omits grout completely and creates a vibrant composition with textural contrasts of heights, shapes, and linear arrangement of white marble cubes.

Notice the crisp textures of cut glass fragments in Mariette Bevington's panels in Chapter 21. Compare it with the play of angular tesserae against rounded forms in Rosalis' window in the same chapter.

Helen Rich contrasts the textures of worn pebbles against smalti, the shiny surface of stained glass against dull copper, the sharp facets of quartz chunks against eroded stones.

The possibilities are innumerable, but we must add a note of caution. We need areas of visual "rest" from textural contrasts, as much as from color contrasts. Do not try to combine too many opposing ingredients in a single mosaic or it will be merely "busy" instead of exciting.

Balance

Let us use an old example of balance and visualize identical twins, dressed alike and of equal weight, on each end of a seesaw. The board floats easily in mid-air. This is symmetrical balance, where like objects are placed equidistant from a central fulcrum.

But suppose we replace one with a fat child. If he sits at the same distance from the center as the thin child, the board will no longer float.

The solution, of course, is to move the heavier person closer to the middle. An alternate solution would be to add more weight to the light side. This type of balance with unlike objects is called "asymmetrical."

To think in terms of vertical balance, we can picture a tight-wire performer who balances the movement of his body with a long pole. As his weight shifts to one side, the pole goes up on the other.

We can apply these principles to the problem of balancing a mosaic design. But first, we must establish the *visual* weight of its elements.

For example, a large neutral area may actually weigh less than a small spot of bril-

Fig. 141. There are many contrasting elements in this sketch for "Winter Landscape," to be executed in black clay cut-outs and the characteristic whites of quartz pebbles, milk glass, frosted glass, smalti, and marble. Notice the textural breaks from large slabs to finely webbed patterns to the solid black shapes of the trees.

liant color. A textured material may be heavier than one with smooth, unbroken surface.

Most persons have an instinctive sense of balance, and if allowed to move and arrange a collection of objects freely, will usually balance them in one way or another.

But there is something immovable about the appearance of objects which are drawn on paper. In spite of the fact that we are all aware of the existence of erasers, we resist erasing a complex drawing even if it seems to be sliding off the page.

Considering our natural reluctance to redo a drawing, try cutting pieces of construction paper to represent the area, value, and intensity of motifs planned for a pattern.

Move them about without sticking them down until the arrangement looks comfortable. Sketch lightly around the paper scraps and use the sketch as a guide for making the drawing.

Movement—Rhythm and Line

Movement in a mosaic comes from anything which leads our eyes from one spot to another. Colors and textures can create movement, and so can the particular means by which the design is balanced.

Rhythm is a kind of movement derived from repetition. In music, it is an emphasized beat at regular intervals. In nature, it is the cycle of life from seed to flower to fruit to seed again. In art, it is an element which recurs throughout the design, either precisely, or with variations.

One has only to think of the many ways we react to musical rhythms to realize the pos-

Fig. 142. This is a formal and symmetrical design for a small stained-glass window. (Pencil lines at the four cardinal points indicate how it can be adapted for a clock.)

sibilities of mosaic rhythms. In Figure 12, the repeated pattern carries us around and around the circular form. In Figure 143, the repetition of superimposed crosses serves to hold us on a two-dimensional plane.

A dot stands still, but a line always goes somewhere. Its manner of moving can stimulate certain feelings, such as excitement, tranquility, or restlessness. Graceful flowing lines produce an atmosphere of peace and serenity. Sharp angular lines arouse us and create tensions.

A dancer uses the lines of his body to tell a story and convey a mood. Study the billboards along a highway to see how advertising artists use line to attract attention and to express some distinctive feature of a product.

WORKING WITH DESIGN

Once we have the tools for design, we must put them to work. And we cannot overlook the usefulness to this end of being able to draw. To the student without previous art training, this single skill appears more awesome than all the others put together.

Anyone can draw if he thinks of it as "writing in pictures," rather than realistic representation. Even primitive peoples and small children write in pictures without any instructions whatever, and their statements are often far more expressive than self-conscious draftsmanship.

We call such drawing symbolism. It is a way of telling a story or expressing an idea without using words. The craftsmen of ancient cultures used symbols on their pottery, graves, and dwelling places to record brave deeds, catastrophes, and tribal history.

Religious art works are rich with symbols which stand for various elements of the faith and for persons and events which were significant in its development.[1]

[1] See Figure 179 for an example of symbols of the Jewish faith. In Figure 342, the symbols are Christian. The ancient symbol of healing was the origin of Ray Rice's mosaic at the San Leandro Medical Center, Figure 435.

Fig. 143. Decorative window of faceted glass in epoxy. For Orco Glass, Inc., by Cecil Casebier.

Fig. 144. The balanced, orderly lines of these weeds and grasses derive from the upthrusting motion of plant growth as it stretches toward light. It is a calm movement that neither disturbs nor arouses.

Fig. 146. The opposition of these crisp lines forces us around the picture in a series of short, staccato dashes. It fairly crackles with excitement.

Fig. 145. Here, the natural motion of growth has been thrown off balance by the wind, and the lines give a feeling of restlessness and impermanence.

Some symbols have been in use for so long that they seem more "real" than reality. Ask a person to draw a star, for instance, and chances are good that he will draw a five-pointed figure, not a sphere.

By its very nature of construction and fragmentation, mosaic art is better suited to symbolic expression than naturalism. This does not mean that we are limited to circles and triangles and sun-faces, but rather that we design in terms of communicating an idea as economically as possible. It means that we select the elements which are most meaningful, and eliminate those which add nothing but superfluous detail.

Emotional Reactions to Color

We have mentioned how color values and intensities are tools for organizing a composition and directing our attention to important elements. This is using color intellectually. We also use color emotionally.

Color associations can cause reactions in senses other than our eyes, or remind us of reactions experienced at some earlier time.

If you tried to describe color to a person who had been blind all his life, you would have to relate your description to his capacity to smell, hear, touch, and taste.

For example, you might tell him that certain greens feel cold and sharp, like ice; that blue is distant, like a summer sky or the echo of your voice in a cave. Gray can be furry and soft like a kitten, or heavy and threatening like a thunderstorm. Brown can be the yeasty odor of decay, or the fresh pungent taste of morning coffee. Pink is the feel of organdy and the smell of an open rose.

We can love a color because it reminds us of a favorite childhood dress, or hate it because of the walls in a hospital room.

Colors have traditional symbolic associations, too. Think of the red, white, and blue of the American flag and try to imagine it in yellow, orange, and purple.

The motivation of the Expressionist movement was to give art a deeper meaning by expressing an emotional reaction to a subject rather than simply reproducing its visual aspects. Toward this goal, artists used color to "say something," rather than to simulate an effect in nature.

All of us are expressionists before we lose confidence in our own ideas and seek the security of conforming to popular taste and opinion.

But this kind of freedom of expression derives from innocence, which would be a pretty difficult subject to teach. So let us try an interesting experiment with symbolic color to discover what it can do for a prosaic subject.

Experimenting with Symbolic Color

Select a large sheet of heavy drawing paper, preferably with a slight "tooth," or texture. Think of colors you associate with some feeling. Loneliness, for example, might be conveyed in shades of blues and purple. Anger in bursts of red and orange.

With oil or wax crayons, coat the paper heavily in the colors you have chosen. Do not try to paint a picture, but do include contrasts of value and intensity.

When the sheet is covered, paint it all over with black waterproof ink. Let it dry, then make a white chalk sketch on the inked surface of some simple scene or symbol which relates to the emotion you expressed in color.

Use a sharp tool, such as an Exacto blade, to scratch through the layer of ink and expose the underlying color. Scrape lightly at first, working from dark values to light, using broad strokes in some parts, thin lines in others. Think of the spots of color as tesserae in a mosaic.

Now, we shall work from light to dark in a different way.

Tear random shapes from colored construction paper and arrange them on a piece of cardboard. Move them about, working only for an emotional effect, then glue them down smoothly with wallpaper paste.

Turn the collage around to study it from several angles. Does it suggest something? Place a sheet of tracing paper over it and spread a thin layer of black poster paint on a saucer. Dip a small, slightly moistened sponge in the paint and, pouncing lightly, build up medium and dark tones. Add a few sharp lines to bring it into focus. Make several trial patterns—a simple portrait, perhaps, or a landscape, or a cluster of seed pods.

When one strikes a spark, remove the tracing paper and transpose it onto the collage, using short brush-strokes and sponge dabs to represent tesserae.

There are countless other ways of exploring symbolic color, and your horizons will be greatly expanded by studying how it was used by such masters as van Gogh, Rouault, Cézanne, Matisse, Klee, Chagall, and Nolde.

If you are inspired to try to transpose one of their works into mosaic, do so. But—consider it a type of exercise, not an ultimate goal.

This is a daring suggestion, because it smacks of the outmoded method of teaching painting through copying the Old Masters. Still, some of van Gogh's most eloquent expressions derived from deliberate interpretations of paintings by Millet, Daumier, Rembrandt, and Delacroix which he admired.[2]

Actually, it would be impossible to reproduce one of these paintings accurately in pebbles or broken crockery. You would be forced to make certain changes and innovations, which in turn would teach you a great deal about the nature of fragmented design.

[2] Edith Hoffmann, *Expressionism* (New York, Crown Publishers, Inc., n.d.), plates 1 and 3.

You would be further forced to analyze the elements of the composition if you were serious about the study. Certainly, this has more carryover value than merely filling in the spaces of a commercially prepared drawing.

And finally, you would gain a new insight and respect for those who have left their indelible mark on the artistic world.

These are pretty significant accomplishments when you stop to think about it.

We are by no means suggesting here that the best path to originality winds through the

Fig. 147. "The Heart of Man," by Henry Matisse, inspired this panel by William Ruder.

Tiny crumbs of cathedral glass and pattern chips become luminous jewels when they are melted. Here they are set in a fired clay form. By Mary Lou Stribling.

Crushed, sieved glass, opaque commercial tiles, and square brass rods. By Mary Lou Stribling.

Polynesian folk art was reinterpreted for this panel by Emmy Lou Packard for the S.S. *Mariposa*. One of eight related designs, it was executed in inlaid linoleum and abalone shells.

F I S H . Cathedral glass fragments fused into the subsurface of a colorless glass blank. They actually become almost inlaid. By Kay Kinney.

K A L I . Mixed media set in sculptured magnesite. The symbolism and violent bursts of color were inspired by the Indian black goddess of destruction and evil—the vengeful consort of Shiva. By Helen Steinau Rich.

creations of the great masters, but *any* exercise which serves to get you started in mosaic design has validity. Even kits may have some limited value for the beginner who needs a temporary crutch, though he would gain more confidence from a simple sand-cast stepping stone.

Everyone has the capacity for original design, for no two human beings react to physical and emotional experiences in exactly the same way. It follows then that no two honest expressions relating to these experiences can ever be identical.

The key word, of course, is *honesty*.

The first step toward releasing the force of your own imagination is to lose your fear of the blank page.

It will help considerably if you use humble brown wrapping paper or newsprint, rather than costly art paper. And the sooner you make a few smears and doodles on it, the sooner you will lose your awe of its purity.

A few experiments follow which may be of help in stimulating ideas. Approach them with an attitude of curiosity. And do not forget that the most valuable designing aid which has ever been invented is—the wastebasket!

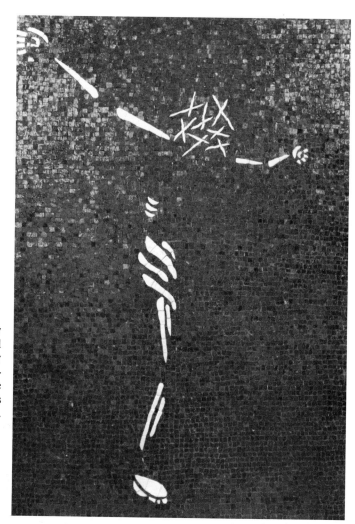

Fig. 148. "The Crucifixion," by Father Stephen Katsaris, derived from a piece of metal sculpture by Mexican artist, Castillios. The translation of the stark, stylized figure of Christ into gold and black tiles produced a mosaic of great power.

Getting Rid of the Blank Page

• Place some object directly in front of you (a bottle, leaf, cup, vase, etc.) and draw its outline. Turn it upside down and draw another outline on the same page. Continue turning the object, drawing large and small views from all directions, superimposing some on top of others. Fill the page comfortably, then tape it to the wall and move away from it.

Without regard for the identity of the subject, accentuate the lines which divide the sheet into interesting spaces, and block out the rest. Work this up in color as an abstract design.

• Wet a cotton string so that it is soft and pliable, then drop it on a sheet of paper. Lift and drop it several times and notice how it falls in curves and bent lines. Trace one pattern with a felt-tipped pen and study it for design possibilities.

Fig. 150. When the cement has completely hardened, paint a coat of black waterproof ink over the entire sheet.

PATTERNS FROM RUBBER CEMENT

Fig. 149. With the applicator brush, lift a mass of rubber cement from its container and dribble it around on white or tinted paper. Let it trail freely, without allowing it to puddle.

Fig. 151. Wait until the ink is dry, then rub the cement to expose the resist pattern. Retain lines which please you, and paint out those which are distracting.

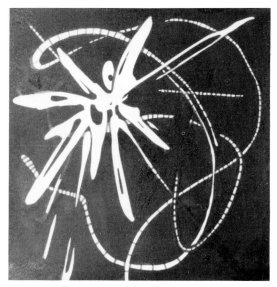

Fig. 152. Some interesting forms may emerge. This could be an expressionistic interpretation of the great star which hung over Bethlehem on the first Christmas.

• Make a reference drawing of a simple flower—a daisy, wild rose, or morning glory. Use strips of paper to frame certain sections as a photographer might crop a photograph. Forget it is a flower and pretend you have moved in close with a magnifying glass. Now see only the interesting pattern of petal veins or textured stamen.

On a sheet of gray paper, block in with white chalk the spots of highlights. Then block in shadows with charcoal, leaving the paper exposed for middle values. Make several small mosaics of the design in light and dark pebbles.

• Thin black and white oil paints with turpentine and drip them on the surface of a flat pan of water. Shake the pan, then lay a sheet of colored paper on the water and lift it straight up.

Dry the paper on a sheet of glass and add line or spots of color to those which suggest something.

Fig. 154. PAINT PATTERNS. The lower right square suggests surf breaking around a reef. Visualize it in pebbles, shells, and frosted glass nuggets, with the darkest area in deep green and cobalt glass.

Fig. 153. "Bug Face" originated from a string dropped on a board. The artist, Chris Hackney, was eight years old.

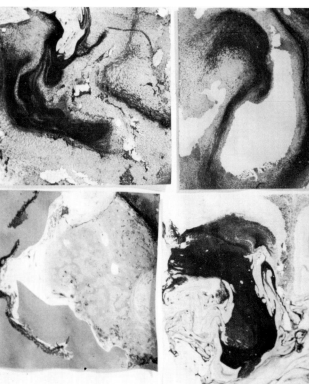

chapter 10.

Developing the Plan

The plan of a mosaic starts with inspiration—a reaction to some visual or emotional experience. If the craftsman could effectively express these experiences in words or some other medium of communication, there would be no motivation for mosaic. Instead, he would write a poem or a story or song. Or he would paint a picture or weave a tapestry.

But if mosaic is his language, his plan for expression moves from inspiration to arranging its elements into tangible form. This includes decisions on size, decorative materials, area of installation, and organization of the pattern.

We discussed some tools for working out this part of the plan in the last chapter. Now there remains the matter of developing the actual mosaic.

There are probably as many ways of doing this as there are mosaicists. Most, however, are variations of three main approaches. Each has special advantages and disadvantages and a choice would depend on the use for which the mosaic is intended, as well as the experience and personality of the craftsman.

WORKING FROM AN ACCURATE CARTOON

A cartoon is a full-size, detailed drawing for a mosaic. It can be made in poster paints, pastels, inks, water colors, or whatever medium best conveys your mental picture. Some artists' cartoons even include the placement of each tessera, and are so complete that execution of the mosaic itself consists primarily of putting the pieces together.

A good cartoon is like stage directions for a play. The manner of expressing the idea is not as important as making the meaning clear.

This is the safest way to work and is essential for large projects or architectural murals where an impulsive decision might be disastrous.

A number of rough sketches are made first, to experiment with organization of textures, values, color, etc., and when one shows promise, it is developed further with regard to the decorative materials. This is the hardest part, for it means designing in one medium—

90

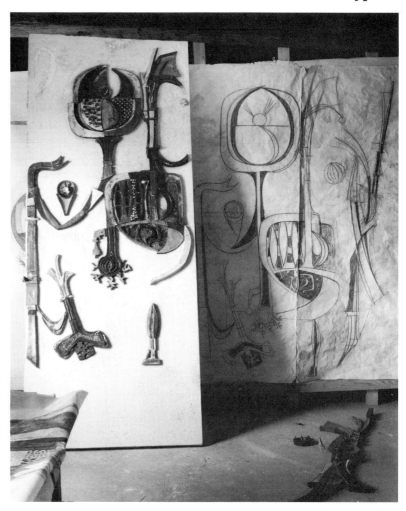

Fig. 155. Cartoon and work in progress for a monumental mural for the Strasenburgh Laboratories (Rochester, New York). By Frans Wildenhain. (See other sections in Chapter 12.)

that of paper, inks, and paints—and thinking in another—that of fragmented glass, clay, stones, etc.

Several fairly complete drawings may be necessary before one is satisfactory enough to enlarge to scale. Further changes will probably be made then, since a pattern in one size will look different in another. The angle from which it will be viewed must also be considered.

When the cartoon is complete, the linear pattern is transferred to the backing or support on which the mosaic will be set, or to heavy paper to which the tesserae will be attached face down for indirect installation.

The cartoon is then used as a reference for the mosaic translation.

Critics of this method of working claim it discourages inventiveness and reduces the actual creation to a dull, mechanical chore. On the other hand, it enables the designer to detect weaknesses in his plan in advance of construction, just as does a blueprint for a building.

We could compare it to cooking by a perfect recipe. The finished dish may hold no surprises, but neither will it waste precious ingredients.

The value of a well-planned cartoon for commissioned work cannot be underestimated, whether the commission be for a small window in a private residence or a monumental mural for a public building. In the first place, it

Figs. 156, 157. Cartoons for two of the fourteen Stations of the Cross for St. Mary's Church, Regina, Saskatchewan, by F. John Miller. Forms, light and dark values, color, and textures are clearly established. Notice particularly in Station Twelve ("The Crucifixion") how exciting contrasts direct attention to the small but powerful scene in the distance.

allows the client to study the concept and make recommendations for alterations.

This is a matter requiring both patience and diplomacy on the part of the artist, for often the layman is unaware of the structural limitations of a prescribed material. But after all, it is far easier to compromise at the cartoon stage than when the work is ready for installation.

An accurate cartoon serves another purpose when the design is executed by someone other than the designer. (This is often the case with companies making commercial mosaics.)

Highest quality work is produced when designer and craftsman work together as a team, each having respect for what the other contributes to the finished product.

The designer must be careful to relate his drawing to the nature of the materials in which it will be executed. For example, if it will be in stained glass, he will not include sections which are impossible to cut, or which would violate the character of the material.

The craftsman is then obliged to carry out the concept as closely as possible, though the translation will include certain original elements.

Fig. 158. "Boy in the Market Place" illustrates how a designer-craftsman partnership can work successfully. The forms and value pattern of Cecil Casebier's original design have been faithfully reproduced by mosaicist Jo Wood. However, the fragmented design has a character distinctly its own. (*Collection of Orco Glass, Inc.*)

WORKING FROM A SKETCH

As a guide for a mosaic, a sketch does not have to be drawn to scale, but it should be drawn to approximate proportions. For example, a sketch which looks fine on a square sheet would require considerable tailoring for a rectangular mosaic. It might be entirely inappropriate.

The essential purpose of the sketch is to capture at the moment of inspiration some idea which will be developed directly in mosaic materials, rather than being put through the stage of an accurate cartoon. It may note only one stimulating aspect of the idea—perhaps the movement of grasses in the wind, or the chesty strut of a pigeon. Perhaps it is simply an abstract pattern of color derived from an emotion aroused by music or the cry of a night bird.

The sketch serves to remind the craftsman of his reaction to this experience. It is seldom actually enlarged and traced onto a backing, but rather is freely transposed as the work progresses.

There are more chances for error in this method of working, but what you may lose in accuracy, you may gain in strength and emotional quality. Even the experienced craftsman, however, is prepared for a certain amount of changing and redoing of his arrangement of tesserae, sometimes to the extent of prying up large areas and starting over.

WORKING FROM AN IDEA

In many schools, beginning mosaic students are assigned a theme, or subject, and told to develop it spontaneously without any preliminary sketch whatever. This is a valuable exercise for learning a process and for gaining confidence in one's ability to create original works. There is a temptation, however, to pretend the results are profound, when they may be simply unintelligible.

Ideally, the mosaicist maintains a delicate balance between enthusiastic expression and selectivity. "Childlikeness" is one thing, suggesting an open, unprejudiced mind and a joy

Fig. 159. This rough sketch of sailboats moored along a pier was as far as the mosaic idea was carried on paper. No color notes were added, though values are suggested.

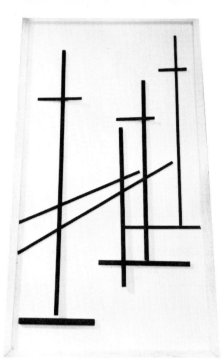

Fig. 160. The linear pattern is formed of wood strips, painted flat black. Several compositions were tried on the prepared backing before a final decision was made. In this arrangement, where most of the lines form right angles, there is no feeling of motion . . .

Fig. 161. . . . but when the rigid order is disturbed and the vertical lines thrown off balance, the original impression of turbulence is re-created (see figures 144, 145, 146). Once satisfactorily positioned, the strips were secured with white glue and weighted with bricks.

Fig. 162. The mosaicist, using the sketch as a guide for value pattern, set vividly contrasting colors of glass tiles directly on the panel.

in new experiences. "Childishness" means simply immaturity, which is a *stage* in the development of maturity.

As we mature, we extend our capacity for study and concentration, and perfect our control over technical processes. With such discipline, the artist has a powerful tool for developing an idea before the edge of inspiration is dulled by overmanipulation. But there is a great deal of difference between the happy accident and the deliberate effect.

Some of the mosaicists represented in this book create intricately detailed and exquisitely organized works without any guidance other than the vision inside them. But in essence, whether the guiding statement is made on paper or in the mind, the plan must be clear before a single tessera is set in place.

The mosaicist who works spontaneously must be equipped with good judgment, some of which may be intuitive. A larger proportion probably derives from training and experience.

Fig. 163. "St. Demetrius, Protector of Children" was displayed in Thomas Hunt's one-man show at the M. H. De Young Memorial Museum in 1963. No preliminary sketch was made. Following a few guidelines on the backing, the artist pressed Venetian glass tiles and smalti directly into wet mortar. *(Photo courtesy of the M. H. De Young Memorial Museum.)*

chapter 11

Inspiration from Other Artists

Our art is the outgrowth of many experiences and influences, for none of us lives in total isolation. We are products of the things we inherit, as well as our environments and the people who share them.

The standards by which we decide that an art work is or is not beautiful are as varied as art itself, and usually incredibly personal. Beauty means different things to different people, and our capacity to respond to it may to some degree be determined by the genes and chromosomes of our ancestors.

It is always safest to evaluate an art work from the distance of a few years. In retrospect our eyes see more clearly and are not distracted by showmanship. Unfortunately, this hindsight has its tragic aspects, as the biographies of some of our greatest artists reveal.

Few significant innovations in form and expression have derived from a single impassioned moment. Rather, they are results of many hours of experimentation toward a calculated deviation from an established order.

The non-creative person may imitate one of these innovations without ever really understanding what it is all about. The creative person listens to and observes and analyzes what is going on around him, and makes an honest effort to decide how it affects his personal philosophies. Then, he rejects what has no meaning for him and assimilates what does. His mosaics are not only fragments of decorative materials but also fragments of influence from other persons.

The mosaic examples in this book have been placed in certain sections to illustrate or make some special point in relation to the text. All of the artists who made them are creative, and not just those who are represented in this chapter.

This group has been selected to show a wide variety of techniques, applications, and design concepts, and to provide a glimpse of the tremendous scope and vitality of contemporary mosaics.

It is a kind of gallery through which we may browse at leisure. No two readers will react to them in the same way, but a great deal will be missed by too hasty evaluation.

Inspiration seldom announces itself with loud proclamations and a bright flash of insight. It often speaks in a small voice which can be lost in the noise of our own.

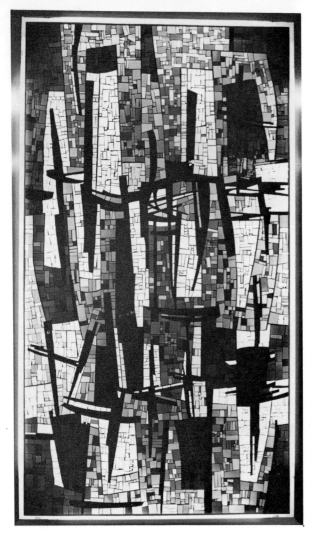

Fig. 164. "Autumn," by Mariette Bevington, is one of four panels in the entrance vestibules of a complex of luxury apartment houses, Park Towne Place, Philadelphia, Pa. The design was inspired by the colors of autumn trees—yellow, gold, olive, and browns—as reflected in a still pool. The materials are stained glass, and the technique of construction is described in Chapter 21.

Fig. 165. "Martyrs and Fighters," memorial mural at the Tucson (Arizona) Jewish Community Center. Praying hands, mosaicked with images of Jewish heroes and heroines, frame an eternal torch, a symbol of hope, freedom, and enlightenment. Decorative materials are stoneware segments, glass, pebbles, and porcelain tiles. By Charles Clement.

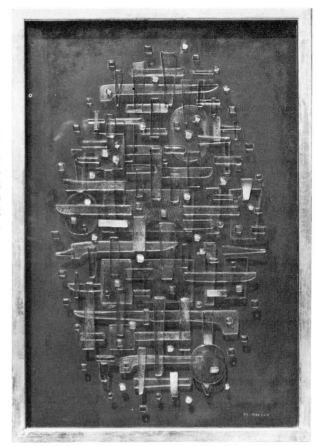

Fig. 166. This construction in yellow and green by Maurice Heaton shows an interesting method of assembling pieces of fired glass, some of which are colored with glazes, some with enamels. Part of the design is cemented on top of ¼-inch-thick base glass, and part attached to the underside. The sheet was then framed ½ inch above a flat black backing and appears to float on black plate glass.

Fig. 167. Detail of a large mural by F. John Miller in the Regina, Saskatchewan, Court House. It was made by the indirect method from nearly 200,000 pieces of Venetian glass and installed in sections by professional tile setters. The central figure is a symbolic God of Laws, holding above him a balance of right and wrong. Figures around him represent jurors and apprentices and Truth and Justice. *(Courtesy of Saskatchewan Government.)*

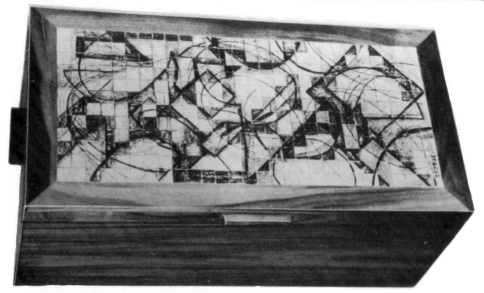

Fig. 168. Chest with a lid of glazed ceramic tiles by Aida and Dan Whedon.

Fig. 169. Many of Marlys Frey's mosaics derive from her interest in organic growth and form and the unchanging cycles of nature. "Cliff-water" was inspired by the movement of water against strata of rocks, and is composed of pebbles, shells, and bones.

Fig. 170. Charles Counts cut tesserae from clay slabs to fit his design for "Spring." They were fired, glazed, and directly embedded into wet cement. The cement is a non-shrinking mixture containing flecks of iron which weather in an interesting manner.

Fig. 171. "Tree Form," by Richard Peeler, is an enameled mosaic in shades of blue and violet on a framework of brazed bronze rods. Each copper form is counter-enameled except for a small point where it is soldered to the supporting structure. (Photo courtesy of Ceramics Monthly. Mosaic in collection of Professor and Mrs. David Maloney.)

Fig. 172. Mural for the Hide-Away Bar in the New York Hilton Hotel at Rockefeller Center is made of precast concrete panels. Natural pebbles, slab glass, and cubes of marble were set directly into wet concrete. By Aleksandra Kasuba.

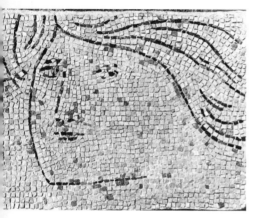

Fig. 173. "Woman's Head," by Leo Lionni, is stylistically contemporary, but materials are essentially the same as those used by Byzantine craftsmen in the eleventh and twelfth centuries. Compare this arrangement of marble cubes and smalti with the Triton's head in Chapter 1. *(Collection of William Ruder.)*

Fig. 174. Section of a 100-foot mural for the Strasenburgh Laboratories, Rochester, N.Y., by Frans Wildenhain. Each clay fragment is carved, modeled, textured, glazed, inlaid, until the richly fabricated whole resembles a monumental composition of jewelry. This area depicts laboratory symbols—bunsen burners, bottles, distilling flasks, etc. Other parts are shown in Chapters 12 and 26.

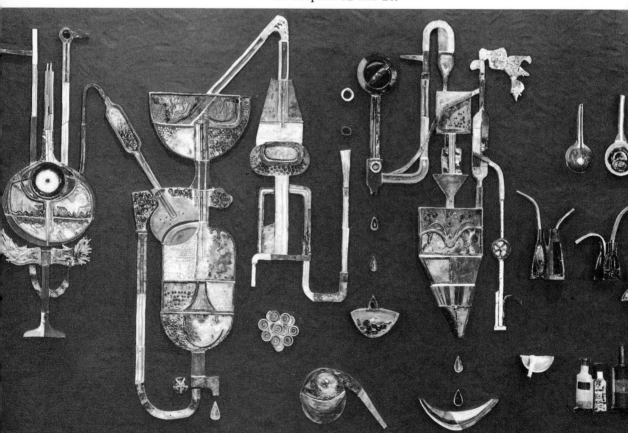

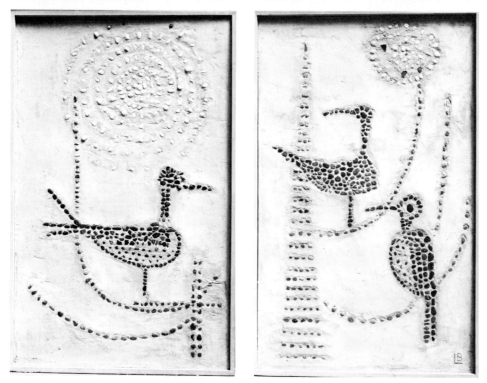

Figs. 175, 176. "Birds," by Lucienne Bloch Dimitroff, were made by the reverse method from beach pebbles and concrete.

Fig. 177. This garden sculpture by Ray Rice was inspired by surf patterns and the small plants and creatures of the sea. The back form was pierced to allow light to pass around the edges of the upper form, which was mounted out on aluminum pegs. Pressed asbestos board was used as a foundation for the concrete bas-relief. *(Collection of Melton Ferris.)*

Fig. 178. "Peasant Caravan" by Bedri Rahmi Eyuboglu. Venetian glass tiles. *(Collection of William Ruder.)*

Fig. 179. "Faith in the Temple," a mosaic wall in the Temple Beth Yeshurun, Houston, Texas, depicts traditional symbols of the Jewish faith. Designed for Orco Glass by Cecil Casebier and executed by Jo Wood in glass tiles. *(Photo courtesy of Orco Glass, Inc.)*

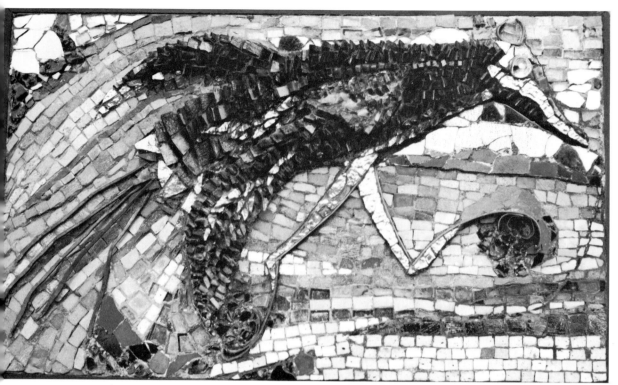

Fig. 180. "Roadrunner," by Helen Steinau Rich, is made of mixed media and has a flash of humor which is rare in mosaic expressions.

Fig. 181. "Fighting Cock" is made of 2-inch-thick carved Japanese ash. The mosaic areas were routed out and inlaid with Italian and Mexican tesserae. By Emmy Lou Packard for the S.S. *Lurline*.

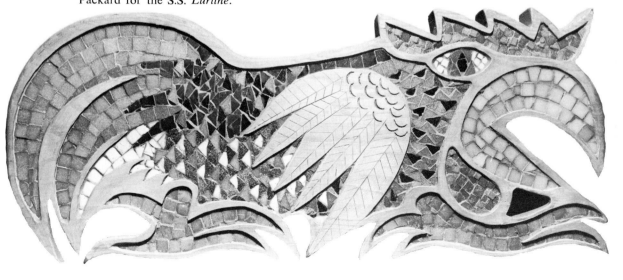

Fig. 182. A non-objective design by Ruth Dunn made of faceted glass set in two colors of epoxy resin—charcoal gray and ochre. It was an award winner in the 1963 Benesco competition. *(Collection of Orco Glass, Inc.)*

Fig. 183. Fireplace panel by Rosalis. Hand-carved stoneware slabs, glazed and unglazed clay tiles in earth and brick colors.

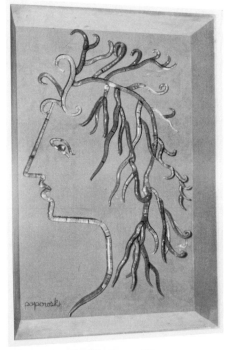

Fig. 184. Fragments of drawn and torch-shaped glass in many shades of sapphire form "Winter" by Stella Popowski. The glass is mounted on gray velvet. *(Photo courtesy of El Presidente Hotel, Mexico City.)*

chapter 12

Starting to Work with Clay

It is but a short step beyond making clay materials to making the separate parts of a mosaic and assembling them in jigsaw puzzle fashion. Before we begin with a simple introductory project, study the following general notes, since some of them were not important when we were dealing with only small tesserae.

NOTES ON WORKING WITH CLAY

• Plaster bats or the fabric side of a sheet of oilcloth make good work surfaces from which clay can easily be removed. Dry rolled slabs or cut-outs between paper towels with a light weight on top to prevent warping.

• Clay loses plasticity quickly with exposure to air and heat of hands. Work should be kept covered with damp rags until modeling is completed, though some trimming and carving can be done after it is dry.

• It is risky to try to add fresh clay to sections which have already started to become rigid, since their rates of shrinkage will be different. If it is necessary, however, wet the joint, roughen it with a tool, and paint it liberally with slip before adding new material. Keep it covered for several days with damp rags and a plastic sheet to equalize the "wetness and dryness."

• Slab pieces more than 1 inch thick should be hollowed out on the underside or they may explode in the firing from the expansion of internal moisture. Be sure to provide a vent for cavities in sculptured forms.

• Red clay and white clay are seldom compatible and if combined on one piece will usually crack apart when they are fired. Glazes will also react differently on them.

• Wedge all moist clay thoroughly on a plaster bat or sheet of oilcloth to eliminate air bubbles before you start to work with it.

Fig. 185. "Earth Colors" is a scale model for one section of a large mural to be installed on a brick wall. Lewis D. Snyder, who is an art instructor at Middle Tennessee State University, started with slabs of clay rolled out on burlap, and attached the wheel-thrown forms while both they and the slabs were still plastic. The colors are inspired by natural earth harmonies and range from warm red-browns to deep blue-green. The lighter warm tones are slip made from the basic clay body with a smaller percentage of red iron oxide. The cool tones were derived from a white translucent boron glaze which becomes blue-green over a red clay body when fired in a reduction atmosphere.

• There will be less shrinkage and warping of cut-outs if the clay contains from 15 to 30 per cent fine grog.

• Be careful not to get crumbs of plaster in your work. They will calcine in the firing and gradually expand, sometimes to the point of causing a fracture.

• Slip should be the consistency of thick cream. Scraps and trimmings may be dried and saved in a covered container. When a good amount has accumulated, crush it with a mallet, soak several days in water, then drain off excess liquid and mix until it is smooth. (A kitchen mixer on low speed is good for small amounts.) Add about 1 tablespoon of 10 per cent solution of sodium silicate per gallon, strain, and set aside to age and de-air. It may then be added to new casting slip in proportion of 1 to 3.

• Rust and particles of steel wool will fire as dark flecks if they get into slip or glaze. All containers for ceramic materials should be rustproof.

• The labels of commercial glazes usually state directions for application. Dilute the glaze with water if necessary so that each coat will flow on smoothly without piling up. If a sponge instead of a brush is used, it must be well saturated or it will retain the glaze, rather than deposit it in an even layer.

• The terms *gloss* and *mat* applied to a glaze indicate the degree of surface shine. Glosses flow freely, and brush marks will be obliterated. Mats flow very little and the application should be smoother.

• If the glaze is too thin after firing, warm the piece in the kitchen oven to facilitate a fresh application, float on another coat, and refire.

• Sandpaper grit left on the surface of clay will often cause a glaze to crawl or pinhole. Reglaze the bare spots, pack pinholes with glaze dried to a paste consistency, and refire.

• There are basically two kinds of underglazes: those which are used for an all-over even coat of color, and those formulated for painting detailed designs. (Underglazes in the first category are sometimes called "engobes.") They cannot be successfully interchanged, and inquiries should be made at the time of purchase.

• The thicker the form, the slower the bisque-firing should be. Preheating the kiln is good insurance against cracking of heavy pieces. Turn the kiln on low for several hours with the lid propped open about an inch. Then close the lid, turn off the heat, and wait over night before starting the actual firing cycle.

• Never bisque-fire hand-made materials in the same kiln with glazed ware. An air pocket may expand and blow bits of clay into the glaze.

• Flat shapes and materials can be stacked on top of each other for a bisque-firing if they are not too heavy. Glazed pieces must be separated and either dry-footed or fired on stilts to keep them from sticking to the kiln shelf.

• Prop the kiln door (or lid) open about an inch for the first few hours of both glaze and bisque fires to allow steam and gases to escape.

• A "soaking fire" is often the answer to a problem glaze which will not flow freely or is inclined to craze or bubble. This means holding it at the molten stage for an extended period of time by turning kiln to medium heat for about an hour after the maturing temperature has been reached.

• Most commercial clay bodies have a flexible maturing range of one or two cones. By examining the bisque, you can determine the precise point in this range where results

are best with your particular kiln. Underfired bisque is soft, chalky, and porous. Overfired bisque is warped and distorted and difficult to glaze.

• Porcelain and stoneware bodies have more critical maturing temperatures than earthenware and must be watched closely during the final stage of firing.

• Your kiln is an important investment. Keep it clean. Paint a thick coat of kiln wash on the bottom so that glaze drippings can be easily removed after each firing. Protect the tops of shelves the same way, but leave the undersides untreated or flakes of kiln wash may sift into molten glaze or glass. Every few weeks, dust the elements with a stiff brush and remove loose materials with a vacuum cleaner.

The most creative way to start working with any material is to make a series of test pieces without anything in mind but investigating its possibilities.

The experiments in Chapters 7 and 8 were designed to serve this purpose in part, and we can move now into using these materials for specific projects.

Written instruction of this kind can be dangerous, for many students will have difficulty disassociating a technique from the particular example presented.

The following project and those in the rest of the book are not intended as ideals, but purely as demonstrations to make the description clear. It is hoped that the reader will study the step-by-step procedures and then apply them to his own ideas.

GLAZED CLAY CUT-OUTS

Trivets are handy for exploring various mosaic processes since they are small enough to be made quickly from a negligible supply of materials.

Frames can be made by the method used for making the cutting board in Chapter 5. The wrought-iron base in the demonstration was purchased from a mosaic shop.

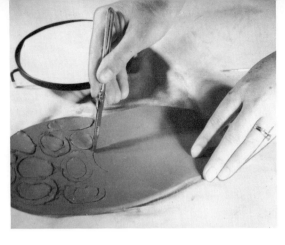

Fig. 186. Roll out an even clay slab ¼ inch thick and cut it into a number of shapes. (If the base is square, elongated forms will be better related than those shown here.) Do not use a pattern. Keep the cut-outs free and varied, and make more than you need. You can return the excess to the clay bin before they dry.

Fig. 187. Separate the cut-outs from the margins, smooth the rough edges with a moist brush, and, while they are still soft, arrange them on a paper liner inside the trivet frame. Push them together into an all-over cellular pattern. A few "holes" from the cut-outs will keep the texture from being monotonous. Place a paper towel over the arrangement and weight it with a small book. When the clay is leather hard, clean it with a damp sponge.

Fig. 188. Lift out the mosaic on the liner and place it on a kiln shelf. (The paper will burn away.) To make sure that it will fuse into a unit, drip a little glaze on the joints. Crackles are interesting on pieces like these. When the drippings are dry, brush two thin coats of glaze over the top surfaces. Dry thoroughly before firing to the maturity of the clay.

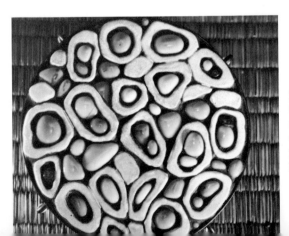

Fig. 189. A wash of concentrated brown pigment was applied to the crackle to bring out a network of fine lines. The clay pieces and bits of yellow, orange, and vermilion melted taillights were pressed into a moist bed of dark-brown wood putty.

If your clay is heavily grogged, the percentage of shrinkage on a small piece will not be great enough for concern and will result only in a margin of from ⅛ inch to ¼ inch between the clay insert and the trivet frame. This can be filled with grout.

With clay which shrinks excessively, it is best to refine each cut-out separately, bisque and glaze them, then reassemble with other tesserae inside the frame.

We shall expand this idea further in the next chapter by using clay cut-outs as frames for little resin windows.

Fig. 190. Detail of "Martyrs and Fighters," by Charles Clement, shows ways of combining sections of incised, colored stoneware slabs with mixed media (see Chapter 11 for the entire mural).

Fig. 191. "Pine, Moon, and Shadows" is made from stoneware cut-outs which were textured while they were still plastic, then colored with engobes. For exterior use, the finished segments were attached to marine plywood with mastic and framed with wrought iron. By Charles Counts.

Fig. 192. Frans Wildenhain starts with small sketches, then progresses to full-size cartoons for his monumental clay murals. The pattern is transferred to thick slabs, and the sections are cut out and assembled on the floor. Each piece is carved, modeled, textured, and colored before being hollowed out on the back to a safe thickness for firing.

Fig. 193. Several firings may be required to get the exact effect he wants. The pieces are often glazed and reglazed for subtle nuances and bursts of color or deep translucent glassy pools. Here and there, jewel-like domes of glass may be pressed into the clay and fired to a point at which they begin to flow and drift over a clay protrusion.

Fig. 194. The finished sun symbol is the central theme of a 100-foot mural in the Strasenburgh Laboratories in Rochester, New York. Chapters 11 and 26 show other sections of this impressive achievement.

Starting to Work
with Polyester Resin

The liquid polyester resins are thermosetting, and the most accommodating of the synthetic resins for mosaic embedments. As to how and why they are solidified through polymerization, nothing further needs to be added to the material in Chapter 4. It should be reviewed, however, before you actually start to work.

Liquid polyester resin is packaged in two components; one is the resin itself, the other is the catalyst, or hardening agent. This additive which initiates polymerization is usually supplied in a small squeeze bottle to enable you to measure accurately the number of drops needed (see Figure 195).

Do not make the mistake of using an eye-dropper instead, because the size of the drops may be larger. Too much catalyst will cause the resin to set up too fast, creating tensions which may ruin many hours of work.

Most manufacturers recommend proportions of catalyst to resin on the labels of their products, but these are generalities only and may need adjusting according to climate, size and thickness of the mosaic, and the nature of the embedments. It will further be influenced by the age of the material. Resin which has been in stock for some time will polymerize much faster than a new batch. It is good economy to "waste" several ounces in a series of tests to establish your own scale of proportions.

Use disposable tools as far as possible to minimize the chore of cleaning up after your work. Resin and catalyst can be combined in paper cups and blended together with wooden tongue depressors, sucker sticks, or hors d'oeuvres picks.[1] Reusable implements should be dropped into a pan filled with hot water and detergent before the plastic has hardened. It can be cleaned away without difficulty at this stage.

Most craft shops carry two kinds of colorants for polyester resins: dyes, which are transparent, and pigments, which are opaque. They are concentrated and suspended in an unpolymerized vehicle for easy blending with the

[1] Avoid plastic, rubber, or copper stirrers. Some react unfavorably with the resin.

114

 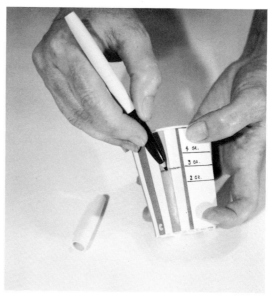

Fig. 195. For accurate measurements of resin, pour an ounce of water into a paper cup (more if needed), and mark the level with a pencil. Empty out the water and dry the cup thoroughly, then fill with resin up to the mark. Add catalyst and stir gently.

Fig. 196. To keep from having to repeat this procedure for every batch, make a graduated scale on a strip of cardboard. If cups of the same size are used each time, the resin level can be quickly determined.

resin. Of the two, the opaque pigments are more stable and fade-resistant.

Additives, such as surface hardeners, promoters, etc., should be mixed with the resin, not with each other or the catalyst, or they can generate enough heat to become explosive.

MOLDS

Although many kinds of containers are suitable for molds, it is important to realize that their textures will be imprinted on the surface of the resin. Irregularities can be ground off and polished away, of course, but there is no reason why they cannot be avoided in the first place.

You can make original molds of your own design from clay. Porcelain has a finer grain and is smoother than earthenware, but in all cases, the clay should be glazed. Watch for undercuts in hand-modeled impressions. Even a small inward curve can permanently lock in the casting.

Slabs and blocks of various sizes can be cast in tin cans, aluminum cake pans, bread pans, and certain types of flexible plastic containers, such as those used for ice trays and mixing bowls.[2] Molds should be coated thinly with mold release, and the excess wiped away with absorbent tissue.

Glass is a superior material for molds, and will produce beautiful castings even without a releasing agent. Burned-out light bulbs and chipped glassware make fine expendable forms for door knobs and paperweights. Use them as waste molds and break them away from the hardened casting.

PROBLEM AREAS

Soft Spots

Soft spots in cured resin are caused by improper mixing. As you drip in the catalyst, notice that fine hairlines begin to form immediately as it reacts with the resin. Stir gently, without whipping, until all these lines disappear, before pouring it. Scrape the stirrer

[2] Always make a test pouring to determine whether or not a plastic mold will warp from the heat of polymerization.

MAKING A MOLD FROM A LIGHT BULB

Fig. 199. Paperweights and door knobs can be cast in broken stemware if the bowls are intact. Set the stems in a block of styrofoam to hold them in a level position. When the curvature of the bowl forms an undercut as shown here, it must be broken away from the hardened form.

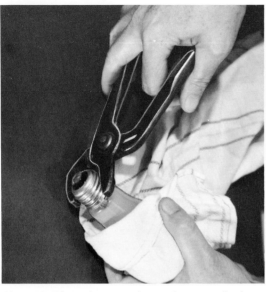

Fig. 197. Place the screw-in cap between the jaws of large pliers and squeeze until the glass fractures.

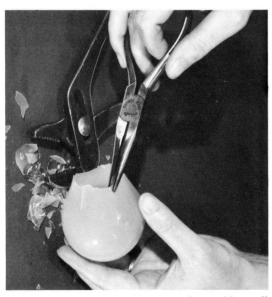

Fig. 198. Draw out the filaments, then, with small pliers, carefully nibble away the excess glass around the broken edge. Cracks can be bound with masking tape to keep them from becoming dislocated. Set the bowl in an upright position on a patty of plasteline.

around the walls of the container just as you would cake batter to make sure the entire batch is blended, not just the middle.

Surface Tack

A sticky residue sometimes remains on top of thick castings, particularly when there has been a low percentage of catalyst. Professional workers usually remove this with electrical polishing equipment. It can be done by hand, starting with coarse emery paper and graduating to finer grades, then to buffing compounds.

This is a great deal of work and not applicable to types of castings where some of the embedments protrude above the surface. In this case, simply paint the surface with a coat of heavily catalyzed resin which will generate enough heat to harden the sticky layer. A small amount of surface hardener in the final pour will also eliminate tack. (These are especially recommended for cap coats which contain opaque pigments.) Use as little as possible, however, for too much can create a cloudy film.

Bubbles

When the catalyzed resin is ready to pour, it will be thick and syrupy. It is easy to trap bubbles in the mix by stirring too vigorously.

Start the pour in the center of the mold so that the resin will pool slowly and push air away ahead of it. Where bubbles form in small pockets, puncture them or slip a toothpick under them and chase them up to the surface. They will be surprisingly resilient and elusive, bouncing around like tiny slippery beads. Sometimes, they must be literally "swept up" onto a strip of cardboard.

Sheet inclusions, such as fibrous glass mat, rice paper, etc., should be punctured all over with a needle. Curl the sheets slightly and lower them into the resin from one edge, rather than dropping them down flat. Use a strip of cardboard to agitate and release bubbles which may be trapped underneath.

Fracturing

It is a common fallacy that resins are non-breakable, and the beginner may be shocked to see an apparently perfect block suddenly begin to crack.

When a block has fractured, nothing can be done to restore it. But if accurate records are kept of each project and test, the problem can be completely eliminated.

As already explained, polymerization is induced by heat. The degree of heat produced is relatively increased by larger amounts of catalyst. When polymerization is excessively fast, expansion and contraction are naturally more abrupt.

On thick pourings, this can be great enough to cause the piece to fracture. The obvious solution is to counteract the heat in some way. The mold can be set in a pan of ice water, or in an unused refrigerator. A simpler method is to decrease the catalyst or pour the casting in several layers, waiting for each to become hard and cold before adding another.[3]

[3] A greater amount of surface is exposed to air on thin sheets. Polymerization is retarded, thereby indicating a need for a larger amount of catalyst.

Since different brands of resin set up at different rates, preliminary experiments will be more valuable than volumes of printed material. We have found, for example, that best results are obtained with some resins by cutting the manufacturer's suggested proportion of catalyst in half. This means, of course, that the cure will be slow and often requires a heavily catalyzed surface coat to eliminate tack. (It is especially important that slow-curing mixes be protected from dust.)

Make a series of test pours at one time so that all factors, including weather and temperature, will be alike. Keep notes of your findings.

Making Test Pours for Thick Castings

Measure 2 ounces of resin into each of 5 paper cups. The cups should be small enough for this to make a layer about 1 inch thick. Start the first test with one half the minimum amount of catalyst recommended by the manufacturer, and increase it in each batch four drops at the time. For example, we shall assume that the label suggests 4 drops of catalyst per ounce for thick castings. Reducing that by half, put 4 drops in the *2 ounces* of resin in the first cup, 8 drops in the second, 12 in the third, 16 in the fourth, and 20 in the fifth.

Stir well and add a few samples of embedment materials.

About every fifteen minutes, check the cups and make notes of your observations. Useful information will be:

1. The gelling time.
2. The clarity and color.
3. The appearance of the embedments.
4. Whether or not heat becomes excessive.
5. The degree of shrinkage away from the sides of the cup.
6. Fracturing.
7. The length of time required for total hardness.

After twenty-four hours, peel away the cups to examine the results more clearly. The surface which was next to the cup will appear slightly frosted owing to the resin picking up a film of wax. This has no real bearing on the tests.

Somewhere in the above scale of proportions you will locate the best catalyst-to-resin mix for thick castings.

Silvering

This is a term which describes the appearance of certain embedments which seem to acquire a silvery skin after polymerization becomes complete. This may occur within a few hours, or be delayed a few days. It can spoil what would otherwise be a beautiful mosaic and, incongruously, occasionally enhance it.

This "skin" is actually a minute separation of the embedment from the resin. It can result from materials which are difficult to "wet" or saturate, such as fuzzy plants, fabrics, or seeds, and can be caused by moisture, grease, or dust.

It most frequently occurs with hard, impervious materials, such as glass, which have different ratios of contraction and expansion from the resin. This can create a cleavage at certain points of contact.

The most reliable way of handling this problem is to use a minimum amount of catalyst and a number of very thin pours. If the embedments are fairly large, they can be pretreated by dipping into a low-catalyzed batch of resin and leaving to "drip dry" for twenty-four hours on a sheet of mylar before embedding.

Now and then, silvering can be attractive, especially where it takes the form of shining rings around glass nuggets.

Unfortunately, the effect cannot be predicted. Sometimes the silver film will completely obscure the fragment it encloses.

Dirty materials of any kind are inclined to silver. Small objects such as cogwheels, metal scraps, glass chips, etc., should be dropped into a jar of acetone and swirled around for a few minutes. Scoop them out into a sieve, then spread on paper towels to dry before using. Handle as little as possible, since even clean hands may leave a deposit of moisture or oil.

A different type of silvering sometimes appears when an embedded mosaic is deliberately left inside a glass casing. (This is described later in the chapter.) As the resin shrinks with curing, it may begin to withdraw from the glass in several places, forming odd mirror-like patches. They will completely disappear once the resin shrinks entirely away, but usually this will not happen without a little prodding.

Place the piece in a pan of very hot water, then in the refrigerator for an hour or so. If one or two spots still remain, repeat the treatment.[4]

CERAMIC MOBILE WITH RESIN WINDOWS

Fired clay cut-outs similar to those used for the trivet in the last chapter can be designed as frames for beautiful little resin windows. The pieces can be put together into room dividers or screens, but we shall explain the process on something less ambitious.

The demonstration project is a mobile of free forms in several sizes. The resin windows are quite thin and poured in two separate layers. The build-up of heat, therefore, is not as great as in thick castings, and the amount of catalyst not as critical. To keep the shrinkage to a minimum, use a little less than what is recommended on the resin labels for $1/4$-inch castings.

For the most part, the mosaic inclusions should be transparent, though a few opaque fragments will strengthen the pattern as long as they do not exclude too much of the light. Brilliant mosaic materials can be made by pouring several thin "puddles" of colored resin on a sheet of acetate. (Use small coils

[4] Wrap the casting in a plastic bag so that the odor will not permeate food.

SUNRISE. Venetian glass tiles attached to a backing with white glue and grouted. By William Ruder.

THE PIER. Wood strips and pressed-glass tiles. By Mary Lou Stribling. (*Collection of Margory Hoya Smith.*)

MOONSCAPE has a light source built inside the frame. Translucent areas are mosaicked with fragments of flattened bottles, antique cathedral glass, and cullet. Plastic steel forms the opaque linear pattern. By Mary Lou Stribling.

GIFTS FROM THE SEA.
Shells, barnacles, moonstones, and Venetian glass set into colored magnesite. By William Justema.

THE POTTER. Smalti, transparent and gold-dusted tiles, and melted glass nuggets. Designed by the author for a cover of POPULAR CERAMICS magazine.

ST. JOHN THE BAPTIST.
By Thomas Hunt.

of plasteline as dams.) When the resin has gelled, trim the edges and slice them with a pastry wheel into tesserae of useful sizes. Let them cure completely before using.

Colored transparent beads, short segments of opaque plastic hors d'oeuvres picks, and melted glass chips are demonstrated, but there are hundreds of other possibilities.

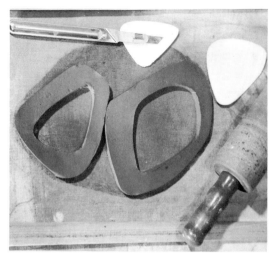

Fig. 200. CLAY AND RESIN MOBILE.
Making the parts of the mobile.

Fig. 201. Roll out a sheet of grogged clay about ¼ inch thick and use a sharp, thin knife to cut out the forms. This can be done freehand or from cardboard patterns. The forms will be more interesting if the outlines and window openings are not exactly alike. Remove excess clay and refine the cut edges with a moist brush.

Fig. 202. When the forms can be peeled from the oilcloth without stretching them out of shape, place them between sheets of grass mats, nubby fabric, or plastic doilies, and roll lightly to texture both sides. Holes for suspending can be pierced now with a toothpick, or with a hand drill after they are dry.

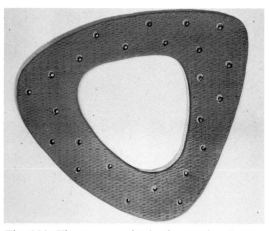

Fig. 203. The top spreader is about twice the size of the other forms. Pierce it all over so that a number of arrangements will be possible. There will be less chance of warping if the clay pieces are dried between paper towels with a light weight on top. Refine the edges with a moist sponge, slightly rounding those which will border the resin. This will create undercuts to lock in the panes. Bisque-fire when dry.

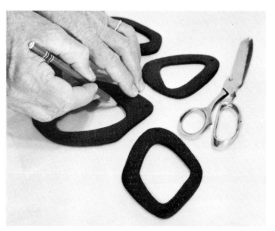

Fig. 205. . . . place the form on a strip of acetate (or Mylar) and draw around the inside of the window. (If frosted acetate is used, be sure to turn it shiny side up or your resin window will be frosted, too.) Cut out the drawing, leaving a narrow margin all around . . .

Fig. 204. You may want to glaze the clay in a separate firing. These pieces were stained black. Place them on a sheet of cardboard, arrange the mosaic in each opening, then lift up carefully to leave the pattern undisturbed. Some of the pieces here are ready to be turned over and filled with resin. To prepare them for this process . . .

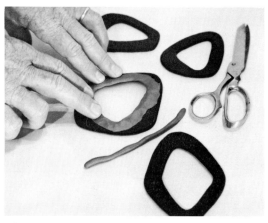

Fig. 206. . . . and replace it over the window. Seal it firmly to the bisque with a tiny coil of plasteline (or florists' clay) so that no cracks remain through which the resin might seep.

Fig. 207. Now turn all the prepared windows right side up on a level surface and press them down so that the plasteline cushions and holds the acetate tightly against the frame. Mix catalyst and resin and pour a very thin layer on the acetate. Use a strip of cardboard to guide it into the crevices. The layer should just cover the bottom.

Let the first layer of resin become completely hard before pouring the anchor layer for the mosaic. In this batch, we shall add a few drops of transparent dye, and mix only enough to fill about three windows at the time.

Pour the colored resin into the windows to a depth that is slightly below the level of the clay, and immediately set in the mosaic arrangement. Use tweezers or a toothpick to

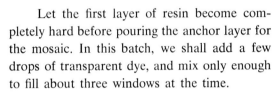

Fig. 209. Suspend the mosaic on rawhide thongs, shoelaces, twine, or, as shown, heavy black cord. Hang the spreader temporarily first, then thread the suspensions through the holes and knot on the upper side. Make final adjustments in the lengths of the spreader strings so that the mobile hangs level. A spot of household cement on the knots will keep them from raveling and becoming loosened.

push the pieces in place. Domed or faceted materials will have more luminosity if their top surfaces are left elevated above the bed of resin.

WINDOWED DIVIDERS

The method described above can be used for striking mosaic curtains or room dividers. Plot the shapes on paper and trim them before firing so that the assemblage will be even. For a flexible curtain, use links of chain or wire to bind the finished pieces together.

Similar forms can be designed for rigid screens. Some allowance should be made for shrinkage of the clay, but the width of the frame can be adjusted as needed. The finished clay-and-resin pieces can be set into a solid bed of resin as described in Chapter 21, or they can be fired in units and framed together.

COMPLETING THE MOBILE

Fig. 208. Wait twelve hours before peeling away the plasteline and acetate. Use a knife to scrape away any residue of resin on the underside, and finish cleaning it with acetone. This will also remove some of the stain from the high spots of the texture, bringing it out more boldly. Cure pieces for several days before hanging.

Fig. 210. CLAY AND RESIN ROOM DIVIDERS.

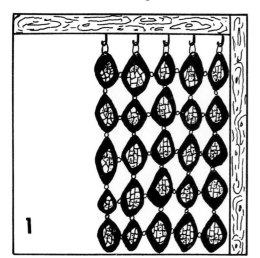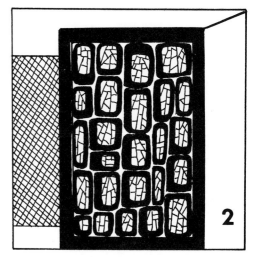

1. Flexible curtains can be hung on small hooks in a board attached to the ceiling.
2. Forms can be bound together with wire and framed, or set in a bed of resin.

THICK CASTINGS

Bookends slabs can be cast in glass or aluminum cake pans, and the finished pieces mounted on wooden bases or metal library-type book supports. Low tumblers are good molds for paperweights, as long as the sides flare outward and do not cup in. You might also try a light-bulb mold as shown in Figures 197, 198.

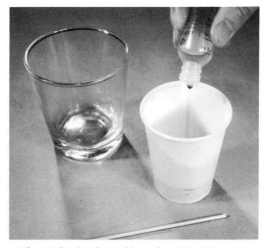

Fig. 211. The spokes of the layered pinwheels were pulled from a molten scrap of glass. Little crumbs of melted cathedral glass were arranged in the middle and at the tip of each spoke. (Other materials may be substituted.) Since this is a symmetrical design, a simple pattern was drawn up as a guide.

Fig. 212. Apply a film of mold release inside the tumbler and wipe away visible residue. An ounce of resin will be enough for the first layer. It will form a clear casing for the mosaic and will have no inclusions. Use a minimum amount of catalyst. Only 2 drops per ounce were used for this demonstration.

Mix the batch well, pour into the mold, then tilt the mold so that the resin coats the sides. Check every few minutes to note when it begins to thicken, then immediately roll the resin around in the tumbler again to leave a heavier deposit. (Do not wait until actual gelaton begins.) This will keep subsequent layers from causing lines on the finished surface.

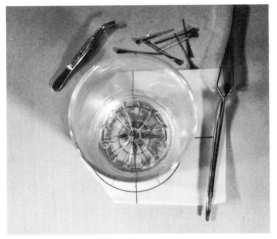

Fig. 213. The anchor layer for the first wheel is added as soon as the casing has gelled. Pour only enough to provide a thin bed, set in the materials, and cover them with the remaining resin. The deeper the layers, the more pronounced the three-dimensional effect will be, but they should not appear totally unrelated.

From here on, to prevent a build-up of heat, let each layer of resin become cold before adding another.

Repeat step 3 until you have built up a casting from 1½ inches to 2 inches thick. Each wheel should be larger than the one before in relation to the increasing diameter of the tumbler. Handsome effects can be obtained with progressively deeper colors of glass.

Keep the casting in a cool place for at least twenty-four hours. To facilitate removal from the mold, place in a pan of very hot water for a few minutes, then into the refrigerator for about half an hour. Pry around the edge with the tip of a knife blade, and the hardened form should slip out. Trim away sharp ledges which may have formed around the rim.

Antique gold paper was glued to the bottom of the paperweight shown for a reflective backing for the mosaic. In the following examples we shall pour opaque cap layers instead.

CASTINGS WITH GLASS CASES

There are often very good reasons for leaving a casting permanently in a glass mold. These can stem from the belated discovery of a small undercut which will not release the hardened form. But beyond an actual necessity, we may find that the glass casing enhances the three-dimensional quality and, for certain uses, provides a more durable surface.

There is no difference between the construction of such objects and the construction of those which are removed from the mold, but they usually require refrigeration to eliminate the silvery patches which may appear as the resin shrinks away from the glass.[6]

If the resin core loosens and falls out during the process of "de-silvering," let it and the mold stand at room temperature until both are completely dry. Replace the core and glue a mat of cork or felt to the bottom to hold it in.

Gelling resin is sometimes said to have a "memory," and you will discover why if you try to rearrange an embedment which has slipped out of place. It will glide around easily with a little prodding, but a few minutes later will return to its original position.

[6] This was discussed earlier in the chapter.

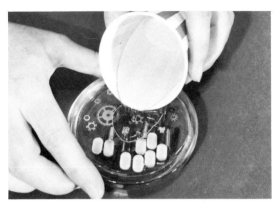

Fig. 214. A number of different materials can be embedded in a cap layer to provide a textured background for the mosaic. Leave at least ⅛ inch between the final decorative layer and the top of the mold, and fill it about halfway with resin.

Fig. 217. Clock parts make up the design of this gold, black, and white paperweight. The thick glass casing is the same as that used in Fig. 216. It has interesting magnifying qualities which cause the decorative materials to appear suspended in space, some floating in front of others. When the weight is turned, there is an illusion of movement as though the inclusions are drifting from one level to another.

Fig. 215. Sift colored sand, gravel, or crushed glass evenly into the bed, tamp it down until it is saturated, then add more resin to fill the mold.

Fig. 216. The colored background is dramatic behind a three-dimensional mosaic of cogwheels, lock washers, aluminum scraps, and glass nuggets, though the photograph does not show the full multi-layered effect. The casting is left inside the cavity of a domed paperweight designed to hold a photograph.

Fig. 218. Five thin pours were required for this effect. The first was the casing layer as described in Fig. 212. The next three contained the decorative materials. By lifting the weight up and studying it from the underside, bubbles trapped beneath the embedments were located and removed with a toothpick.

Fig. 219. The fifth layer was a cap coat of opaque white. The same catalyst-to-resin proportions were used, plus 2 drops of surface hardener. Opaque pigments were added a drop at the time until the mix had the desired density.

TESSERAE FROM WASHERS AND GLASS JEWELS

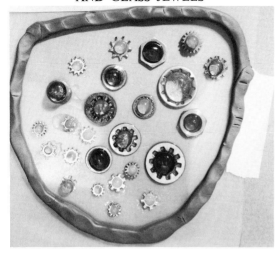

Fig. 220. These jewel-like objects are actually lock washers and nuts set around small gold-backed glass nuggets. If we tried to embed them in one layer, they would undoubtedly float apart. To hold them together, arrange them on a sheet of acetate and, with a toothpick, drip a few drops of catalyzed resin in the center of each. (The coil of plasteline provides a dam in case of an overflow.) When the resin has gelled, peel away the acetate and trim surplus resin from the edges with a sharp knife.

Fig. 221. The jewels are arranged upside down in layers of wet resin. Agitate them gently from side to side to encourage bubbles to rise to the surface. Leave ⅛ inch of space between the last pour and the top of the mold for an opaque cap. White was used again here to complement a color scheme of silver, greens, and turquoise.

Fig. 222. This little metal pan was certainly manufactured for another purpose, but it exactly fits the piece shown in Fig. 221. We'll epoxy it in place . . .

Fig. 223. . . . then epoxy a flat metal cabinet-pull on the back, and install it on the door of a storage cupboard.

When changes are necessary after gelling has begun, lift the piece completely out with tweezers, wait a few seconds, then press it carefully back into the resin.

The small objects we have shown on the previous pages were designed as introductions to polyester resin. They have, however, other uses aside from paperweights. Without an opaque backing, they can be made into "eyelets" for a garden wall.[7] A little sleuthing in the hardware stores will uncover all kinds of fittings with which they can be converted into handsome cabinet pulls or decorative knobs for doors and storage chests. Some caster caps, for example, can be used as frames.

Unless the knobs are quite heavy, they can be mounted on flat metal door pulls with epoxy cement. Epoxy is entirely adequate for forms such as those shown above in which the castings exactly fit.

[7] Use them in place of the eyelets which are outlined in Chapter 20.

chapter 14.

Starting to Work with Fused Glass

Mosaicists have been working with glass for centuries, though it has been more usual to join fragments together with lead or mortar, than to fuse them with heat.

The Roman mosaic wares were mentioned in the first chapter, and we shall investigate a similar technique later here. This type of fragmented design illustrates the important difference between cemented and kiln-fused mosaics. In the first group, decorative materials and foundation remain physically unchanged by the method of attachment. In the latter, both are altered and reshaped when the glass is softened by heat.

The thermoplastic qualities of glass open up many new areas of mosaic design. For example, a composition assembled on a flat backing can be molded into a three-dimensional form at the same time at which its separate parts are fused together.

Chapter 8 is a necessary introduction to the work which follows, since it explains many mechanical techniques as well as decorative possibilities. It will also provide you with a certain basic understanding of glass craft without involving you in large projects and a quantity of materials.

We shall review a few general notes with the reminder that haste and negligence, the two enemies of good work with clay and resin, also lurk behind most failures with fused glass.

NOTES ON WORKING WITH GLASS

• The work table on which glass will be cut should be cushioned with an old blanket, carpet, or pad of newspapers. Keep a wide brush handy for sweeping away sharp crumbs.

• Glass is cut by scoring a line with a cutter, then applying pressure to it on the opposite side. For thick glass, this is best done with the ball end of the cutter. Uncomplicated scores on thin glass can be snapped apart with the hands, and the breaks will be cleaner than those obtained from tapping.

• Allow at least ½-inch margin around cut shapes or they will be difficult, even impossible, to remove from the sheet.

• Bearing down too heavily on the cutting tool can either break the glass sheet or so bind the wheel that it scores a skip-miss-drag line which will cause a ragged fracture.

• Straight lines and gentle curves are easy to cut from glass. Avoid narrow "peninsular"

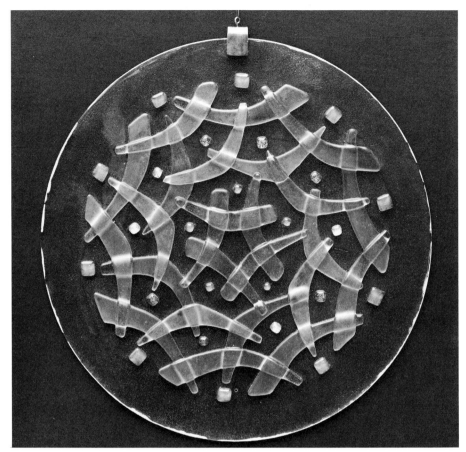

Fig. 224. "Roundel," by Maurice Heaton, is designed with shards and small tesserae of glass colored with transparent enamels. The pieces were fused to a 14-inch circle of glass at 1350° F.

shapes, or V wedges which arrow inward.

• To prevent edges from slanting, keep the cutting wheel perpendicular to the glass.

• Textured glass is scored on the smooth side, mirrors on the uncoated surface.

• Dirty glass is not only hard to cut accurately but also may scum or cloud in the firing. Clean it in hot soapy water, rinse thoroughly, then polish dry with a lint-free cloth. Traces of detergent can leave a scum, too.

• Some very soft glass will scum even if it is clean. (Firing too high is another cause of this fault.) If your tests have indicated such a tendency, brush on a *very* thin film of low-fire flux or clear glass glaze before firing.

• Opaque enamels applied to the sub-surface of glass will pick up a layer of separator. This is acceptable for certain types of materials, but dictates the need for a thicker than normal application of separator. The enamels will sometimes stay clean if fired on special foundations, such as sheet mica.

• Annealing, or "heat-soaking," of layered materials, large sheets, and bent forms will make them harder and less subject to cracking.

• Pretest for compatibility all glass to be laminated or fused together, as well as all other materials which are to be fused between layers.

• Sharp pinpoints on the edges of fired glass can result from thin ledges or tiny protrusions left on cut forms. Before firing, remove imperfections with an emery-tipped electric grinder, coarse emery paper, or a carborundum stone. Even perfect cuts may pinpoint if the glass is overfired.

128

• The only times you can be absolutely sure two adjacent pieces of glass will fuse together is when you don't want them to. Large pieces, especially those which do not fit precisely, have a perverse tendency to pull away from each other, resulting in a weak, unsightly seam which will fracture from the slightest jar. These points should be reinforced with a "patch" which is related to the design and fused over the joint (see butterflies in Figure 121).

• Fire important projects only where they can be visually observed. Use the rest of the kiln space for compatibility and color tests, and for making materials.

• Always use a separator between glass and the support on which it rests. Nearly all separators will stick to glass if it is overfired.

• Even small scraps of glass are useful, but they are harder to identify than large sheets. Save them in marked containers to eliminate the chance of using them on an incompatible base.

Fig. 225. Fused glass trivets are not recommended for hot dishes, but may be used as an accent for flower arrangements, or to add a ring of glowing color around containers for nuts and candy. Several disks of different sizes and color combinations could be grouped for wall decorations.

LAYERED FRAGMENTS

No pattern is necessary for this introductory project unless you prefer a particular motif rather than the all-over pattern illustrated. Since the trivet is made of two layers of transparent fragments, we must first choose colors which can successfully be superimposed.

Think of overlaying glass colors in the same way you would of overlaying washes of transparent watercolors. Related hues—blue, blue-green, green; or yellow, orange, red—will be safe. Sharp contrasts, such as orange over green or violet over yellow, will produce muddy or neutral shades.

The second layer will go faster than the base structure since it is not necessary to fit the pieces closely together. A more pleasing texture will be obtained, however, if the fragments are reasonably uniform in width.

Arrange them on top of the underseams, thus reinforcing the joint and bonding the structure together.

ARRANGING THE BASE LAYER

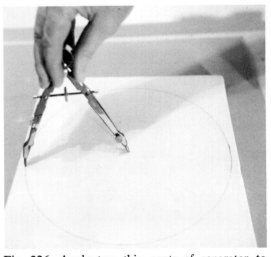

Fig. 226. Apply two thin coats of separator to the kiln shelf and let it dry. Then with a compass (or plate of suitable size) mark off a circle which comes no closer than ½ inch to the edges of the shelf.

Fig. 229. To ensure a certain unity, it is best to go completely around the circle with one color, though the width of the band can be irregular. Continue until the circle is filled, securing each piece to the wrap with a dab of rubber cement. A symmetrical pattern can be followed, or a random mix of sizes.

Fig. 227. Protect the shelf with a sheet of cellophane wrap to keep any particles of separator from sifting between the pieces of glass. Use a section several inches larger than the shelf, smooth it over the surface, pull edges to underside, and secure with cellophane tape. Both tape and wrap will burn away in the firing.

THE UNFIRED TRIVET

Fig. 228. Start assembling the base layer at the outside edges of the circle. Close fits are important, and some cutting will be necessary. To trim small fragments, mark the line of fracture with a glass pencil, score with the cutter, and snap away margin with square-jawed pliers. Nippers can be used on very narrow strips.

Fig. 230. There may be hairline separations between the strips of the bottom layer, which adds an interesting texture. The second layer will hold them together. Both heating and cooling cycles should be as gradual as possible, and the fused unit must be annealed.

MAKING A GLASS MOLD

Although excellent commercial molds for shaping glass are available, most craftsmen enjoy the experience of making their own. The process is neither complex nor expensive, and with the exception of a kiln, requires no special equipment.

Any kind of mold involves two separate forms we can distinguish as "negatives" and "positives." The positive, or core form, is the shape of the depression into which the glass will sag. The negative form is the mold itself, an imprint of the outside of the core.

Original core shapes can be carved from wood or plaster blocks, or modeled in clay. Many household items can be used as starting points, becoming "originals" as they are altered, textured, and provided with a wide rim to accommodate blanks of various designs. Metal, plastic, or pottery bowls make good cores if they have simple flowing contours without undercuts, and do not slope too steeply from rim to bottom.

Molds made from 2 parts plaster of Paris and 1 part of fine river sand will hold up for one or two firings. But their fragility, due to calcination of the plaster from heat, makes them impractical except as waste molds for one-of-a-kind pieces. For this purpose, they are excellent, since they can be made fairly thin and chipped away from undercuts.

Patching asbestos, soft firebrick, and metals have certain specialized uses for the mold maker, but clay is best of all.

Terra cotta molds will last indefinitely if properly handled. The clay should contain 15 per cent to 30 per cent fine grog and be thoroughly wedged to eliminate air pockets.

Roll out a slab ½ inch to ¾ inch thick and about 12 inches in diameter. (If you cannot obtain an oversized rolling pin, use a broom handle or length of pipe.) Puncture with a toothpick any air bubbles which may rise to the surface and place a damp cloth over the clay to keep it from drying out while you prepare the core.

We have chosen a plain china bowl for the positive form. Center it upside down on a plaster bat or pad of newspapers.

Fig. 231. Some kind of separator must be used between core and clay to facilitate its removal before the mold shrinks and cracks around it. A slightly damp square of cotton jersey or cheesecloth may be stretched over the bowl with a minimum of wrinkles. Strips of paper towels will also serve. Use a moist sponge to press them against the bowl. Let them extend an inch or so beyond the rim.

Fig. 232. When the bowl is covered, lift the slab in its oilcloth "sling" and drape it clay side down over the core. Center it, and peel away the oilcloth. Without stretching the clay, press it firmly against the core, adjusting it as necessary to eliminate folds.

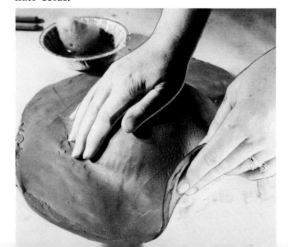

When the clay is firm enough to handle, the core can be removed. Slide one hand beneath the bat, place the other on top of the clay form, and flip it over. Remove the bat and core, and peel away the newspaper strips. Refine the rim and turn it upside down again on the bat to stiffen.

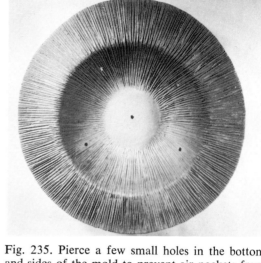

Fig. 235. Pierce a few small holes in the bottom and sides of the mold to prevent air pockets from being trapped under the sagging glass. Dry it slowly and thoroughly before firing one or two cones lower than for full maturity. This will leave it absorbent enough for easy application of separator. Being less brittle than completely matured bisque, it will be less inclined to crack from weight of glass and repeated exposure to heat.

Fig. 233. Refine the shape with modeling tools and trim away excess clay. Leave a margin of at least 2 inches around the core.

Fig. 234. When the clay is almost leather hard, smooth and clean the inside with a moist sponge, then texture it with a blunt tool. Try several different kinds of texture prints on a clay sheet. If radiating lines are used, divide the rim into equal parts as a guide for keeping them even. Brush away loose crumbs and soften the sharp edges of the texture with a sponge.

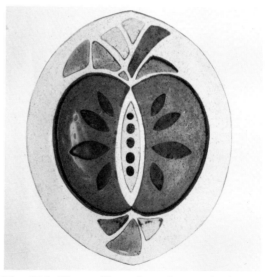

Fig. 236. The mold we have just made formed this bowl, though the glass blank was cut into a pointed oval. The stylized fruit motif of cathedral-glass cut-outs was designed to fit the depression, with leaves and stem extending up into the rim. Prefired jewels with metallic undercoatings were used in the middle.

It is important that the bottom of the mold be level so that the glass will sag evenly into the depression. Smooth it with a rolling pin, then check it with a carpenter's level. As an alternate measure, place two jars or boxes of equal height on each side of the mold and rest a strip of wood (or heavy cardboard) across them. By measuring the distance from the strip to several points on the bottom of the mold, you can determine where to add or subtract clay.

The edges of the mold will dry faster than the center unless they are covered with a damp cloth. Place several small weights around the rim to prevent it from warping.

MOSAIC WARE FROM GLASS NUGGETS

The mosaic wares of the ancient Romans were made in solid cast molds rather than open molds such as that in Figure 235. One half of the mold shaped the outside of the form, the other half shaped the inside.

To describe very briefly their process, slices of patterned glass canes were arranged to line the depression in the outside section of the mold. The inner section was then positioned on top, and the unit fired until the glass fused together and assumed the shape of the mold.

Irregularity in thicknesses of the cane slices meant that before firing, the top part of the mold was slightly raised, held up by thicker segments. As the glass softened, it dropped into level position, squeezing the molten material into all the interstices to form a solid dish. When cool, the glass was removed, refined with grinders, and put back in the kiln for fire-polishing.[1]

Picking up this idea and greatly simplifying it for limited equipment, we can make a type of mosaic ware from glass chunks either broken at random or prefired into rounded nuggets.

[1] This and other techniques of ancient glassmaking were described by Frederic Schuler in *Craft Horizons,* March–April, 1960.

The slippery chunks would slide on a steep slant, so the mold must be fairly shallow. Even if they remained in place during construction, as they became plastic the upper rim of a deep bowl would probably fold over and collapse into the bottom.

You can make a mold from a glass, metal, or china plate by the method just described, or use a commercial mold such as shown in the following demonstration.

Only a clean, dustless surface will enable you to arrange and rearrange the glass to your satisfaction, so a liquid separator must be used on the mold. You may begin work while it is still damp, but it should be completely dry before firing.

Several related colors may be used if they are compatible, but since the ware will be textured by both the mold and the fragmentation, subtle harmony, rather than sharp contrast, will be most effective. (Acutely delineated motifs or geometric patterns should be made in a slightly different way, which will be shown later.)

Chunks, broken or nipped from thick bottle bottoms, are used for the first project. Light colors will show the fragmented pattern to the best advantage.

Fig. 237. Starting at the bottom of the mold, arrange glass chunks as close together as possible. As you progress up the sides, a dab of rubber cement on the edges of tesserae will hold them in place.

When you reach the rim, some shaping of the nuggets will be necessary to obtain an "evenly uneven" edge. Nip a few chunks into tiny bits and drop them into crevices which are larger than the end of a match.

When the mold is covered, fire it just high enough to fuse the fragments together—about 1425° F. is usually sufficient for bottle glass.

On another shelf, or in the corners not filled by the mold, place a few thick pieces of the bottle glass. (We shall use them to make a kind of glass grout.)

After firing, leave the glass undisturbed on the mold and prepare the filler for the crevices.

Heat the fired scraps in the kitchen oven and drop them in a pan of ice water. Return to the oven to dry, then wrap them in a heavy cloth and pulverize with a hammer. Sieve to remove larger granules. The glass should be about the consistency of sugar, and you will need several spoonfuls.

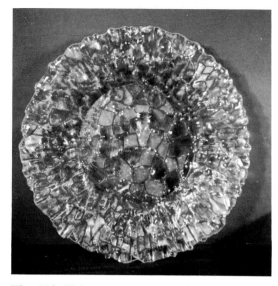

Fig. 239. Take care not to overfire, or the mass of glass will slide down into the bottom. 1500° F. can be used as a rule of thumb for bottle glass.

The fragmentation of the design is still apparent, but now it has the fluid, half-melted quality of cracked ice.

Fig. 238. Moisten the powder with a few drops of water and sprinkle the paste over the entire plate. Sweep it into the crevices and tamp down firmly with the fingers. Brush away excess. In the final firing, which should be high enough to round the fragments and fuse the piece solidly, the pulverized glass will liquify and seal the spaces between nuggets.

All such ware should be fired slowly, annealed, and cooled slowly, since the grouting mixture of pulverized glass will be molten before the larger fragments are fused. If it returns to a rigid state too quickly, the piece may fracture.

Stunning bowls, plates, ash trays, trivets, etc., can be made in this manner with the antique gold nuggets described in Chapter 8.

It would be quite difficult to organize glass chunks into a rigidly controlled pattern on a concave surface. If such design is desired, cut a glass blank to fit the mold and arrange the nuggets on it. (Naturally, they must be compatible.) Eliminate the procedure of grouting the crevices with pulverized glass. Fire until the nuggets are fused and the blank has sagged into the mold.

We can also use scraps of colored sheet glass for this purpose, though the effect will be entirely different.

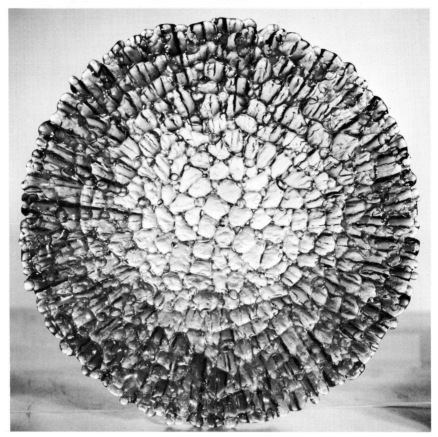

Fig. 240. Prefired nuggets will give a different textural effect. In this example, green bottle nuggets were used for the basic arrangement. Small spaces in between were filled with pale amber crumbs, which melted into glistening droplets.

Fig. 241. The depression into which softened glass will settle is an important factor in the mosaic design. Decoration and form should always be related. Mark guide lines on the cut blank to indicate the shape of the cavity. (As shown in Fig. 236, it is not necessary for the blank to follow the lines of the mold exactly.)

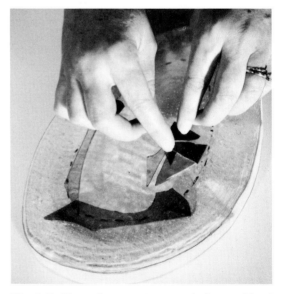

Fig. 242. Try a few spontaneous designs, without working from a predrawn pattern. Sometimes margins and random shards will suggest a striking arrangement you would never have produced with a pencil.

COBBLED GLASS

This is a coined name for a reverse-method type of mosaic lamination which is obtained by sagging thin sheets of glass over thick, prefired domed tesserae. Many different kinds of these decorative materials are explained in Chapter 8. Marbles can be fired until they are half flattened, and they are compatible with some sheet glass. Similar commercially prepared products are available which fuse beautifully with cathedral glass as well as certain brands of soft window glass.

The seeded "cobbles" for the birds in Figure 243 were made by laminating transparent copper enamel between pieces of scrap window glass.

Fusion of large glass sections which have wide variations in thickness and thinness can be tricky, but the depth and luminosity more than compensate for a little extra attention to firing and preparation of materials.

Fracturing from uneven tension is the problem, of course, and it can be delayed for some time after the piece is removed from the kiln. An examination of breaks will show that they occur at points of greatest strain, that is, where a thin area sags and stretches over a thick cobble.

This is a logical reaction, for naturally, heat will penetrate a thin layer of glass quicker than a thick layer. If the difference in their rates of expansion and contraction is great enough, the pull of one against the other can cause the glass to break at its weakest point.

As previously explained, the answer is to reduce tensions by tempering. And in this case, we should temper the decorative materials when they are formed, as well as the fused structure.

If a particular type of glass proves stubborn (as occasionally we find true with certain brittle sheets), we can tame it by prefiring the cut sections of a pattern along with the decorative materials. Often, they will then fuse agreeably together.

Large cobbled panels can be fused in sections and reassembled in a bed of mortar

Fig. 243. Pale-pink cobbled birds are combined with olive-green leaves, deep pink berries, and a few antique gold jewels. The bird in the foreground is mounted out slightly from the backing and secured with concealed bolts. Other elements are attached with epoxy.

Fig. 244. Cobbled glass motifs have greater dimension if they are mounted out from the backing so that more light passes through them. This also enables you to overlap certain elements. One-inch clear plastic boxes can be used as mounts, and are shown in Chapter 21. Short segments of dowels with holes drilled through the middle to accommodate a bolt were used in Fig. 243. Matching holes must also be drilled in both glass and backing and the bolt head countersunk so it can be concealed by a nugget. Mounts should be buttered with epoxy at points of contact with glass and backing.

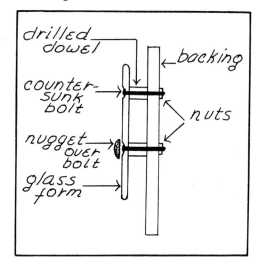

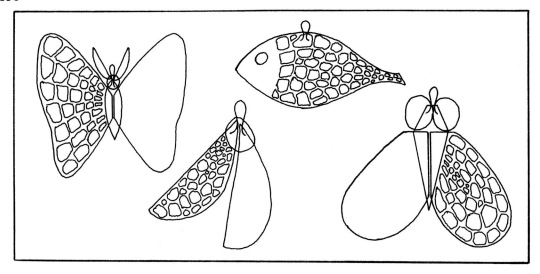

Fig. 245. Cut out all sections of the motifs first so that the scraps can be used for making cobbles. (The fish can be cut in one piece.) These drawings show several ideas for arranging pattern parts. Notice how reinforcements are planned for the seams, and the way loops of Nichrome wire are laminated for suspensions.

or other adhesive. To become familiar with the procedure, however, we shall start with a single motif—a stylized bird, flower, or fish—which can be hung on a wall, used as an insert in a tiled counter or splash-back, or suspended as a mobile.

Cobbled Butterfly Mobile

To make the cobbles, cut the leftover glass into pairs of matching pieces and laminate mica flakes between them. Fire to 1475–1500° F. and temper. Cut the fused fragments into strips, then nip into irregular chunks from ½ inch to ¾ inch in size.

If you like, arrange these bits on a kiln shelf so that they are not touching and refire until they are rounded.

Clean all the glass cut-outs and place the sections to be cobbled bottom side up on your work table. (They may be edged with black glass color, left plain, or the finished piece bound with lead or lead tape.) Small parts, such as the butterfly body and head, may be painted black or with metallic overglazes.

The cobbles are arranged face down about ⅛ inch apart and secured with rubber cement.

For suspensions, laminate a small nichrome loop bent to form undercuts. The metal will not stick to glass and must therefore be embedded in such a way that it cannot be pulled out.

When the cement is dry, turn the pieces over and assemble them sheet side up on a prepared kiln shelf. First position uncobbled sections (such as bodies, stems, etc.), then overlap the other pieces on top with joints aligned. The under-sections will partly compensate for the thickness of the cobbles. Study the pattern diagrams to see how these parts are planned.

Single units, such as the fish, need only to be turned over and placed on the shelf.

Fire to about 1500° F., or until edges are rounded and the overlay has sagged smoothly over the cobbles. Prop kiln lid open an inch until the temperature drops to 1250–1300° F. Close lid. Turn on low or medium heat and leave for a full thirty minutes before turning off.

For an effect which equals the beauty of gold-dusted Venetian glassware, make laminated cobbles from sieved, roasted vermiculite instead of mica. Liquid gold overglaze should then be substituted for platinum.[2]

[2] See Chapter 8.

Fig. 246. Shapes of this kind cannot be cut from glass in one piece. They must be designed in sections, with reinforcements to strengthen the seams. This example is in crystal, silver, and black, with thickly seeded cobbles. Its pure "glassiness" is quite elegant. Single-strength window glass, mica, liquid bright platinum overglaze, and black glass color were the materials used.

chapter 15.

Miniatures

Few craftsmen will be inclined to restrict themselves entirely to the art of the miniature, but there are practical advantages to at least a few exploratory experiences. They are adaptable to extremely limited working space, and involve little expense. Uninhibited by the cost and time required for large projects, we can experiment freely with techniques which may later be adapted to more ambitious pieces.

All over Europe we find mosaic miniatures ranging from hand mirrors, bracelets, desk sets, and jewelry chests to elaborate portraits and scenes no larger than a sheet of note paper.

Italian craftsmen have been producing miniature jewelry for many generations, using magnifying glasses to enable them to fit slices of mosaic canes and ribbons into patterns so perfectly blended that they appear to be delicate tapestry.

Although the style and motifs of many of these wares have become stereotyped and somewhat dated for contemporary tastes, we must admire the artists' patience, as well as their eyesight.

JEWELRY

A design which is easily mosaicked in one size may be impossible in another. Unless you have the endurance of the European craftsmen, you will work for bold, decorative effects, rather than intricacy. Contrasts in colors and textures are important elements, for at a short distance, subtle nuances are lost.

Geometric designs are the easiest. With a little experience you might move into fanciful abstractions or adaptations of Egyptian, African, Indian, and Peruvian symbols.

The miniaturist must learn to "think small" all the way through his plan to execution. He cannot, for example, simply draft a small pattern and then try to execute it in bulky materials.

Most commercial tiles are too thick for jewelry. There is, however, considerable varia-

Fig. 247. "Head of Christ," by an
unknown Italian craftsman, measures
only 9 × 12 inches yet is as carefully
detailed as a large portrait. The tiny
tesserae, which are ⅛ to ¼ inch in
size, are cubes of opaque glass and
marble. *(Photo courtesy of the Cavallini Company.)*

Fig. 248. Italian pill-box and brooch sprigged with naturalistic floral motifs made of mosaic canes and splinters of colored glass.

tion in vitreous glass tiles, and some of them are thin enough to be usable. Italian ribbon glass, pattern chips, melted glass scraps, and slivers of pearl chips are more appropriate and less frustrating to arrange. Seed beads can be effective, especially when embedded for pebbly contrast to smooth materials, but avoid the temptation of commercial faceted "stones" unless you can introduce them discreetly. Mosaic jewelry has a unique character of its own which is cheapened if it attempts to imitate something else.

Mountings

Rigidity without bulk is the primary requirement of a backing for mosaic jewelry. The lids of small plastic boxes may be used, as well as ready-made silver and copper mountings.

These preformed frames, however, are usually limited to rectangles, squares, or circles, and eventually you will want to make your own shapes. Persons with a knowledge of metal craft have the advantage here, though there are suitable substitutes.

Hard, firm cardboard can be treated with several layers of spray plastic to preserve it and reduce absorbency. Additional rigidity will be supplied by grout and decorative materials. Sheet phenolic, a synthetic product widely used in the electronics industry, is better. Lightweight phenolic sheets are non-porous and easily cut with shears.

Fig. 249. Craftsmen in the eastern Mediterranean countries produce many kinds of miniature mosaics. This detail of a jewelry chest is made of minute chips of wood and mother-of-pearl.

MOSAIC PENDANTS

Fig. 250. Sections of lemon-yellow cathedral glass were decorated with torch-pulled orange "seeds" and gold-backed jewels, which were then kiln-fused together. By the author.

Fig. 251. Leaded fragments of stained glass could be used to ornament window shades, light pulls, Christmas trees—or necks. By Rosalis.

Fig. 252. A thin melted slice from a green bottle formed the frame for this interesting pendant. Melted glass chips were sealed in the center with a layer of tinted polyester resin. By Bernice Brown.

MAKING JEWELRY WITH PLASTIC MOUNTINGS

Fig. 253. Nip miniature glass rods, ribbon glass, and narrow strips of cathedral glass to fit pattern and arrange inside a small plastic box-lid. Hole for cord may be made with a heated ice pick or a hand drill. Secure tesserae with transparent glass adhesive.

If your outline is simple and has no angles which arrow inward, glass can be used as a backing. The thinner areas of flattened bottles make beautiful jewelry mountings which, when mosaicked with transparent tesserae, have the richness of tiny stained-glass windows.

One-eighth-inch lead stripping can be shaped and cemented to backings where an edge is needed to frame the decoration. Plastic metals can also be used for this purpose and be given special patinas to complement the design.

Plastic steel is a dull gunmetal color when it has cured, but will pick up highlights of whatever metal is used to burnish the hardened surface. Rub it vigorously with a strip of copper or brass and it takes on the warm color of hand-cast bronze. Polished with the back of a silver spoon it has the sheen of old pewter.

For antique silver effects, plastic aluminum should be given a wash of stain or black paint before being polished.

Fig. 254. When the glue has hardened, fill crevices with black grout. A stiff brush will help work the grout into narrow openings. Clean surface after grout has set up.

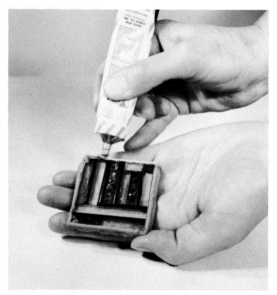

Fig. 255. Squeeze a band of plastic aluminum around edges and spread a layer over the back. Pat it down with a spatula. When the plastic is hard, apply a wash of black paint and polish the high spots with a silver spoon or knife blade.

Fig. 256. 1. Green and dark blue cathedral glass, slices of transparent turquoise glass rods. 2. Orange and dark blue ribbon glass, amber cathedral strips, miniature rods, and chips of red and orange Venetian tiles. 3. Turquoise miniature rods, yellow ribbon glass, yellow and turquoise pattern chips.

Ceramic Forms

With a small kiln and a few pounds of clay we have the capacity for creating jewelry forms of almost unrestricted design. For example, make a few simple outlines with tiny clay coils and join the tesserae with resin by the method described for the mobile in Chapter 13.

Modeled or carved forms are even more interesting. Since considerable time and effort might go into a beautifully perfected model, it is practical to make a mold of it, either before or after it is fired. It could then be duplicated quickly and would have good commercial potential.

A separator of shellac, liquid soap, or light oil should be applied to fired models to facilitate release from the plaster. Being flexible, unfired models require no special treatment.

Cast forms are useful for experiments since they cost practically nothing and an unsuccessful creation can be discarded without sharp pangs of conscience.

Several jewelry forms can be cast at one time in a single block of plaster. If only one model is ready for reproduction, arrange it in a corner to save the remaining blank surface for carved motifs.

Plaster molds should dry at least a week before they are used, longer in damp climates. Moist modeling clay can be pressed into the impression, or it may be cast with liquid slip as illustrated.

Refer to the instructions in chapters 7 and 12 on rolling, cutting, drying, and firing clay forms.

Fig. 257. Plaster is easily carved while it is still slightly damp. Incise the lines lightly at first, increasing the depth a little at the time. Bevel the edges to make sure no undercuts remain.

Fig. 258. With a jar or rolling pin, flatten a small lump of clay into a very thin pancake.

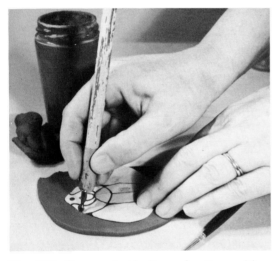

Fig. 259. Go over inside lines of pattern with a blunt pencil, pressing gently to indent the clay. Cut around outline and remove the margin.

Fig. 260. Roll out a tiny coil about ⅛ inch in diameter . . .

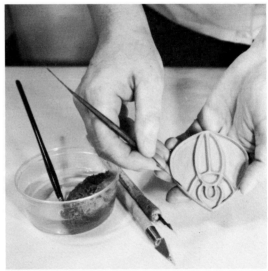

Fig. 261. . . . and, using slip as glue, attach the coil to all lines in the pattern.

Fig. 262. When the clay has stiffened so that it may be handled without distortion, flatten and bevel the coil-framing with a sharp tool. Refine the model with a moist brush and sponge.

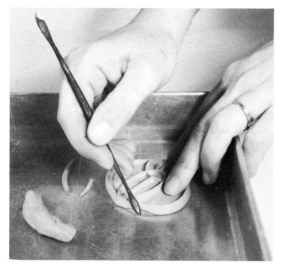

Fig. 263. Press small strips of clay around the model to seal it in one corner of an aluminum cake pan. Brush light oil over bottom and sides of the pan.

Fig. 265. . . . then stir gently to keep from trapping air bubbles in the mix. Bump the bowl several times on the table, and most of the bubbles will be released.

Fig. 264. Sift plaster evenly into water until it rises in dry islands above the surface. Let it slake . . .

Fig. 266. Pour plaster over the model first. Fill pan to a depth of about 1½ inches, and tap against table top until it is level. Remove mold from the pan when it has completely hardened, and pull away the model.

Fig. 267. Fill the impression with slip. When the clay is firm and has shrunk away from the plaster, tap around the edges of the mold with the side of your hand to release the casting. Clean and polish it, drill hole for cord, and fire to maturity.

Fig. 269. Nip miniature glass rods or narrow rounded strips into even slices and arrange in a bed of white glue.

Fig. 268. Use dark stains or flat black paint to color the bisqued form. Areas to be decorated with transparent glass are left white or coated with gold for reflection.

Fig. 270. This piece is in shades of cobalt and turquoise. The back of the scarab is undercoated with gold.

chapter 16

Small Functional Objects

WOOD VENEERS WITH ANTIQUED COPPER

Many small useful objects can become "decorator's pieces" when they are designed with taste and imagination. Natural wood veneers may be purchased in long strips about an inch wide. Being flexible, they are easily shaped to rounded surfaces which would be difficult to inlay with clay or glass materials.

Wood veneers combine agreeably with other thin materials. Leather, metallic papers, self-adhering vinyl, even cured citrus rinds are possibilities where the crevices will be left ungrouted. Antiqued copper foil is especially effective, and provides a rich contrast to the texture of the wood. Thirty-six-gauge (medium weight) is suggested for small pieces.

You might try the following instructions on electrical switch plates, escutcheons, album covers, jewelry chests, bookends, wastebaskets, or desk sets.

The form selected for demonstration was an inexpensive lacquer-ware lighter and urn set. To obliterate its original shiny gilt finish, the lighter insert was removed and surfaces to be left exposed were sprayed with several thin coats of flat black paint.

Mosaic materials were prepared next. Although the veneers can be used in their natural colors, they can be treated in various ways for striking effects.

Cut several strips of paper to fit the basic form and experiment with simple patterns. Do not use naturalistic motifs. Approach it as a problem in dividing a given area into shapes of interesting proportions and values. The separate sections may be planned for close fits as in Figure 273, or allowance may be made for grouted crevices. Figure 274 was inspired by the grain in the wood veneers.

Fig. 271. Translucent tints can be obtained with washes of oil paints diluted with turpentine, or, as shown here, the grain pattern can be intensified with wood stains. When dry, buff the strips with fine steel wool and seal with two coats of satin-finish varnish or plastic.

Fig. 272. Burnish a few scraps of copper foil with steel wool and apply antiquing solution until the desired color is obtained (see Chapter 6 for instructions). Rinse in clear water and dry.

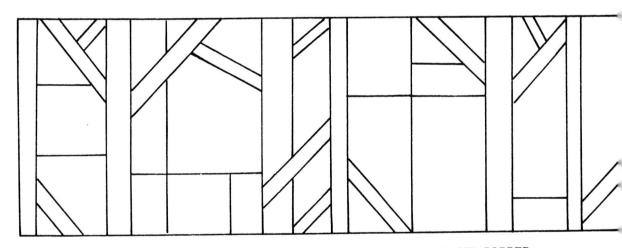

Figs. 273, 274. SIMPLE PATTERNS FOR WOOD VENEERS AND COPPER.

C—Copper   M—Mahogany   W—Walnut   O—Oak

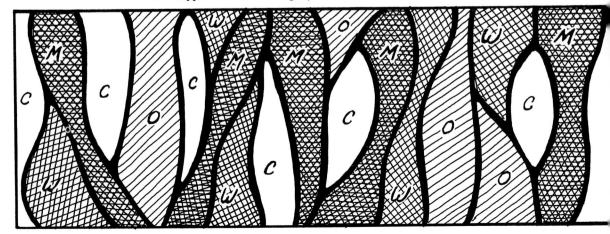

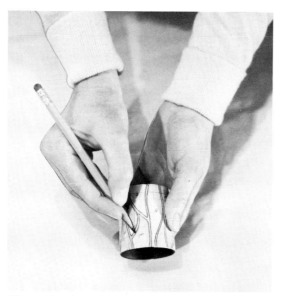

Fig. 275. Place a strip of white dressmakers' carbon under the pattern and transfer it to the form.

Fig. 277. Apply a heavy coat of wax to the mosaic to facilitate cleaning away grout. If the copper color becomes dulled, brush it lightly again with antiquing solution and wipe with a damp cloth. When the grout is dry, add a final coat of wax and buff to a soft sheen.

Fig. 276. Straight lines are easier to cut than curves, but both are possible with perseverance and sharp scissors. To simplify final assembly, lay each piece in its proper place on the pattern. They may then be removed one at the time and attached to the form with mastic. Let the mastic harden over night.

DECORATIVE BOTTLE STOPPERS

CORK, CITRUS RINDS, AND SCRAP ALUMINUM

Printed legends or brand names would spoil an attempt to elevate discarded bottles to the status of decanters, and often require special treatment. Paint solvents and a razor blade will remove certain types of lettering. Metallic printing is more difficult to eradicate, but usually a few dabs of Gold-Off, or other products used by ceramists for erasing fired gold, will dissolve it like magic.

Forms for mosaicked bottle-stoppers can be made in a number of ways. Clay is always a good choice, but interesting things can be done with segments of broom handles, wooden dowels, or small blocks of wood. A cork should be attached with epoxy to the chosen form and sanded to fit snugly inside the neck of the bottle.

Fig. 279. The list of materials used to decorate these stoppers sounds like an inventory of the contents of an incinerator, but they are surprisingly handsome. This one is made of aluminum scraps and tiny gold-backed glass jewels. They were attached to the wood stopper in Fig. 278 with white glue, and the crevices filled with dark-brown grout.

Fig. 280. Cured lemon and orange peels and brilliant crumbs of melted smalti are combined with sections of mahogany-stained cork. A layer of light-brown mastic was spread on one side of the cap at the time and the materials pressed into it deeply enough to squeeze the mastic up into seams. (Any flecks of mastic which may accidentally get onto the surface of the tesserae should be removed immediately with solvents.) Two coats of spray acrylic will help preserve the color.

Fig. 278. Sometimes we can salvage an existing cap, such as that on the left bottle. These should be roughened with coarse steel wool for better adhesion of the mosaic. The wood stopper in the foreground was purchased from a mosaic shop.

BRASS TUBING AND GLASS RODS

Fig. 281. Small medicine bottles can be converted into decanter caps. In this case, the large end of a cork was coated with epoxy and wedged inside the rim of a little bottle.

Fig. 283. A random mix of colors was more interesting than regular stripes. The crevices were filled with green grout, and a thin wash of olive-green oil paint used to stain the cork.

Fig. 282. The cap is decorated with short lengths of blue and green glass rods, pale-green opaque rods, and tiny brass tubing. They were secured to the rounded surface with white mastic, which also provided reflection for the transparent materials. A circle of thin cork was glued on top, and another cut to fit as a "sleeve" around the neck of the stopper.

MISCELLANEOUS MATERIALS

Fig. 284. Entire bottles can be mosaicked, as well as the stoppers. These decanters by Rosalis are "collector's items." They are decorated with fragments of stained glass, transparent Venetian tiles, and domes of melted glass.

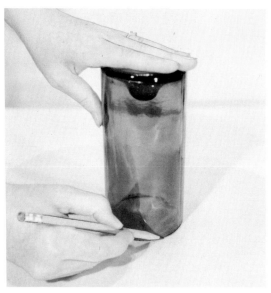

Fig. 285. On tracing paper draw around the rim of the form, then cut out the circle and fold it into quarters. This will establish the center and the radius. Make allowance for the thickness of the walls and, with a compass, draw a smaller circle as a pattern for the inside lip of the glass lid. (Place it over the container to make sure it fits.) Draw a larger circle for the top section, making it ⅛-inch wider than the container rim.

GLASS LIDS FOR CONTAINERS

Lids can be made out of glass to fit coffee cans and sections of bottles so that they can be used for canisters, humidors, and various kinds of storage containers.

The following project shows forms in Figure 42 (Chapter 3) converted into covered jars.

Fig. 286. Cut the two circles from window glass and join them with glass adhesive. When it is dry, bind the outside edge with self-adhering lead tape. Go around the tape on both sides with a smooth wooden tool to iron out the wrinkles and press it against the glass. Tape the container rim in the same way.

Fig. 287. You can leave the lid flat, or add a handle. This is a simple twist of brown stoneware. We shall mosaic around it with some of the clay materials described in Chapter 7.

Fig. 288. For another jar, we shall make a handle with polyester resin. This is a thin glass mold designed for casting artificial grapes, set on a patty of plasteline. For grapes, only the bulbous section is filled . . .

Fig. 289. . . . but we shall use the entire mold. The resin is tinted blue-green to match the container. As it shrinks, the resin may be inclined to crack at the junction of neck and bowl. Use as little catalyst as possible and leave it in the refrigerator overnight to gel slowly. (Set it in a covered jar to eliminate odor.) Cure it at room temperature for twenty-four hours, then wrap it in a cloth and tap lightly with a knife to break away the mold.

Fig. 290. Glue a circle of silver foil to the top for reflection of glass materials, and attach the handle in the center with epoxy.

Fig. 291. This lid was mosaicked with scraps of stained glass and melted nuggets in several sizes. The silvery undercoat gives a brilliant luminescence against the black grout.

DRAWER PULLS FROM RESIN FORMS

Fig. 292. The little grape mold can also be used as a form for unusual drawer pulls. This time, it was not completely filled, leaving a flat area for attaching a disk-shaped plastic pull.

Fig. 293. The knob was decorated with melted slices of mosaic canes and tiny scraps of taillights in shades of opaque yellow, orange, and vermilion. It was left ungrouted so that with light, the transparent orange resin form casts a soft glow in the interstices between tesserae.

chapter 17.

Mosaics for Special Occasions

A lot of physical and mental energy goes into the creation of a serious mosaic, and it deserves the dignity of durable materials. But a great deal of joy would go out of our work if we felt compelled to design every effort as a timeless masterpiece.

Materials which may be beautiful for a limited period of time are logical choices for mosaics intended only as decorations for special occasions. We would place colored acetates in this category, as well as unfired lacquered glass and certain kinds of colored papers.

Although there is no real reason why mosaics we bring out only once a year are not worthy of our best efforts and most precious tesserae, tastes and styles in seasonal decorations are fickle. We may be more inclined toward originality where the element of thrift is present.

Stained glass of high quality has depth and brilliance that cannot be equalled by substitutes. It is relatively expensive, however, and an inexpert slip of the glass cutter can spoil an entire sheet. It is more practical for the beginner to work with something cheaper until he has acquired a reasonable degree of skill and confidence.

Projects of the kind which follow offer the opportunity to practice cutting techniques and glass design as well as using resin as a setting bed for large sections of glass.

This is a useful process which can be an answer to certain problems involved in securing large glass forms to an opaque backing.

To illustrate why this can be troublesome, paint a scrap board with flat white, then glue several large pieces of scrap glass to it with different kinds of adhesives.

Glue pools as it hardens. It does not simply go away. Transparent though it might be, its very substance will appear under the glass as bubbles, crystals, or a shadowy mottling.

This is not noticeable under small tesserae or where light passes through the mosaic. Where light is reflected or bounced, it can be quite unpleasant.

The white casein glues harden by evaporation. If they are kept airtight, they will remain

Fig. 294. "The Holy City," by Jean Dunlap, is made of fragments of broken bottles and mirrors pressed deeply into a bed of magnesite. (*Photo courtesy of* Better Homes and Gardens Christmas Ideas.)

fluid almost indefinitely. Under large pieces of glass the air is excluded except around the edges, and toward the center the glue may remain milky until such a time as the solvent is absorbed by the backing. Even then, the dried solids are visible.

Epoxies harden through a molecular reaction which will come about even if they are not exposed to air. But here again, we are left with a tracery of the resin itself between glass and backing.

An obvious solution is a material which will not shrink into puddles as it cures and which is thick enough to act as a cushion for the glass. If the frame is deep enough for a bed of adequate thickness, we could use white magnesite or a white cement such as Crest Tile-Set.[1]

For thin panels, paste or liquid polyester resin is more suitable. The latter was used for the following project.

LACQUERED GLASS SET IN POLYESTER RESIN

Frame a plywood or pressed-board backing, and finish the frame with flat black paint. (If a smooth board, such as Masonite, is used, arrange it with the rough side up.) Mix enough catalyzed resin to fill the panel to a depth of about ⅛ inch and add opaque white pigment to color it solidly.

[1] A product of the Kaiser Company.

Fig. 295. "Tannenbaum," by the author.

Place the frame on a level surface and pour in the resin, then protect it from dust with a sheet of clean paper or cellophane.

Glass lacquers dry quickly and are difficult to apply evenly to a smooth surface. Textured glass can be colored more successfully. Intermediate hues can be obtained by mixing the lacquers or applying one color over another after it has dried.

Design the mosaic for sections which will not be too difficult to cut, and enlarge it to scale. Indicate the colors for each piece, and go over the lines with a ¼-inch felt-tipped marker to represent the crevices between sections.

When the first coat is dry, study the composition before applying a second. Unsatisfactory colors can be peeled away after soaking in very hot water for a short time.

The lacquer should harden at least twenty-four hours before the glass is set in the panel.

Mix enough uncolored resin to pour a very thin layer over the opaque backing. Use a strip of cardboard to spread it evenly, then, starting at one edge, arrange the glass in place. A slight downward pressure will force out the larger bubbles. Tiny ones are not unattractive.

Work quickly to finish the arrangement before the resin starts to gel, and keep the crevices between sections as even as possible. Be careful not to get resin on the top surface or it will dissolve the color.

Let the panel cure for at least thirty hours, more if the temperature is low.

The process of cleaning grout from the glass would either scratch or remove the lacquer, so we must use an alternate method of filling the crevices.

Mix dry wood putty with black pigment, using about 1 part of color to 15 parts of putty. Keep the basic batch in a covered jar and mix small amounts at a time with water. It should be very soft, but not runny.

Spoon the wet putty into one corner of a small plastic bag. Snip a tiny hole in the bag so that the mixture can be squeezed out in the manner of icing from a pastry tube. Pile it up slightly in the crevices to give the glass an appearance of being deeply inset.

As a final touch to the panel in Figure 295, diamond-shaped bits of glass were backed with gold tea paper and attached to the tree motif with epoxy.

Fig. 297. Clean the glass blanks and place on the cartoon textured side up. Use a wide, soft brush to float on the lacquers quickly. Do not go back over thin or uneven layers after they have become tacky. A second coat will smooth out the color.

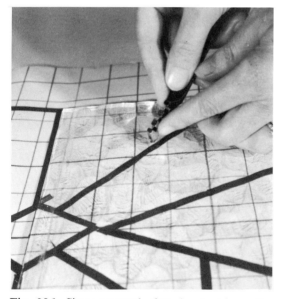

Fig. 296. Since textured glass is scored on the smooth side, the cutting patterns must be reversed or the finished design will be exactly opposite. Hold your drawing to a mirror to determine whether or not this difference is significant. Use the inside edges of the black lines as cutlines.

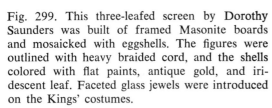

Fig. 298. Mrs. R. D. Rawn mosaicked this Christmas angel with bits of colored papers. Sheet acetate, antiqued metallic foils, fabric scraps, and self-adhering vinyl are other possibilities for this type of decoration. (*Photo courtesy of* Better Homes and Gardens Christmas Ideas.)

Fig. 299. This three-leafed screen by **Dorothy Saunders** was built of framed Masonite boards and mosaicked with eggshells. The figures were outlined with heavy braided cord, and the **shells** colored with flat paints, antique gold, and iridescent leaf. Faceted glass jewels were introduced on the Kings' costumes.

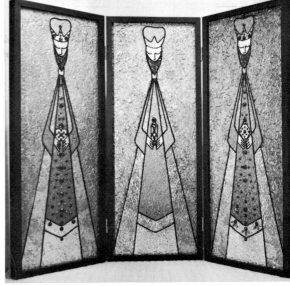

Fig. 300. Colored sheet acetate, cut into rectangles of varying sizes, can be attached to cylindrical lamp chimneys for seasonal lighting effects. Plastic metals or self-adhering lead tape will conceal the joints and give the effect of leaded glass.

Clocks

The evolution of structural and decorative design from the use for which a work is intended is so completely accepted today that it is hard to imagine it was ever controversial. Yet, one has only to study the clocks which were popular in earlier periods to see how it has affected accessories for the modern home.

Not many years back, clocks were set into everything from sculptured plaster waterfalls and castle turrets to bronzed baby booties and the stomachs of porcelain dancing ladies. Now, we no longer apologize for a clock which looks like a clock, nor do we find its functional nature a hindrance to imaginative design.

The plan for the decorative aspects of an object should grow out of how it will be used, and this includes both basic structure and applied ornamentation. But it must also incorporate methods of construction.

Execution may include a number of purely mechanical techniques, but these are no less important than the aesthetic concept. Regardless of the sound principles upon which a design is founded, there remains the matter of directing our hands to put it into effect. With most mosaics, we can permit ourselves a certain freedom in the final assembly. But a clock design must be executed precisely or it cannot serve the function for which it is intended.

DESIGNING THE FACE

The hands of a clock move at a regulated speed around a central shaft or axis. It is up to the designer, then, to arrange in some manner twelve hour spots spaced exactly thirty degrees apart around this axis.

These points can be positioned at varying distances from the center, but until some better means of dividing the day into hours is invented, we cannot argue with the thirty degrees.

Use a very sharp, hard-lead pencil for this work, and learn to twirl it lightly as you draw to ensure an even width to your lines.

Fig. 301. The case for this clock by Rosalis is made of mahogany, and the backing is covered with gold Japanese tea paper for reflection of light through the glass. About 6 feet of square brass rods and 180 transparent Venetian tiles in shades of green, olive, and amber were required for the mosaic. Crinkled mirror-tiles were scattered for random accents and arranged gold side up on the hour points.

Fig. 302. A collection of clocks by Aida and Dan Whedon was exhibited in 1961 at the Museum of Contemporary Crafts (New York). "The Riders" is made of turquoise, blue, and black hand-made ceramic tiles, with accents of red. The stylization of the design is reminiscent of early American samplers.

Fig. 303. The Whedons used an entirely different approach to the design of "The Reach," which is also made of clay. Notice that the curved lines of the sculptured figures repeat the movement of the clock's hands and act as a frame for the face.

The clock itself can be installed in any location on the face of the case as long as the weight is reasonably balanced so that the mosaic will hang straight. Figures 301, 302, and 303 have works in the center. Figure 308 shows works set in the upper left of the case.

Once this part of the design is established, you have a starting point for the decorative pattern. Geometric arrangements are always appropriate, and probably the easiest. But as exemplified by the Whedon's clocks, they are by no means the only possibilities.

The area where the clock will be displayed should, of course, be considered. A design for a professional office, for example, might be entirely out of place in a kitchen.

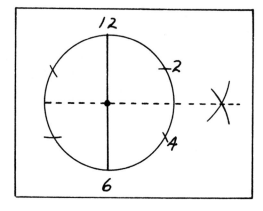

Fig. 304. DIVIDING A CIRCLE INTO TWELVE EQUAL PARTS. Establish a center point to represent the axis of the hands, and scribe a circle. Draw a vertical line through the center to mark the hours of 12 and 6. With the compass set to the radius of the circle, start at either point and cut arcs around the circumference to divide it into six parts. Swing crossing arcs from adjacent points to divide the segments in half as shown.

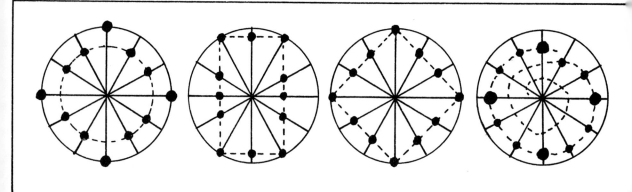

Fig. 305. ESTABLISHING THE HOUR POINTS. Use the length of the short hand as a radius to mark the distance the hour points should be placed from the center. They should not be set so far beyond the tip of the hand that they are confusing, but they can form squares, rectangles, circles, or even meandering lines, without sacrificing function.

BUILDING THE CASE

Clockworks are manufactured with shafts of various lengths, but unusual requirements can pose a real problem. It is best to determine approximate needs and buy the works before constructing the case.

Electric works can be purchased in sizes which will accommodate fairly thick backings, but most battery-operated works have a shaft slightly longer than ⅜ inch. Allowing for the depth of the decorative materials, the backing must not be more than ¼ inch thick or the hands will drag.

Hard pressed boards have considerable rigidity in this weight, and, if braced on the back, can be used for clocks up to 2 feet square.

Not all mosaic clocks have to hang, of course, and a simple easel-type frame will equip them for a table or desk.

Fig. 306. Stylized fruit, vege-
tables, and seed pods can be
adapted for kitchen and dining-
room timepieces. Floral motifs
can be used almost anywhere, as
long as they are treated decoratively, rather than realistically.
Some of the elements in Figure
308 are combined with a different background in the bottom
drawing.

Fig. 307. WAYS OF BUILDING CLOCK CASES.

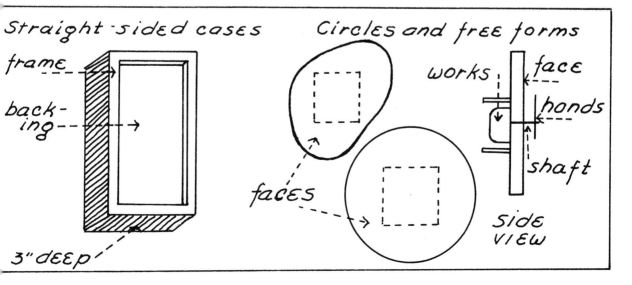

Straight-sided cases   Circles and free forms

frame   works   face

back-   hands
ing

                                                                    shaft

                          faces   side
                                                                   view

3" deep

MAKING THE MOSAIC

The melted glass chips used in Figure 308 were made by dabbing ½-inch to ¾-inch scraps of double-strength window glass with glazes and firing them to the point where the edges rounded.[1]

A cartoon was prepared with careful attention to the accurate spacing of the hours. The drawing was blacked on the back with pencil lead so that it could be transferred to the face of the case.

The cartoon was traced onto the face of the case and a hole drilled for the shaft of the works. The brass rods were cut with a hack saw to fit the pattern and set in place with white glue.

The rest of the tesserae were attached with white glue and the mosaic was finished with black grout before the installation of the clockworks.

[1] See Chapter 8.

Fig. 309. Quarter-inch pressed hardboard was set into an 18-inch wrought-iron frame. The square frame built on the back serves as a brace, as well as a housing for the clockworks. It is painted black to match the iron frame.

Fig. 308. The decorative pattern of this clock by the author was made of ¼- and ⅛-inch-square brass rods, stained glass, melted glass chips, and both opaque and transparent Venetian tiles. (*Collection of Mr. and Mrs. Matthew Dooley.*)

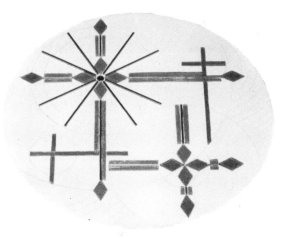

Fig. 310. Positions of the rods were checked for accuracy after the glue began to harden. They were then weighted with heavy books for twenty-four hours. The sections of cathedral glass were cut, buttered on the back with paste polyester resin, and arranged in place. Gentle pressure squeezed bubbles and excess plastic out around the edges. This was removed with a sharp knife after the resin gelled.

Fig. 311. This kitchen clock was made by Joy Schendel when she was a student of the author. Decorative materials are Venetian tiles, brass stripping, and cogwheels retrieved from a discarded timepiece.

Fig. 312. An 18-inch circular brass frame was used for this clock by Robert Stribling. The hour points and border were marbleized with ceramic gold floated on water (see Chapter 8). The large brown and amber cathedral-glass sections which form the "star" were backed with gold tea paper. Other glass sections are cobalt and turquoise. The mosaic is embedded in resin as described for the Christmas panel in Chapter 17.

chapter 19.

Functional Surfaces

No instructions for designing mosaics will apply to all situations. Functional surfaces, however, must meet rigid structural requirements, and a few general guidelines may prevent costly mistakes.

GENERAL NOTES

The amount of wear the mosaicked area will receive and the location of installation are primary considerations. Will it be walked on? Must it withstand heavy traffic? Will it be cleaned frequently, or exposed to water and severe climatic changes? Must it be absolutely level, or will its function be unaffected by a textural unevenness?

The answers to these questions will influence the selection of decorative materials and determine whether the mosaic should be done directly or indirectly.

Although different surfaces will have unique peculiarities requiring special solutions, we can note a few generalities which will apply to most of them.

1. Only permanent and impervious decorative materials should be used.

Certain rocks and clay tesserae which have a limited degree of porosity are acceptable in areas where they are not exposed to stains from chemicals, smoke, or greasy fumes. They should, however, be periodically treated with a good waterproofing compound.

2. The crevices between tesserae should be filled.

This does not necessarily involve grout. By either the direct or indirect method, the mosaic can be pressed into the setting bed deeply enough to force mortar into the joints. For special effects on walls, counters, or tables, the tesserae may be sealed in with resin, or sandwiched between layers of glass.

The most evident reason for this requirement is to create a cleanable surface. It will also reduce the danger of moisture seeping into the foundation and causing it to deteriorate. In geographical areas subject to temperatures below the freezing point, there is the added risk of ice forming in open cracks and exerting enough pressure for serious damage.

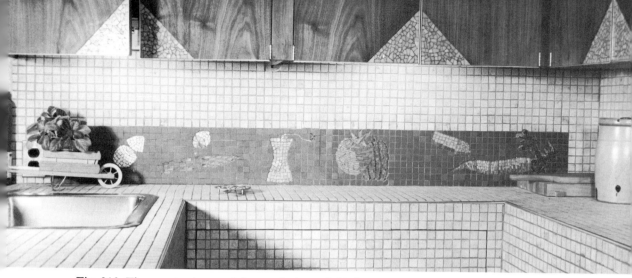

Fig. 313. The counter tops and drawer facings of this handsome kitchen designed by Jean Burton are surfaced with unglazed porcelain tiles to match the floor. Bright glass accents in the wall insert are repeated on the cupboard doors. The door decorations provide "cleanability" to areas which are constantly handled.

3. Where tesserae are not set in mortar, the adhesive must be adequate for the conditions to which the mosaic is exposed.

There is a great deal of difference between "waterproof" and "water resistant," as many beginners learn the hard way. The white glues will be resoftened if they become saturated with water. Mastic or one of the reactive adhesives should be used for all exterior mosaics.[1]

4. The foundation upon which the mosaic is laid must be strong enough to support its weight.

It would seem unnecessary to mention such an obvious truth, yet appearances can be deceptive. Glass has such a fragile appearance that one is astonished to discover how heavy it is. In spite of the indestructible look of concrete, it is quite brittle, and should be reinforced with metal mesh or rods for mosaics of any size.

[1] See Chapter 4.

5. The decorative pattern should be visually flat, even though in actuality it might be somewhat uneven.

This important point often gets lost in the periodic revivals of wallpapers and floor coverings which "fool the eye" with three-dimensional effects. It is far easier to change a rug or wallpaper which has become tiresome and disturbing than to eradicate with hammer and chisel a composition of mortar and tiles or stone.

Optical illusions of depth and movement can be created by arrangements of lines, light and dark values, exaggerated perspective, or the juxtaposition of vibrant colors. These are useful techniques for certain purposes, but fall more within the territory of the painter or "Op" artist than the mosaicist.

A floor may be perfectly level, but if it appears to be built of cubes and spheres, we

Fig. 314. OPTICAL ILLUSIONS FROM VALUES AND LINES. Rectangles, yes. Blocks, no. Curving lines are fine—unless they upset our equillibrium by undulating into hills and valleys.

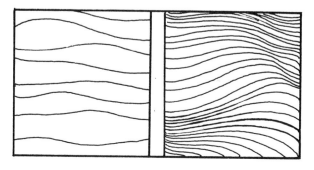

find ourselves walking uneasily across it, looking for horizontal planes on which to step. A wall which seemed to undulate or recede as we approached it would be equally disturbing, even dizzying. The bottom of a swimming pool which gave an illusion of depths or shallows which did not actually exist could be extremely dangerous.

WALLS AND INSETS

Wherever the indirect method is used for mosaics of considerable size, it is wise to have them installed by a professional tile setter. If possible, the artist should supervise this work, since sometimes minor adjustments or changes are necessary.

Small wall insets or pavings made in sections can easily be handled by anyone who has acquired experience with basic mosaic techniques.

These may be done directly on a properly prepared surface, and will be fairly level if decorative materials of uniform thickness are used.

Where inlays are planned for new structures, they may be made in advance of construction and installed flush with the surrounding area. On existing structures, the surface must either be routed out to the depth of the mosaic or built up to its level.

Figure 315 is one of four insets in a masonry wall behind the swimming pool at the James Sloan residence in Redlands, California. The personal crest of gunsight and camera was mosaicked with smalti, quartz, pearl chips, and hand-made gold tiles on a field of melted glass and smalti.

The tesserae were set directly into a bed of Crest Tile-Set on cast concrete slabs. More Tile-Set was tinted turquoise and green to match the bubbled glass and the tiles of the swimming pool, and used as grout. The completed insets were secured to the wall on stainless steel ledges, and textured mortar was built up around them.

When it is not objectionable to have the mosaic slightly elevated, the installation is very simple. A tile mural behind a counter-top stove is a good illustrative project.

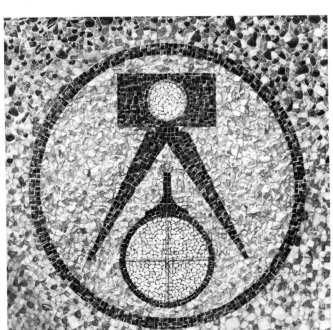

Fig. 315. "Sloan Crest" by Mary Lou Stribling.

Draw a cartoon to the exact size of the area and indicate the colors with crayons or poster paints. If the existing wall is wood and already well sealed, the cartoon can be traced onto it and the decorative materials set in place with mastic. (Start at the bottom and work upward.) Now and then, before the mastic completely sets, place a board over the completed section and tap lightly with a hammer. Finish the edges with wood strips or right-angle tiles

(see Figure 316). Grout and clean, then seal all the joints between frame, wall, and mosaic with a caulking compound. After several days, waterproof both frame and mosaicked surface.

If the existing wall is sheetrock, it is best to provide the mosaic with extra reinforcement. We can use a different procedure which is easier than that just described, though it will elevate the decoration a little more.

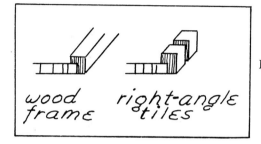

Fig. 316. EDGINGS FOR MURALS

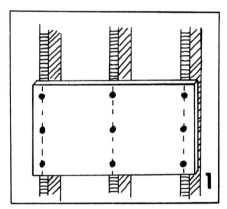

Fig. 317. INSTALLING A WALL PANEL
1. Cut a sheet of ⅜-inch Masonite or marine plywood to size. Locate the studs in the wall and mark them on the backing. Drill several holes along the stud lines for screws to install the panel.
2. Seal the backing and transfer the cartoon. Use mastic or white glue to attach the tesserae, leaving small areas around the holes clear. Secure the panel to the wall with heavy screws and mosaic over the spots. Frame the edges, grout, and caulk as previously described.

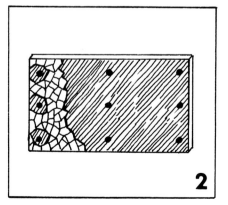

Fig. 318. Detail of a shower-tub enclosure by Wilma Harris. Glass tiles and unglazed porcelain tiles were attached directly to the waterproofed wall with mastic. Several colors of grout were used to blend with the decorative pattern.

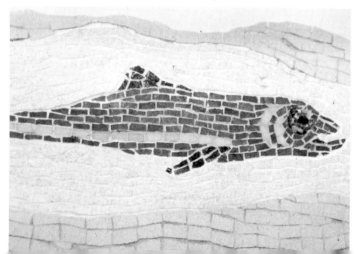

FLOORS AND PAVINGS

Exterior floors should be set on a foundation of crushed rock or packed sand 4 or 5 inches deep. The mortar bed itself, reinforced by wire mesh and metal rods, should not be less than 2 inches thick.

Forms for stepping stones and walkways may be built of wood and removed after the concrete has hardened. If non-rusting metal or redwood is used, the frame may be left in place as a part of the decorative effect.

Mosaic entryways have become popular in contemporary homes because they require little upkeep and will withstand constant wear. Before designing such a floor, the substructure should be checked to make sure it will hold the weight of tiles and mortar. The area to be decorated should be recessed about 1½ inches to accommodate ⅛-inch tiles, and be floored with plywood. (Marine plywood is best.)

Most tile setters build the foundation in two layers. The first is about an inch thick and is given a rough scratched finish. When it is firm but not dry, the second layer is troweled on and leveled to a depth of a little more than ⅜ inch. The mosaic is then laid into the fresh mortar a section at the time and tamped with a board until it is level (see the indirect method in Figures 328, 329, 330, 331).

If only part of the floor is laid at a time, excess mortar should be trimmed from the edges of the installed sections so that subsequent additions will fit smoothly.

The mosaic should be grouted and covered with damp rags or newspapers for about twenty-four hours to keep it from drying too fast. Shrinkage of the grout will be reduced if 1 part of fine sand or molding plaster is mixed with 3 parts of grout and a product such as Grout-Tite is added to the water.

Fig. 319. "COSMATI" FLOOR INSERTS. The Italian Cosmati mosaics were made by inlaying recessed areas with fragmented patterns, and a similar process was used for floors in the Church of the Holy Cross, Belmont, California. Lucienne Bloch Dimitroff made the insets by the indirect method, and they were installed flush with the surrounding area by a professional tile setter. Materials are unglazed porcelain tiles in a subtle blend of muted colors.

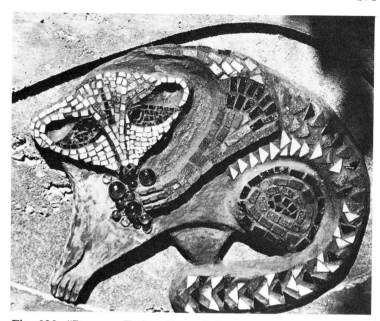

Fig. 320. "Raccoon Eating Grapes," by Emmy Lou Packard, is set in the wall of a private garden where raccoons visit to do just that. The mosaic was attached to cement with epoxy, then grouted with cement. Decorative materials are marbles and Venetian glass.

Fig. 321. "Flower Beds" by William Justema. Poolside pavings for a private residence made of glass tesserae by the indirect method.

POOLS AND FOUNTAINS

The indirect method just described is the usual way of installing mosaics in pools and fountains. It does limit us, however, to materials with a relatively flat surface. For example, if rounded nuggets of glass were attached face down to paper, the mortar would leave only a small spot exposed, unless we went through the laborious process of digging around each separate piece before the setting bed hardened.

In Chapter 4 we described an interesting direct method of flooring a bird bath so that many different kinds of materials could be used. The same technique was used by Rosalis for the insert in Figure 325.

We must point out again that although white glue is used to attach the tesserae to a net foundation, it does not serve to secure the mosaic permanently.

The arrangement is pressed into wet mortar, which oozes up in between the threads of the net to enclose each separate piece snugly. The mosaic should be well cured and thoroughly waterproofed before the pool is filled.

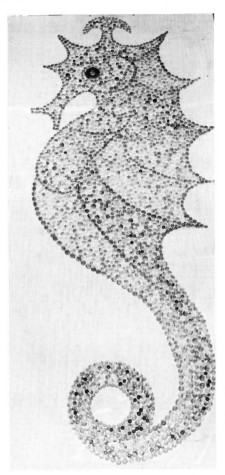

Fig. 322. A mosaic frog stretches across the bottom of a childrens' play pool. His warts are smooth, rounded rocks, and he views his domain through taxidermists' fish eyes, backed with gold leaf. By Emmy Lou Packard for the Berkeley (California) Day Nursery.

Fig. 323. This large, stylized seahorse of domed glass nuggets in blues, greens, and turquoise is ready for installation on the bottom of a swimming pool. The glass has been attached to coarse net as described in Figures 45 and 46, and will be embedded face up in mortar. *(Home of Mr. and Mrs. Orlando Conti, Jr.)*

Fig. 324. Ray Rice mosaicked this wall fountain for the Redwood Building in Palo Alto, California. Water flows into a trough behind the decorative fascia and spouts out through small openings to fall into shallow runnels below. *(Photo courtesy of Lawrence Halprin and Associates, Landscape Architects.)*

TABLES AND COUNTER TOPS

It is not always necessary for tables and counters to be completely level, though unevenness should be consistent enough so that objects placed on them will not rock. The indirect method illustrated in Figures 328, 329, 330, 331 will produce a flat surface, as will a direct application of materials of uniform thickness. But in many cases, a table will not relate well to its surroundings if flatness is given priority over decorative effect.

Counters are usually attached to a wall on one side and are approached from a single direction. It is permissible then for the design to have a top and bottom. On the other hand, tables are movable pieces and the pattern should be equally effective from all viewpoints. As illustrated by the tables in Figs. 326, 327, this need not restrict us to symmetrical compositions.

Extra reinforcement of the setting bed for small mosaic tables is not necessary. A few carpet tacks hammered into the backing far enough to leave the heads slightly raised above the surface will serve to lock mortar and backing together. Exterior magnesite is recommended over ordinary mortar for beds less than an inch thick.

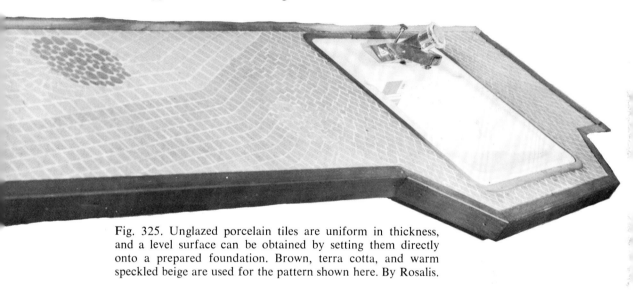

Fig. 325. Unglazed porcelain tiles are uniform in thickness, and a level surface can be obtained by setting them directly onto a prepared foundation. Brown, terra cotta, and warm speckled beige are used for the pattern shown here. By Rosalis.

Fig. 326. Helen Steinau Rich's tables are such fascinating nature studies that owners often use the tops for wall decorations at the end of the season for outdoor dining. In "Fish Pond," pebbles and heavy copper wire enclose a vivid central composition of water lilies and goldfish. Mirrored glass, smalti, Venetian tiles, and other decorative materials were set directly into mortar. (Collection of Mr. and Mrs. Harold Freemon.)

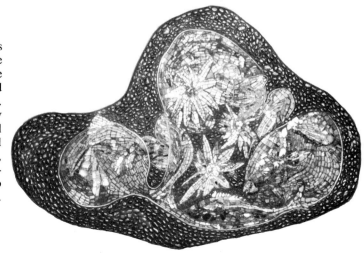

Fig. 327. Individual tables can be designed to form a unified pattern when they are fitted together. Transparent Venetian tiles and melted glass were combined with brass stripping for the two shown here. The focal point on the right table is a melted bottle ring. By Rosalis.

SMALL TABLES BY THE INDIRECT METHOD

Fig. 328. A water-solvent glue is used to attach the tesserae face down on heavy paper. The finished mosaic is then flipped over into a prepared bed of mortar and leveled by tapping a board across the surface.

Fig. 329. Excess mortar is squeezed over the sides of the frame, which has been protected with masking tape. The setting bed should be allowed to harden several hours before the paper is dampened and peeled away. The mosaic may be partly cleaned at this time, but final scrubbing with rags and scouring pads should be reserved until the mortar has lost flexibility.

SETTING BEDS FOR LARGE TABLES

Fig. 330. Large tables require a thicker setting bed and the reinforcement of wire mesh. To elevate the mesh slightly so that mortar will flow beneath it, staple small nails or shims to the underside at regular intervals. The first coat of mortar is troweled on firmly to force it through the screening.

Fig. 331. Color has been added to the second layer of mortar and the mix is somewhat thinner. It is built up to the top edge of the frame and leveled with a strip of wood. The mosaic will be cut into sections and assembled face down into the mortar. Some of the dry tinted mortar has been reserved for filling small cracks or pinholes which might be left between tesserae.

RELATED MOSAICKED SURFACES

All of the bathrooms in this home were decorated with the same materials, but they were arranged in different ways.

Fig. 332. For a children's bathroom, gloss and mat Japanese tiles in earth colors and muted greens have been used to line the tub and shower area. The amusing tree form might have been drawn by the children themselves.

Fig. 333. The dressing counter in the same room has a different plant motif. By Rosalis, for Cleon M. Arnold, architect. (Tiburon, California.)

Fig. 334. Game table, by Bernice Brown. Unglazed porcelain tiles in shades of speckled brown, set in a simulated marble frame.

chapter 20.

Sand Casting

The indirect method of making mosaics is usually associated with the need for obtaining a level surface or with the installation of large floors and murals. Sand casting, however, is one way of working indirectly for a special kind of textural effect.

Two types of sand casting are described in this chapter. One is for the molding of forms, the other for indirectly embedding a fragmented pattern.

SAND MOLDS

Packed damp sand makes an excellent mold for free-form stepping stones, low plan-ters, and bird baths. Since they can be made quickly, you might like to work outdoors, but choose a spot out of the sun and wind.

Your container for sand can be a wooden crate, a stout cardboard box lined with Pliofilm, or four boards fastened together at the corners (see Figure 335). Fill it with fine moist sand and pack it down level. We shall make a stepping stone first, using prepared mixes for concrete and mortar.[1]

The cured stone should be installed on a bed of sand to cushion it from irregularities in the earth foundation which might cause it to crack under weight.

[1] Concrete mix has an aggregate of coarse pebbles which eliminates the need for reinforcing small slabs with metal strips or mesh.

Fig. 335. SAND-CAST STEPPING STONES

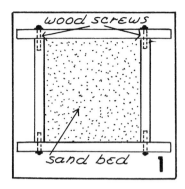 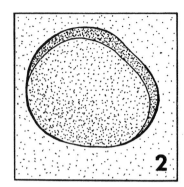 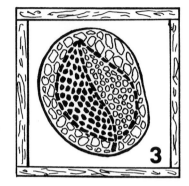

1. Join four boards at the corners with long wood screws so that they can be taken apart and reassembled for a number of sizes. One- × 4-inch boards are adequate for slabs. (Bird baths and planters which are scooped out require a depth of at least 8 inches.)

2. Cut a strip of thin pressed hardboard or plywood about 4 inches long and 2¾ inches wide as a guide for the depth of the sand cavity. Sketch a free-form shape on the sand and scoop it out with a spoon, spatula, or smoothing trowel. Check the depth from time to time and keep the edges as straight as possible. Tamp down the finished mold with a small wooden block.

3. Pour a 2-inch layer of concrete mix into the mold. When it has firmed slightly, hammer it all over by striking a mallet against the wooden block.

Cover with fresh mortar up to the level of the sand. Test for density. If decorative materials can be set into it without sinking, you can make the mosaic.

It can be simply rows of pebbles of different sizes which follow the contour of the slab. Stylized leaves or flowers are attractive for gardens, and smalti or strips of Venetian tiles will add a crisp contrast to rounded materials. Press them in deeply enough to be secure in the mortar, then cover the slab with a layer of damp newspapers.

After twenty-four hours, lift the slab carefully from the sand bed, and, if necessary, refine the edges with a stone rasp. Hose off the loose sand and scrub the mosaic with a brush. Cover with newspapers again and cure in a cool place away from the sun.

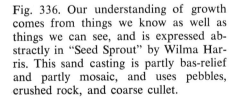

Fig. 336. Our understanding of growth comes from things we know as well as things we can see, and is expressed abstractly in "Seed Sprout" by Wilma Harris. This sand casting is partly bas-relief and partly mosaic, and uses pebbles, crushed rock, and coarse cullet.

Bird Baths and Garden Planters

Use boards 8 to 10 inches wide to make a container for sand and fill as previously described. Scoop out a shallow bowl shape and pack the walls firmly with the back of a spoon or rounded trowel. Mix enough stiff mortar to line it with a layer about an inch thick. (If the sides slope steeply, you will have to let the bottom section get firm before building higher.)

When the mortar has set, cut a section of medium-weight hardware cloth several inches larger than the circumference of the sand cavity. Press it into the form, shaping it to an exact fit by slashing the screening where necessary and overlapping it. Trim away the excess mesh in the overlaps and around the upper edges. The screening should be recessed about ½ inch below the rim.

Remove the shaped wire and cover the foundation with a thin layer of fresh mortar, then set the wire back in place. Press it down firmly before adding mortar on top of it to make the form between 1¾ and 2 inches thick.

Use a trowel, spoon, or rubber spatula to refine the inside surface. For bird baths, use a sharp stick to roughen the mortar and provide a "tooth" for the mosaic bed. The sand will leave enough texture on the outside of the casting for mosaicking planters.

The decorative materials can be attached to a dry form with epoxy or mastic, though mortar is very appropriate for pieces of these kinds. In this case, the mosaic is best done as soon as the concrete is hard, though some products (such as Crest Tile-Set) will bond well even to dry masonry. Cement additives are also available to improve bonding qualities.[2]

Sketch the pattern on the form or transfer it from a paper drawing. Wet the concrete thoroughly, then butter a small section at a time with fresh mortar and press the tesserae in place.

Waterproof both inside and outside surfaces when the mosaic is dry.

[2] See Chapter 4.

Rounded bowl forms will rock without a stand of some kind. Three smooth rocks or half-bricks can be attached to the bottom with mortar to serve as legs. (Do this on planters before the mosaic.)

Bird baths can be installed by digging out a small depression in the ground, filling it with mortar, and setting the bath on top. Both earth and casting should be damp to keep the mortar from becoming desiccated. Even if the bath does not actually stick to the base, it will be held securely in place.

SAND-CAST PANELS

Projects of more elaborate nature should be made indoors away from the drying action of sun and wind. A thick layer of sand will stay damp for some time if it is covered with a sheet of plastic between work sessions. Should it start to get crumbly, spray it gently with water, using a plunger-type sprayer sold with window cleaners.

A temporary frame for panels can be made as shown in Figure 335. Place it on a plastic sheet and fill with about 2 inches of very fine, damp sand. Smooth the surface with a board, but do not pack.

Before starting a panel, experiment with textures from imprints of shells, rope, bottle bottoms, or other objects around the workshop. Try carving out shapes, keeping in mind that the casting will be reversed, that is, depressed areas will be raised, elevations will be indented.

After this experimental session smooth the sand again and make a small trial panel with plaster of Paris.

Making a Test Panel

Draw a simple pattern to size on wrapping paper or newsprint. Position it on the damp sand, then go carefully over the lines with a blunt pencil.

Arrange decorative materials without permanently seating them so that changes can be made if necessary. When they are all in place, press them about halfway into the sand.

Spray the entire surface lightly with water to reduce its absorbency, then mix plaster of Paris to a fluid, but not watery, consistency. Spoon it over the sand to a depth of about ¾ inch, using a rubber spatula to guide it into the corners and over the elevated tesserae. A light up-and-down patting motion will encourage air bubbles to rise.

When the plaster is firm, place a matching sheet of wire mesh on top and bind two loops of picture-hanging wire to the mesh, arranging them about halfway between the middle and top of the panel. Add an inch layer of fresh plaster, making sure that the loops are not buried.

Leave the panel undisturbed for forty-eight hours, then remove screws from the frame and tap the strips away from the plaster. Attach a wire across the two loops for hanging.

Fig. 337. "Fuchsias" has a swirling pattern of Venetian glass tiles around the flowers. Petals are fragments of milk glass and crockery. Centers are pebbles and necks of mauve-tinted bottles collected from desert refuse heaps. By Wilma Harris.

Perforated Insert for a Garden Wall or Gate

This unusual project incorporates both the indirect and direct methods of making a mosaic. It is, in fact, two mosaics, since two sides of the wall for which it is planned are exposed to view. If your own version is installed where it can be seen from only a single direction, you need but one decorated surface.

Refer to Chapter 8, Figure 111, for a picture of a test block made by the process which follows, and for directions on cutting bottles either by hand or with a hot wire. It is a good idea to make one of these blocks before starting a large piece.

Cut a number of cylinders 2½ inches thick in related colors. Diameters can vary from quart beverage bottles to slim medicine containers which are just tall enough to provide one cylinder. They do not all have to be round, and you can make fascinating perforations from kiln-stretched slices.[3]

The stretched forms will already be fire-polished. The edges of cut glass should be ground on coarse emery paper, then polished further with a finer grit. You can bind them with lead as described in Chapter 24 if you prefer.

Mark lines ¼ inch inside the cut edges of the cylinders as a guide for equalizing the distance the rims should extend above the mortar.

Cure the insert for several days between layers of damp newspapers, then remove it from the sand bed, hose away loose material, and scrub both sides with a stiff brush. Let it dry another week before waterproofing and installing.

[3] See Chapter 8.

Fig. 338. MAKING A PERFORATED INSERT

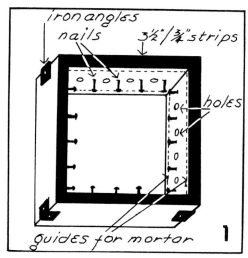

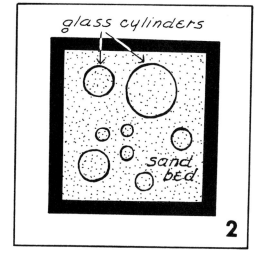

1. Cut the sides of the frame from 3½- × ¾-inch wood boards, preferably redwood. (If more perishable wood is used, it must be well sealed and waterproofed.) Before assembling the frame, partly drive in nails or heavy staples along the middle of the inside surface as shown, then drill a few shallow holes between them. These will form locks to secure the mortar block to the frame.

Put the frame together and reinforce the corners with iron angles. Draw guidelines ¾ inch inside each edge to indicate the space to be filled with mortar. This will ensure that the decorated block will be evenly recessed on both sides.

2. Stretch a sheet of mylar or pliofilm over a level work surface and set the frame in the middle of it. Fill with screened damp river sand up to the bottom ¾-inch mark, distribute it into an even layer, and tamp lightly. You can preplan a pattern for the mosaic, but use it as a reference, rather than a precise cartoon. Arrange the bottle slices, then press them in the sand up to the ¼-inch bottom guidelines. Check to make sure they stand straight.

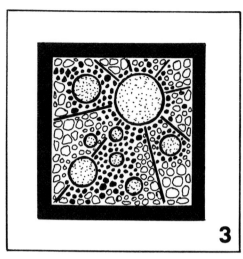

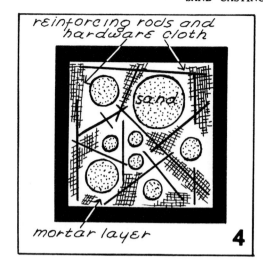

3. Imprints from a blunt tool, jar lid, forked twig, etc., can be part of the design, as can be strips of metal. (Copper and brass weather beautifully.) Set pebbles, melted glass nuggets, shells, cracked quartz, or other materials in place. Press them well into the sand, but leave enough exposed surface to create an undercut in the mortar.

4. Spray lightly with water, then cover with a fairly thin mix of mortar to a depth of about ¾ inch, spooning it carefully over the surface so that the sand is not disturbed. Pat it down with a small wood block to make sure it is forced into all crevices.

Tamp again when it has started to get firm. When the mortar is set but not dry, lay a crisscrossed structure of metal rods or coat hangers and thin strips of hardware cloth between the cylinders (but not touching them) and around the inside of the frame.

Pour mortar around the glass forms up to the ¼-inch guidelines. This should make the level approximately even with the margin marked on the frames. Set another pattern of decorative materials into the wet mortar, and sift a thin film of sand on top without tamping it down.

Fig. 339. This sand-cast panel by Wilma Harris was made by pressing decorative materials deeply into the sand so that they extend far out from the finished surface. "Daisies" are Venetian glass tiles with a background of colored glass shards.

chapter 21

Windows, Translucent Screens, and Lighted Panels

WINDOWS

Mosaic art was the forerunner of the art of stained-glass windows. The early stained-glass windows were, in fact, translucent mosaics, their designs being composed of distinctly separate pieces of color. The relationship was weakened later and eventually dissolved, when windows were made of painted sections, with fragmentation a structural necessity rather than a decorative concept.

Perhaps it is poetic fancy to visualize stained-glass art as rising phoenix-like from the ashes of mosaic. Yet history indicates that artistic inspiration and inventiveness is cyclical, blazing up brightly during one period, then flickering down, dying, and remaining inactive for a time before springing back to life with renewed vitality. And sometimes the apparent death of one form stimulates the birth of another.

The ancient churches were dim and poorly illuminated. Mosaic murals covered much of the wall space and served to brighten the interiors by reflecting back from faceted tesserae what light existed.

But walls began to disappear in the Middle Ages. Windows in the Gothic cathedrals became larger, finally almost replacing the walls. With little or no space left for frescoes or mosaics, the windows themselves naturally offered the best possibilities for decorative treatment.

The early mosaics and early stained-glass windows were flat patterns of color. No attempt was made for an illusion of perspective or naturalism, and they were closely related to architectural design. Abandonment of these principles was the death blow to both arts, and their ashes lay virtually undisturbed for several hundred years.

The renaissance of mosaics and stained glass in the past decade has come about through the restoration of the ancient relationships of medium to design. And a part of the renewed vigor of contemporary stained glass derives from the re-establishment of its ties with mosaic, which dictates a rejection of painterly ideals.

183

Fig. 340. From a vantage point of a few hundred feet above the ground, one discovers that the face of the earth is one enormous mosaic. Its separate pieces are mountains and rivers, fields, fences, and trees, bridges and roads, and the tiny tesserae of buildings inhabited by man.

Fig. 341. This sliding glass wall designed by Cecil Casebier for the Mercedes Civic Center in Mercedes, Texas, bears a remarkable resemblance to the aerial view in Figure 340. Look at it from the right side and you can almost pick out freeways and shopping centers and wide areas of open country.

Fig. 342. These magnificent windows in the chancel of the Kit Stewart Chapel, Calvary Presbyterian Church, San Francisco, were designed by Harold Halbrook for Cummings Stained Glass Studios.

The pattern is made of faceted glass set in exposed aggregate concrete, and is based on symbols which are significant to the Church.

The Celtic Cross is the dominant symbol in the center window, flanked by Alpha on the left and Omega on the right. Behind the cross is the circle of eternity, and the free-flowing lines which unify the design stand for freedom, eternity, and ever active thought.

Although the brilliance of the rich orange-reds, blue-reds, and ruby which dominate the color scheme cannot be suggested in a black-and-white photograph, the emotional impact and jewel-like quality of the composition are clearly evident. *(Photo courtesy of the Calvary Presbyterian Church.)*

Some of the credit for this change is owing to the development of new structural materials which allow translucent patterns to become an integral part of the wall itself. Up until this century, the separate pieces of colored and painted glass were bound with channeled strips of lead called cames. The cames were soldered to form a tight bond and reinforced with heavy metal rods and bars.

This process limited the artist to sheet glass. But improved concretes and the formulation of epoxy resins meant that walls could be pierced without being weakened and glass could be set in the apertures.

Sheet glass was too fragile for such construction, and its lack of visual density was out of character with the rest of the wall. Faceted glass slabs proved to be a beautiful solution,[1] since light rays passing through the boldly textured dalles bend and dart off in many directions, enlivening the pools of color as though they are agitated by some inner force.

Each piece of the translucent mosaic pattern is actually a tiny window, snugly encased in concrete or resin. The material does not lend itself to paint or superfluous detail. The artist is forced to explore the decorative qualities of the glass alone, and to move from sentimentalized, naturalistic subjects to symbols.

As was discussed in Chapter 9, symbolic expressions are often stronger than realism, for they leave full interpretation up to the observer's imagination.

Our religious symbols are deeply rooted in the past, though certain modifications are often made for the sake of design.

[1] See Chapter 8.

Fig. 343. Back lighting focuses interest on the composition of brilliant stained glass, with lines formed by the leading and opaque shapes becoming negative elements in the pattern. Front lighting reveals the rich mosaic of gold, copper, and bronze tiles in the opaque areas.

The tiles, imported from Germany, were attached to shapes cut from Masonite. They were then treated in the same manner as the glass sections and glazed into the structure. (*Collection of Orco Glass.*)

Contemporary stained-glass designers have by no means abandoned sheet glass for faceted glass, but as the preceding example by Cecil Casebier demonstrates, they are exploring new ways to use it. At a casual glance it might seem far removed from the early windows, yet in feeling for the medium it is very close.

Stained-glass decorations for homes were immensely popular during the latter part of the nineteenth century. Their effectiveness was considerably diminished, however, by the ornate Victorian clutter of the rest of the furnishings. Curiously enough, many of these original pieces are being restored for homes today, and new ones are being made from the old designs.

Windows are replacing more and more of our wall space, which means we have fewer areas where paintings can be displayed. We observed earlier that in the Middle Ages, a similar situation in the cathedrals led to the creation of decorative windows, and the modern parallel is obvious.

Since our color preferences and tastes in furnishing change from time to time, it is not always practical to install a decorative window permanently. It is best to make the mosaic separately, and secure it with wood stops over the existing window.

Suitable backings are discussed in Chapter 3. If the window is exposed to the direct heat of the sun, glass is recommended over plastic. Double-strength or crystal window glass can be used for small areas. Large windows should be made on plate glass.

The tesserae can be attached with a transparent adhesive and grouted, or they can be kiln-fused to a compatible base. The latter method would mean cutting the mosaic into sections small enough to be accommodated on a shelf, then reassembling it with strips of wood or lead came.

Little is gained for the trouble of this second method, however, for the rounded effect of the tesserae can be obtained by firing them separately, then gluing them to a base.

In any case, grouting is strongly recommended for both functional and decorative reasons. It not only provides extra support for the tesserae but also greatly strengthens the design, since black lines serve to intensify and separate each color. Without such divisions, the eye blends them together into intermediate hues which lack the brilliance of the individual components.[2]

[2] See Chapter 9, Figure 139.

Fig. 344. Melted bottle rings, glass chunks, and stained glass, in brown and amber tones with sparks of red and orange. The tesserae were attached to $\frac{3}{16}$-inch plate glass with clear epoxy. After grouting, the pane was installed against the existing window with narrow wood stops, so that it can be removed or replaced if the need arises. By Rosalis for the residence of Mr. and Mrs. James Rutledge, Mill Valley, California.

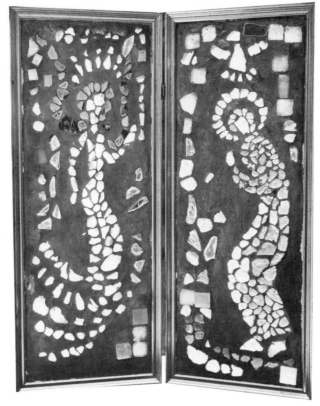

Fig. 345. "The Annunciation" is an experimental two-leafed folding screen by Lucienne Bloch Dimitroff. Translucent Venetian tiles and frosted "beach" glass were attached to plate glass with acrylic cement. A layer of cement and sand was poured over the surface to fill the crevices and create the opaque areas. It was kept damp for forty-eight hours to cure it slowly.

TRANSLUCENT SCREENS

Ordinary picture frames can be turned into small folding screens by fastening them together with butterfly hinges. With a translucent mosaic pattern, they become versatile accessories to serve as decorations in their own right, or as dramatic backdrops for sculpture, pottery, and plants.

A sunny window will provide beautiful illumination, but for a touch of evening glamour, they can be lighted by a bank of vigil candles placed a few inches behind them.

The increasing popularity of open floor plans over complexes of small rooms has created a demand for dividers to define and provide privacy for certain areas without completely closing them off.

The polyester resins may be preferable to glass for these purposes, since they are lighter in weight and the hazard of breakage is eliminated.

Even when it is cast in fairly thick sheets, the resin has a degree of flexibility. If a large divider is needed, such as that in Figure 346, it should be made in several panels so that framing will provide reinforcement. Further strength will be added by inclusions of fibrous glass mat, or a foundation of Plexiglas.

In most cases, it is easier to pour the panels right in their finished frames and join them together after they are cured. As a precaution against the resin shrinking away from the frame, it should be grooved or drilled with small holes on the inside to lock in the casting.[3]

Choose a dry, cool, well-ventilated area for working. If an exhaust fan is not available, place a small fan to one side of the work table so that fumes will be blown away.

Assemble within easy reach all materials which will be needed. Include among these a large sheet of thin plastic to cover the panel so that it will not collect dust before it is hard.

[3] See frame diagram in Figure 338.

Jars can be placed outside the four corners of the frame to elevate the cover above the plastic surface.

Your work table should be level, or the pouring will be uneven in thickness. As a guide, set a measuring cup filled with water in the middle of the table. If one side of the table is low, force pieces of cardboard under the legs.

Decorative inclusions must be dry. Where large areas of color are needed, tissue paper or sheet acetate can be combined with other materials if the divider will not be exposed directly to the sun. Theatrical gelatin, which is used for colored filters for spotlights and floods, is richer and less subject to fading.

Be sure to purchase a brand of resin which is recommended for projects of this nature. (As we have mentioned, boat resin is better for boats than mosaics.) As a rule of thumb, you will use about a quart of resin for every square foot of a fairly thick panel.

If the panel will be thicker than ½ inch, pour it in several layers, allowing each to become firm and cool before adding the next.

We shall describe two methods for making large translucent resin screens. The first is suggested for mosaic designs which can be quickly assembled. The second will cost more but enables you to take all the time you need to arrange the pattern. Temporary or permanent frames can be used for either.

Fig. 346. A translucent room divider, designed and executed by Ray Rice for a private residence, uses mah jong tiles and counters as a part of the decorative pattern. Tesserae were embedded in tinted polyester resin which was textured by sprinklings of dry pigment and crushed quartz.

Method 1 for Making a Translucent Screen

1. A temporary casting frame can be made of smooth wood strips held together at the corners with screws. Coat the frame with mold release or a heavy layer of wax.

2. Cut a sheet of wrapping paper the size of the panel and arrange decorative inclusions on it without sticking them down.

3. Place a sheet of glass (preferably plate glass) slightly larger than the frame on your work table and coat it thinly with wax or mold release. (Cellophane or mylar, which may be "ripply" is not recommended here. Glass will give the best surface.)

4. Position the frame in the center of the glass and caulk the outside edges with masking tape, florists' clay, or plasteline, so that no cracks remain between glass and frame.

5. Cut a sheet of fibrous glass mat to fit the glass area inside the frame exactly. This is required to reinforce the plastic and reduce warpage. Three-quarter-ounce to 1-ounce mat is adequate for small or medium-sized panels. 1½-ounce mat is suggested for large panels. The mat will appear white when dry, but becomes transparent after it is saturated with resin. Puncture it all over with a needle or ice pick to keep from trapping air beneath it.

6. Mix the resin and catalyst and stir them well. You should have enough for a layer ⅛ inch thick inside the frame.

7. Reserve a small amount of the resin and pour the rest in the frame. Use a square of cardboard or a thin metal spreader to distribute it evenly. Make sure the edges and corners are filled. Bubbles can be brought to the surface with a gentle up-and-down motion of the spreader.

8. Carefully position the glass mat on the layer of plastic, dribble the reserved plastic over it, and brush the spreader back and forth across the surface until the mat is saturated and bubbles are eliminated. Let this layer gel before arranging the mosaic.

9. Mix enough fresh resin to cover the surface of the cast layer with a thin coat. Remove the decorative materials one at the time from the sheet of wrapping paper and set them in place.

10. There are alternatives for the final layer of resin. It may be poured over the mosaic to a depth which will completely cover it and make a flat surface. In this case, a sheet of mylar or sized surfacing mat can be placed on top to prevent surface tack and to improve the finish.

If you prefer to pour it only to a depth which will leave the tops of the tesserae slightly elevated, add a few drops of surface hardener to the mix. When the sheet has set, brush it with a highly catalyzed mix of resin.[4]

11. The panel will cure more slowly if kept below 70°, but the results will be better than if it cures too fast. Remove the caulking and tap the edges of the frame lightly with a hammer to release the resin from the glass, then remove the temporary frame. Thin ledges which may result from resin seeping under the frame can be trimmed with a sharp knife, then sanded smooth.

The panel should cure about a week before being framed. Turn it over from time to time to expose both sides to air.

Method 2 for Making a Translucent Screen

1. Cut a sheet of Plexiglas to size and buff both surfaces with fine steel wool or sandpaper until they are well frosted. (This improves bonding qualities and will not be noticeable after the resin is poured.) One-eighth-inch Plexiglas is suitable for small panels. One-quarter-inch is best for large sizes.

2. Frame the Plexiglas so that the back is recessed about ¼ inch and the top recessed a little more than the planned thickness of the finished panel. Pour a thin layer of catalyzed resin over the back side. This will help to equalize tensions and greatly reduce possibility of warpage.

[4] See Chapter 13.

3. When the back layer is hard, tape the mosaic pattern to it face down, and turn it over. Attach the tesserae to the Plexiglas with a transparent glass adhesive. (A small drop is sufficient.)

4. Pour a layer of catalyzed resin over the mosaic to the desired depth as described in step 10 above, and cure. (Since this layer of resin may be fairly thick, it is best to reduce the catalyst according to the suggestions in Chapter 13.)

LIGHTED PANELS

Tiny panel lights, even Christmas-tree lights, can be wired in series and mounted inside the frames of translucent wall panels. A better distribution of light will be obtained if the frame is painted gloss-white on the inside, or plated with aluminum foil.

Since incandescent lights become quite hot in an enclosed area, adequate ventilation must be provided. If the wall against which the panel will hang is a light neutral color, the back of the frame can be left open and a few small holes drilled around the back edges. If the wall is dark, a perforated removable white backing should be installed.

Thin fluorescent tubes stay cool and burn much longer than incandescent lights. On large panels, a tube mounted in the center of each side of the frame will provide good light if recessed back several inches from the edge of the translucent area. An even better distribution can be obtained with a construction of the kind shown in Figure 347.

For certain designs, the light can be deliberately uneven. In "Moonscape," (see color plate), the effect of moonlight filtering through trees and becoming fainter as it touches the landscape was obtained by mounting a single thin fluorescent tube 12 inches long inside the upper right section of the frame.

Tape-Lite, a new product by Sylvania, may have possibilities for back-lighting mosaics, though at the time of this writing adequate experiments have not been made for unqualified endorsement.[5]

The light source is laminated in plastic tape which produces a soft glow. It may be operated from batteries or household electrical service.

[5] Inquiries may be made of their Western Region Sales Engineer, Distribution Center, 6505 East Gayhart Street, Los Angeles 54, Calif.

Fig. 347. CONSTRUCTING A LIGHTED FRAME.

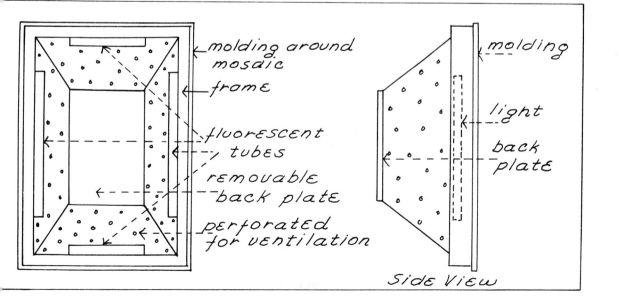

molding around mosaic

frame

fluorescent tubes

removable back plate

perforated for ventilation

molding

light

back plate

SIDE VIEW

Fig. 348. The inside of the frame for "Moonscape" was coated lightly with white glue, then covered with aluminum foil. For better diffusion, the foil was crushed then pressed out flat before being glued down. The fluorescent tube was mounted against the upper strip of the frame, and the cord stapled around the side to emerge at the bottom.

Reflected Lighting

By mounting a translucent mosaic out from a wall or backing, it can be illuminated by reflected light, rather than a direct light. Brilliant effects can be obtained with light sources positioned above or below the panel so that they flood the backing and bounce back a glow through the mosaic.

If such arrangements are impractical or make awkward installations in the room, the panel can be lighted from one side with an ordinary table lamp. In this situation, translucent areas will cast colored reflections on the backing, but opaque elements will receive enough surface light to make a positive contribution to the design.

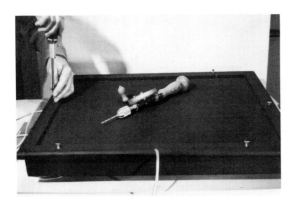

Fig. 349. A back plate was made to bounce light through the glass. It is a sheet of ⅛-inch pressed hardboard, painted glossy white on the inside and edged with molding. Several holes were drilled for ventiliation. It was secured to the panel frame with wood screws which can be removed when the tube needs replacing.

Fig. 350. Pack ice floating in the Hudson River was the inspiration for "Winter," by Mariette Bevington. The individually fitted pieces of stained glass are dark violet, royal blue, and other blue tones suspended in cold colors. To relieve the monochromatic effect, there are chinks of lemon and orange as are seen when the sun strikes fiery sparks from a facet of ice. The fragments are attached to plate glass with a transparent adhesive and the crevices filled with a black glazing compound. The panel stands in front of a polished white marble wall, giving an even distribution to the tube lighting concealed in the frame. (See Chapter 11 for another panel in this commission.)

MAKING A LAMINATED GLASS PANEL

Fig. 351. This translucent panel of stained glass and smalti is mounted out an inch from a backing so that light can pass through and around the glass. It was inspired by patterns of lighted windows in a city night-scene. Glass colors are deep cobalt, purple, and blue-green. Opaque accents are shades of yellow, gray-mauve, blue, and dark green.

Fig. 352. Draw pattern to scale, reverse it, and trace it on double-strength window glass with a felt-tipped pen.

Fig. 354. Elevate the base on jars or boxes and test the bolts in the holes to make sure the heads do not extend above the surface. Fasten the bolts in place with epoxy.

Fig. 355. Cut all the glass sections by the pattern . . .

Fig. 353. Turn the glass over and drill holes for mounting-bolts, keeping the bit moving around in a circle to bevel the edges. This will allow the head of the bolt to be countersunk.

Fig. 356. . . . butter the back sides with epoxy, and arrange on the glass base.

Fig. 358. Set small squares of glass and smalti in place, then attach them with epoxy. Wait twenty-four hours before mounting the panel.

Fig. 357. After twenty-four hours stretch strips of narrow lead by placing one end in a vise and pulling the other with pliers until you feel it give slightly. This will make it lie flat in a straight line against the glass. Coat the backs of the strips with epoxy and arrange them over all the joints in the glass. A wooden paddle can be used to press the lead snugly against the glass.

Fig. 359. Mark the position of the bolts on a prepared backing and drill matching holes in it. Thread the bolts through dividers (which in this case were 1-inch plastic boxes) and through the holes in the backing. Attach the nuts on the back side and tighten them with pliers.

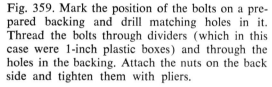

chapter 22.

Lights

There are two basic kinds of mosaicked lights. The first is a decorated structure which *supports* the source of illumination, such as Figures 360, 361, and 362. The second is a structure which *shades* or *contains* the source of illumination, such as Figures 364, 370, and 376.

Each serves a different purpose, which will influence a choice of materials, adhesives, and forms. For example, light is reflected from the surface of a lamp base, and almost any kind of tesserae may be used for the mosaic as long as they are harmonious with its size and shape and the area where it will be displayed. But when we design a shade or cover, we are working with the quality of the light itself, changing it from unobscured illumination to a decorative pattern made up of shadows and translucent color.

Since few technical problems are encountered with lamp bases, we shall primarily direct our attention to ways of designing actual fixtures, or containers.

LAMP BASES

A number of different kinds of forms for lamp bases were suggested in Chapter 3. You can add large bottles to that list if you have acquired enough skill with the glass drill to make holes in the bottom to accommodate a lamp cord.

Not all lights made from bottles have to be wired, as can be seen in the beautiful examples by Rosalis in Figures 361 and 362.

The wrought-iron candelabrum is a commercial item with removable arms which can be arranged for three or five candles.[1] A rubber "stopper-insert" at the base can be adjusted for several sizes.

[1] Trade name: Liquor-Lite.

196

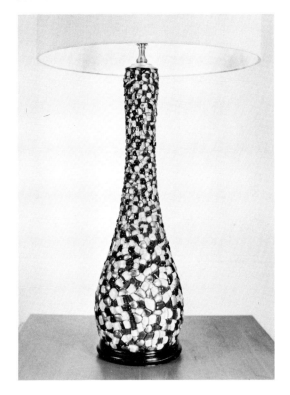

Fig. 360. A bisqued clay form was used for this large lamp base. The all-over pattern is made of bottle nuggets in ivory, light and dark olive, and antique gold. Notice how the texture changes to conform to the shape. By Robert Stribling.

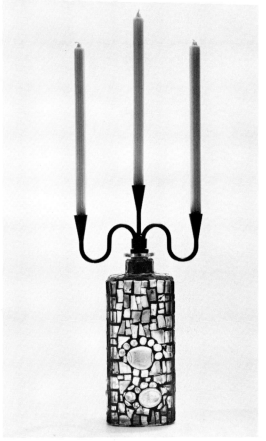

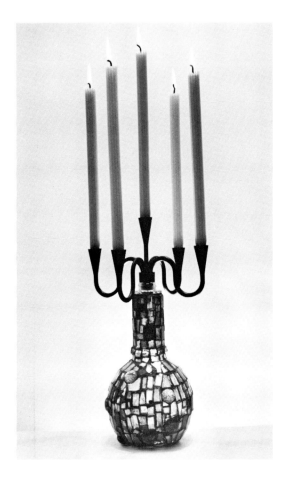

Figs. 361, 362. Adjustable candelabra for bottles may be purchased in gift shops. By using appropriate motifs and colors for the mosaic the artist can make them into prized accessories for special holidays.

LIGHT FIXTURES

Obscure glass or plastic fixtures suitable for mosaics may be purchased from electrical companies or hobby shops. However, finding exactly the right size and shape within a reasonable price range is a different matter. It is not only cheaper to build them yourself, but they can then be tailored to your own decorative and functional requirements.

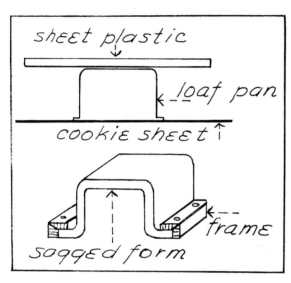

Fig. 363. Sheet Plexiglas (or other thermoplastic resin sheets) can be sagged over molds in the kitchen oven to make translucent wall fixtures. Some allowance should be made for shrinkage. Large metal loaf-pans or Pyrex dishes which have no undercuts in the exterior walls may be used as molds. Frame the edges with grooved strips of wood and drill holes for screws to attach the fixture to the wall.

Lanterns

The directions for building a wooden frame of the kind used for Figure 364 will apply to any lantern with straight sides. Simply change the top and bottom boards from squares to triangles, rectangles, hexagons, etc., and alter the angles of the upright supports to fit the corners.

The mosaic panels can be either removable or stationary. Double-strength window glass can be used for removable panels, since the entire lantern would not have to be dismantled in the event that one side was accidently broken. Where the mosaics are permanently installed, Plexiglas or Lucite sheets are more practical choices for backings.

If the pattern has large transparent areas, some diffusion of the light will be needed. This might be solved with a textured glass foundation, or by coating the inside with one of the spray products manufactured for obscuring windows. Sheet plastics may be obtained in translucent white as well as clear, and will filter the light beautifully.

Clear Plexiglas was used for the demonstration project, since the tesserae are fairly small and part of the pattern is opaque.

A design for the sides was drawn on graph paper with allowance left between each piece for grout. Margins were marked off on all four sides to represent the area which would slide into the grooves of the frame.

Materials were prepared next. The hourglass shapes of scrap aluminum are interspersed with tiny bits of melted emerald-green glass. Blue and turquoise rectangles were cut from cathedral glass and fired until the edges were rounded. Circular tesserae are melted marbles in shades of amber and lemon-yellow.

Fig. 364. This large lantern measures 9 inches square by 20 inches long. Designed to provide a soft glow at an entryway, rather than bright illumination, the decorative pattern is made of aluminum and kiln-fired glass. By day, the aluminum fragments are the positive elements in the pattern. By night, they become negative elements which intensify the brilliance of the tiny pinpoints, circles, and rectangles of colored light. By Robert Stribling.

Fig. 365. When the materials were ready to be assembled, the pattern was taped to the underside of the Plexiglas and the tesserae attached with epoxy. The panels were installed in the frame, the top set in place, and the frame covered with masking tape to protect it from being stained by grout. Black grout was used to fill the crevices.

BUILDING THE FRAME

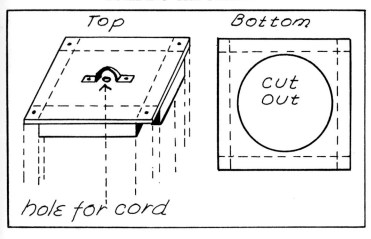

Top   Bottom

cut
out

hole for cord

Fig. 366. Matching squares of ¼-inch Masonite were cut for the top and bottom. A hole was drilled in the top for the light cord, and a large circular opening cut in the bottom to cast light downward and provide a means of changing light bulbs.

Fig. 367. The uprights were made of 1-inch square strips, grooved on the two inner sides to accommodate the thickness of the panels. Four uprights were cut to the length of the lantern. Eight more strips were cut to fit between the uprights at top and bottom as indicated in Figure 366.

Fig. 368. The horizontal strips were attached to the top and bottom sections with wood glue and held with clamps until the glue was dry. Uprights were then attached to the bottom only, and a porcelain light socket installed inside the top. (Right-angle clamps shown here will ensure tight, accurate joints on all kinds of frames and clock cases.)

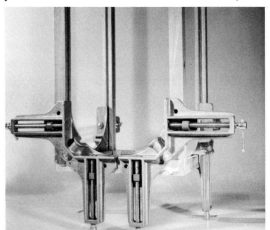

Fig. 369. The top of the lantern will not be secured until the mosaic panels are ready to be installed. Since the top carries the full weight, screws as well as glue will be used in all four corners. (For removable panels, omit the glue and reinforce the structure with four thin steel rods just inside the uprights. These should be threaded on the ends, slipped through matching holes in the top and bottom, and secured on the outside with nuts.) The frame was finished with flat black paint.

Fig. 370. This lantern by Rosalis has a wrought-iron frame and glass sides. It may be wired for electricity and suspended, or used to shield a candle on a patio table. Decorative pattern is made of random cuts of stained glass.

Pendants from Bottles

Owing to the heat which is generated by a light bulb, nothing smaller than a half-gallon bottle is recommended for fixtures designed for good illumination. For decorative lights which might simply brighten a shadowy corner, small bottles can be wired for tiny candle-lamps and hung singly or in clusters.[2]

As far as breakage is concerned, the glass of the base pendant would probably be unaffected by a moderate amount of heat. However, it may have a different ratio of contraction and expansion from the adhesive used to attach the tesserae. This can set up a situation similar to that we described in connection with kiln-fusing incompatible glass, and in time may cause the mosaic to separate from the base form.

The supporting "honeycomb" skeleton of grout on the pendant in Figure 376 adds considerably to its durability.

Trimming the Bottle

Large bottles often have thick-and-thin spots which may cause them to break unevenly. Since a fracture will follow the line of least resistance, we must influence its path by weakening the glass with a scored line.

Two ways of cutting bottles are explained in Chapters 2 and 8. The neck may be severed at any point to create pleasing proportions for the pendant. It may, in fact, be left intact as shown in Figure 41, and the rim plated with plastic metal to cover threads or cap lip.

Cutting large bottles is asking a great deal

[2] Adapter-sockets can be purchased so that miniature bulbs, such as Decor-Lites (by Sylvania), may be used in ordinary sockets.

of the little hot-wire slicer diagrammed in Chapter 2. However, it was used for all projects in this book which involve trimming bottles to specific measurements. It is very important that you practice on small bottles and experiment with ways of controlling the breaks before risking a prized acquisition.

The common uncolored jug which was converted into the form for the following hanging light snapped clean without our having to resort to unusual measures. Other types of containers have required dripping cold water on the point of contact between hot wire and glass, as was mentioned in Chapter 2. This can be risky, since it sometimes starts vertical cracks.

The important point to remember when you are working for accurate breaks is to *score a line around the bottle*. If it fractures all around but remains attached, run very hot water over it, then plunge it in a pan of cold water. A light tap with the ball end of the glass cutter, and the pieces will usually separate.

Fig. 371. Remove the neck first, then the bottom. Cleaner breaks are obtained when this is accomplished by manipulating the off-on switch of the slicer, than when the method involving water is used.

The pattern used for the pendant light in Figure 376 was derived from a section of a dragonfly's wing as it appeared under a magnifying glass. To keep the texture from becoming monotonous, heavy vertical grout lines were designed to divide the lower part of the cylinder into six sections.

A better relationship of applied decoration to form will be obtained if we adapt the mosaic to the problems of attaching flat tesserae to a curved surface, rather than fight them.

Obviously, wide pieces of glass would be impractical. By using long narrow strips on the straight walls and moving into small nuggets where the cylinder narrows sharply into the neck, adhesion and grouting are greatly simplified, and the texture is in agreement with the basic shape.

The strips were cut from medium-brown, amber, and pale-yellow glass. The irregular nuggets are chips of dark brown and olive green. Touches of orange are used sparingly for contrast.

The small chips were arranged in the hottest part of the kiln, where they melted into cabochons at the same time as the edges of the strips were rounded.

Before any of the tesserae were attached to the bottle, the entire exterior surface was buttered liberally with epoxy cement and left overnight to set. There are important reasons for this measure. Unless the tesserae are well sealed on the edges by the adhesive, the dark grout will run underneath and spoil the pattern. Further, when fresh cement is applied to the individual tesserae and pressed against the undercoating, it will "grab," thereby minimizing their tendency to slide out of place on the slippery curved surface.

It is wise to wire the bottle before mosaicking so that work can be checked against interior lighting from time to time.

When the mosaic is finished and the glue completely hard, mix tinted grout a little thicker than is used for opaque projects and rub it into the crevices.

Let it become partly set, then wipe the surface with paper towels and a damp sponge so that the grout is slightly recessed below the tesserae. Wait twenty-four hours, then mix a smaller amount of grout to a thin consistency and go over the entire pendant again. This two-layer method of grouting will fill any tiny pinholes or hairline cracks and provide clean, smooth joints.

Fig. 372. PARTS FOR WIRING AND
          HANGING.

1. Finial.
2. A vase cap which fits the outside of the bottle neck.
3. Short length of threaded pipe.
4. A vase cap which fits inside the neck of the bottle.
5. A nut which fits the threaded pipe.
6. Parts of the socket.
7. Plastic lamp cord.
8. Chain for suspending the light.

ASSEMBLING THE FIXTURE

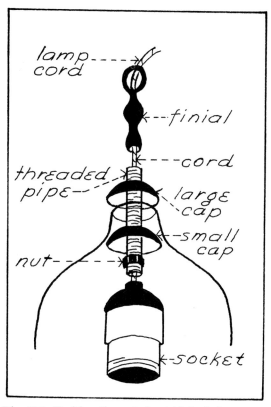

Fig. 373. Position the nut about ¼ inch from one end of the threaded pipe. Thread the lamp cord through the pipe, attach to socket, then fasten the pipe to the socket. Slip the inside vase cap in place above the nut, and arrange in the neck of the bottle. On the outside, secure the vase cap and finial. Readjust the nut against the inside cap so that the fixture is rigid.

Fig. 374. The bottom of the form can be bound with narrow lead came or finished with flexible gold plastic edging. The first method will be explained in Chapter 24. For the second, apply a ribbon of epoxy to the outside rim of the bottom, wrap the edging around it, trim to fit, and use heavy paper clips and alligator clips to hold it in place until the cement hardens.

Fig. 375. Draw the outline of the bottom on a sheet of tracing paper and fold the circle into quarters to establish the center. With compass set to the radius of the circle, mark six equidistant points on the circumference. Vertical lines can then be drawn from these spots. They should end just below the point where the cylinder curves into the neck.

Fig. 377. An oversized brandy snifter becomes a patio lamp when it is mosaicked with stained glass and melted marbles. By Rosalis.

Fig. 376. THE FINISHED HANGING LIGHT.

Fig. 378. Cylinders cut from straight-sided bottles can be set into shallow cans for hurricane lamps. If colored bottles are used, polish or bind the top edges and mosaic the can. Clear chimneys can be mosaicked in the manner of the hanging light.

chapter 23

Soldered Frameworks

In this chapter and the next we shall investigate ways of supporting mosaics with metal skeletons. Each process has its own character, and certain structural limitations should be clearly understood before planning the decorative pattern.

In the first two examples, sections of glass are bound to steel frameworks with plastic metal. Several coats are applied on each side to lock the glass securely in place. All exposed metal is plated, even segments which extend past the edge of the glass.

When drafting the design we must consider:

1. The difficulty of accurately shaping a fairly rigid wire to curved lines.

2. The need for strengthening the basic structure with a few diagonal lines.

3. An arrangement of soldered joints where as few wires as possible meet at a common junction.

The reason for the third point may not be immediately evident to persons having limited experience with soldering, and a few notes may be helpful.

NOTES ON SOLDERING

• Considerable heat is required to solder two pieces of metal together. When a third piece is joined at the same place, there is danger of melting the solder in the first attachment, thereby reopening the joint. Where this complication is unavoidable, insulate the outside edges of the first joint with a paste of powdered asbestos and water, or a small pellet of clay. When soldering is completed, clean away the protective coating with water and a stiff brush.

• Only clean, dry metal can be bonded together successfully, and all paint, lacquer, and other finishes should be removed.

• Flux lowers the melting point of solder and greatly facilitates its flow. Paint it on with an inexpensive brush, heat the joint with the iron, then add the solder. If the metal is too cool, the solder will roll off instead of adhering.

• A "cold joint" is a seam on which the solder is melted but not actually fused to the metal. It is weak and will break apart easily.

• If flux or acid core solder is used, scrub the finished piece with soap and water or the metal will deteriorate.

• Beginners often have difficulty controlling the amount of solder which the iron may melt away from the coil. Try snipping the solder into small crumbs and placing them one at the time on the heated fluxed joint with tweezers. Hold the iron on the crumb until it melts, and add more solder until the joint is sufficiently sealed.

FRAMEWORKS FROM COAT-HANGER WIRE

If properly soldered and braced, coat-hanger wire is substantial enough for mosaics up to 2 feet square. The cells should, however, be kept fairly small. This type of project moves considerably faster where two craftsmen work together as a team.

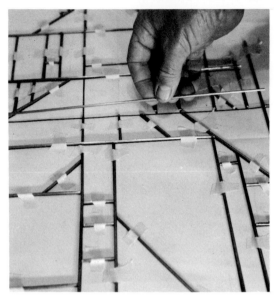

Fig. 380. Clean paint or varnish from the coat hanger and cut into lengths to fit the pattern lines. Tape each strip in place on the drawing.

Fig. 379. Make several small sketches in color until you have one that is balanced and not too complex. Enlarge it to scale, using a straight edge and triangle to keep the lines accurate. (Notice the diagonal lines which serve as braces.) This cartoon will be used only to build the framework. Patterns for the glass insets will be drawn from the metal structure.

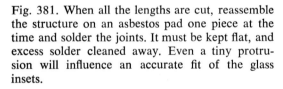

Fig. 381. When all the lengths are cut, reassemble the structure on an asbestos pad one piece at the time and solder the joints. It must be kept flat, and excess solder cleaned away. Even a tiny protrusion will influence an accurate fit of the glass insets.

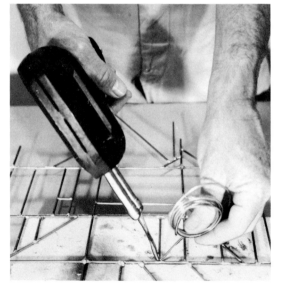

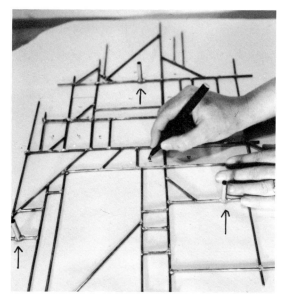

Fig. 382. On the back of the finished framework, solder three 1¼-inch segments of brass tubing to hold the mosaic out from the wall. (Note arrows.) Place the structure on a sheet of paper and draw around the inside of each section to make cutting patterns for the glass. Number the sections to simplify final assembly. Cut out the glass pieces and mark them to correspond to the pattern. Nip away corners as needed to make a snug fit against joints which are slightly rounded with solder.

Fig. 384. Squeeze plastic steel around the edges of the cells first, being careful to extend the plastic at least ⅛ inch over the glass, then cover the wire itself. Use a knife blade to press down the plastic gently so that it clings to the glass and fills the crevices. Several solid coats will be needed. Let the back side cure at least twenty-four hours before turning the mosaic over and repeating the process on the front. All of the metal is plated and given a rough, troweled finish.

Fig. 383. Wrap a length of heavy monofilament line around a horizontal wire near the top and tie two loops on the back for hanging the finished piece. (See arrows.) Place the framework face down, clean glass insets, and position them. Notice here that a few openings have been planned for variety in the shadow patterns.

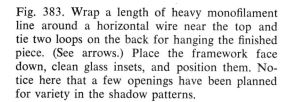

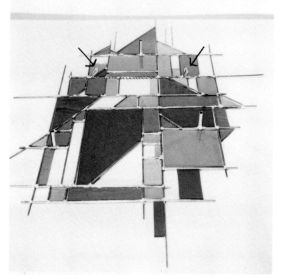

Fig. 385. Let the piece cure several days until the plastic is no longer flexible, then burnish with the back of an old spoon or knife handle.

Fig. 386. With side lighting, "County Fair" casts luminous reflections. By Mary Lou Stribling.

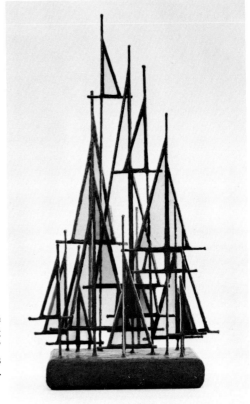

Fig. 387. The individual units should be composed of straight-sided segments, but vary the proportions and sizes. "Marina" is an arrangement of triangles which was developed from a sketch of a fleet of sailboats. By Mary Lou Stribling.

FREE-STANDING STRUCTURES FROM WELDING RODS

Free-standing structures need more support than the preceding wall decoration, so we shall use tough, resilient welding rod instead of coat-hanger wire.

This is an exciting approach to fragmented design since intermediate colors are produced by building up the pattern in layers of glass shapes.

Only the separate forms are planned on paper. The final three-dimensional arrangement is determined as the work progresses.

Cathedral glass was used for the demonstration, though window glass tinted with glass glazes could be substituted.

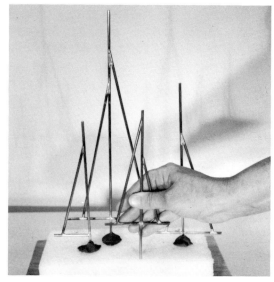

Fig. 388. Cut the welding rods to fit the patterns and solder the joints. Make the uprights a little longer than necessary, since it is easier to saw off a few inches than to try to solder an extension on a piece which is too short. Make a number of frames, then experiment with combinations on a block of Styrofoam. Use pellets of plasteline to keep them from tilting.

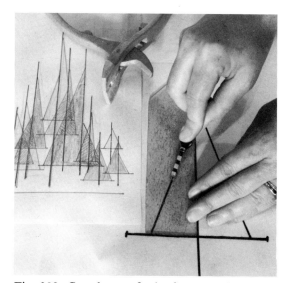

Fig. 389. Cut glass to fit the frames and seat the pieces with plastic steel as described in Figure 384. After the plastic has cured, give it a bronze patina (see Figure 391), then reposition the units on the Styrofoam and study the effect against a lighted background or window. Color adds new elements to the design and changes may be necessary. When a final decision is made, trim the Styrofoam to a compatible shape and size for a base, then mark holes and units with matching numbers.

Fig. 390. Diagram on paper the exact location of each hole and pierce the spots with an ice pick. Tape it over a block of wood which has been cut to the measurements of the Styrofoam block. A dot of white paint in the perforations will indicate where holes should be drilled in the permanent base.

Fig. 391. Drill holes of the same diameter as the welding rod in the wooden base, and plate it heavily with several layers of plastic steel. (Short lengths of rod inserted in the holes will keep them clean.) When the plastic has hardened, give it a thin uneven wash of dark-green oil paint diluted with turpentine. Buff the surface lightly with fine sandpaper, then burnish with a length of brass tubing to pick up bronzy highlights.

Fig. 392. Using epoxy as an adhesive and the paper diagram as a guide, mount the framed units. Pack small crevices around the base of the uprights with plastic steel and burnish to blend in with the rest of the plating.

FORMS FROM COPPER STRIPPING
AND POLYESTER RESIN

Quarter-inch copper stripping is flexible and easy to shape, permitting the construction of a different type of framework from those just described. It is especially useful for making forms which can be hung separately, or grouped together into an arrangement of overlapping planes. The fish demonstrated below are planned for a wall decoration behind an aquarium.

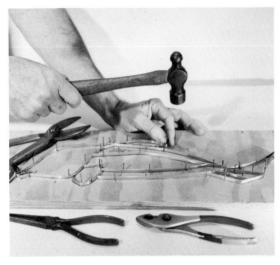

Fig. 393. Trace the pattern onto a scrap of plywood or sheet asbestos, and shape the strips of copper to fit the lines. Sharp angles and curves can be bent around metal rods, the edge of a table, or the handles of paint brushes. Position each strip as it is shaped and hold it upright with small nails on alternating sides.

Fig. 395. Place the form on a board and arrange the tesserae. These are melted smalti and beach pebbles. The eye is a melted glass nugget with a reflective gold backing. Carefully lift the framework straight up, leaving the mosaic arrangement in place.

Fig. 394. Solder the joints. Now we have an open framework, consisting only of metal outlines.

SOLDERED FRAMEWORKS   **211**

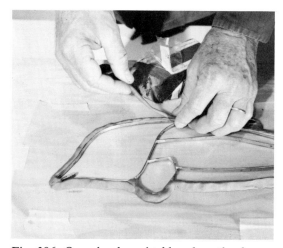

Fig. 396. On a level worktable, place the framework on a sheet of acetate overlay, Mylar, or glass, and seal the outside edges with small coils of plasteline. (If glass is used, coat it with wax or mold release.) Mix enough catalyzed resin to fill the cells to a depth of ⅛ inch. This will be the backing for the mosaic. Let it cure for at least twenty-four hours before removing the sheet plastic or glass. Trim if necessary.

Fig. 397. You may leave the copper in its natural state or antique it. Here, the forms are being sprayed flat black. When they were dry, the top edges of the metal were buffed with a cloth dampened in turpentine to expose copper highlights. Color catalyzed paste polyester resin with black pigment and spread it about ⅛ inch thick into one cell at the time. Press decorative materials in place.

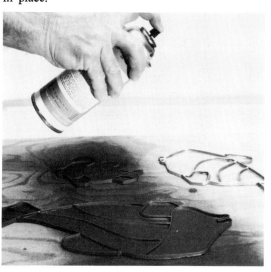

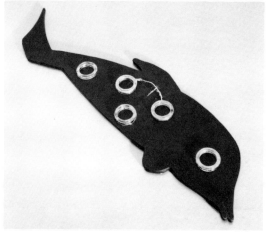

Fig. 398. When the resin has cured, hold the form between thumb and forefinger to determine the point of balance. Mark it on the back with chalk, then, at equal points on each side, glue separators to hold it out from the wall and provide a means of hanging. Segments of wooden dowels, notched to keep the wire from slipping, are suitable. These separators are two plastic curtain rings glued together with epoxy. The hanging wire is twisted tightly in the crevices between them. Other separators hold the fish level against the wall.

Fig. 399. One fish is finished. Others can be arranged to swim behind him or around him . . .

Fig. 400. . . . or, by varying the thicknesses of the separators, the designer can project them at different elevations from the wall, and hang so that they overlap each other.

chapter 24.

Metal Bindings

LEAD CAME

Although the technique of binding glass with lead has remained essentially unchanged for hundreds of years, the character of the designs has changed considerably. Projects of the scope produced by commercial studios require special equipment and engineering know-how, but simple designs can be made by anyone who can use a glass cutter and a soldering iron.

Lead came (sometimes spelled *calm*) can be bought in a number of widths with a channel depth which accommodates the thickness of standard sheet glass. (Special depths can be obtained for laminations.) U-channel is used for binding exterior edges of unframed motifs, H-channel for holding the pieces of glass together. Some imported leaded work is made with H-channel alone, but a combination of the two types will give a neater, more professional appearance to projects of the kind demonstrated in this chapter.

Came must be stretched to prepare it for smooth, tight binding. Some workers secure one end of a strip in a vise and pull on the other with pliers. We find it easier to simply step on one end of the lead, grasp the other with gloved hands, and draw it upward until it is straight and firm without any give. A 6-foot length will stretch nearly 6 inches.

Bend the flattened tip into a loop and hang the strip over a nail until you are ready to use it. The weight of the lead will keep it straight.

A piece of scrap plywood makes a good work surface. A sharp knife or scroll saw will cut readily through the soft lead. Smooth wooden modeling tools or orange sticks can be used to widen the channel lips before inserting the glass. (Metal tools will scratch the binding.)

Small nails can be hammered lightly into the plywood to brace the glass temporarily during assembly. Figure 402 shows how Margory Smith uses this technique for assembling a leaded fish mobile.

Lead joints should be overlapped and pressed down smoothly where extra strength is required. For lightweight pieces, butt joints are less bulky, but the lead must be trimmed for close fits. Solder will flow readily into narrow crevices, but it will not bridge a wide gap.

The technique of soldering lead differs slightly from that of soldering hard metals. Lead

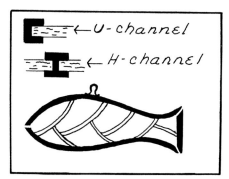

Fig. 401. Leaded outlines should be simple, with as few joints as possible. Notice that the fish shape shown here has only three. U-channel came would be used to bind the edges, and H-channel between the sections of glass.

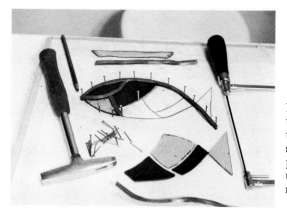

Fig. 402. A length of came was cut and shaped to the upper outline. Starting at one end, a glass section was slipped into the top binding and an inner strip of lead positioned against it. As adjacent pieces of glass were set in place, small nails were used to brace them temporarily. The nails are moved as needed to secure new additions.

will melt almost as quickly as the solder, and you must be careful not to hold the iron too long in one place. Resin core solder, such as is used for electronic work, is preferable to acid core, which must be washed away to prevent deterioration of the lead.

Clean the joints with a small wire brush before soldering. Hold a stick of solder against the joint, melt a droplet into the seam, then run the iron back and forth over it. If further refining is necessary, use an electric grinder or file.

After the unit is soldered on both sides, a glazing compound must be forced under the came to strengthen the structure and eliminate any "play" in the separate pieces. Commercial products can be purchased in hardware stores, but we prefer a mixture which is easier to clean from the glass. For small amounts, combine 1 tablespoon of linseed oil, 1 tablespoon of turpentine, 2 tablespoons of plaster of Paris, 2 tablespoons of whiting, and 1 teaspoon of black mineral pigment.[1] (Increase proportionately for large amounts.) Add a few more drops of turpentine if the paste is too thick. The dark color keeps the packing from being obtrusive and gives the lead a dull, antique finish. Store the putty in a jar with a tight lid and it will keep indefinitely.

Wear rubber gloves for puttying-up. Dribble the prepared mix around the came and force it into crevices with a flexible spatula and an old toothbrush. Go over the lead with a wooden paddle to press it firmly against the glass. Turn the form over and repeat on the other side. Wipe lightly with paper towels. After twenty-four hours, sprinkle dry whiting over the surface and scrub it clean with paper towels and rags.

Leaded windows or large structures require extra reinforcement, which should be planned as a part of the linear design. Welding rods can be soldered directly to the binding in several places, but aluminum must be attached to it with wire. Solder the wires to the came, wrap them tightly around the bars, and solder the twisted ends. Windows should always be framed and the supports fastened to the frames.

[1] This is a variation of a recipe in *Stained Glass Craft* by J. A. F. Divine and George Blachford (Peoria, Ill., Manual Arts Press, 1940).

Leading a Simple Design

Colored glass alone can be used for this introductory project. More unusual effects are possible if glass is combined with mosaicked hardboard. One-eighth-inch Masonite is about the same thickness as standard stained glass and can be bound in exactly the same way. (Use the rough side for the mosaic.) It will provide extra strength, and simplifies the problem of installing a hanger.

Draw a pattern for the mosaic and go over the lines with a felt-tipped pen to make about $\frac{1}{16}$-inch allowance for the core of the came. Stretch the lead, cut out all the pieces of glass and Masonite, and arrange them close at hand.

The heat from small soldering irons will not penetrate through the back of the came and you can assemble the design directly on the paper pattern.

Fig. 403. Cecil Casebier combined white opal glass with brilliant translucent colors of rust, blue, olive, orange, and yellow in this contemporary leaded window. The reinforcing rods have been incorporated into the design. (Collection of Orco Glass.)

LEADED DAISIES

Fig. 404. Bind the Masonite center with H-channel came and place it on the pattern. Set in a glass section, then arrange strips of H-channel lead on each side. Continue until pattern is filled. One section remains to be positioned here.

Fig. 405. Bind the outside edges with U-channel came and solder the joints on both sides. Pack the crevices between lead and glass with glazing compound. Go over the lead with a wooden paddle and press it firmly against the glass. Turn form over and cement the other side. Clean as described in text.

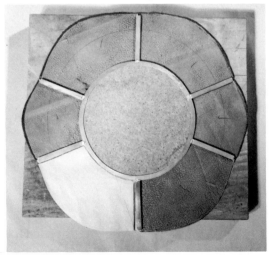

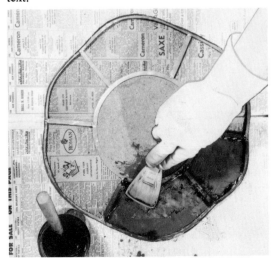

Fig. 406. Drill a hole in the upper center of the Masonite, insert a short bolt, and fasten with a nut on the back. Tie a loop of braided wire around the bolt and secure with a second nut. Epoxy three matching dowels (½ to 1½ inches long) around the hanger to hold the form out from the wall. A narrow wood strip or dowel can be epoxied on as a "stem."

Fig. 407. Mix paste polyester resin with catalyst and color it black with plastic pigment. Spread a bed of resin on the Masonite and press decorative materials into it. Large glass beads, melted smalti, and polished pebbles are shown here.

Fig. 408. Make several stylized daisies in different sizes. Use dowels of varying lengths on the backs so that they can be overlapped on the wall. This arrangement uses amber, chartreuse, and emerald glass. Centers are in shades of yellow, orange, green, and brown.

SHEET COPPER

BINDING GLASS WITH COPPER FOIL

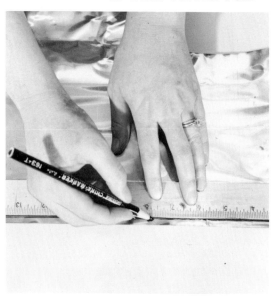

Fig. 409. Mark a margin ¼ inch wide on the foil with a grease pencil. Draw another line to represent the thickness of the glass, which in this case was ⅛ inch. Draw another ¼-inch margin and cut along the line with scissors. Cut off a length to fit one edge of the glass.

Fig. 410. Place a straight edge on one margin line and, with a soft wooden tool, crease it to a right angle.

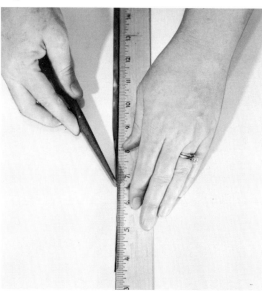

A different technique for metal bindings was developed in our workshop for use where the binding itself becomes a colorful, decorative element in the design.

Copper came is commercially available, and is recommended for large projects where the structure must support considerable weight. It is quite expensive, however. Aside from considerations of economy, 36-gauge copper foil can be cut into strips of any width and shaped to accommodate materials of any thickness. This opens up possibilities for binding fragments of certain materials which cannot be soldered with ordinary equipment (such as aluminum), and combining them with shapes of bound glass.

It is evident that the foil has less strength than came, which means that supports must be a decorative part of the design. Welding rod is suitable, but brass rods or tubing are richer and just as easy to solder.

We use a type of "open flame" soldering to deposit tiny silver pinpoints on the copper binding.

Copper foil does not have the elasticity of lead and cannot with any success be shaped around curved edges. This restricts the mosaic pattern to straight-sided fragments.

Work from an accurate cartoon which defines all the separate pieces of the pattern as well as the supports. Allow for the widths of the supporting rods so that they will fit closely against the bound sections. You will have to use your own judgment as to how many will be needed, since this will depend on the weight of materials. As a rule of thumb, two lengths of ⅛-inch brass tubes or rods are adequate for a glass area about 3 × 8 inches.[2]

Cut out all the decorative materials by the pattern, including the supports. Each separate piece should be bound and the corners soldered before the mosaic is put together. The foil is

[2] Brass rods can be purchased from mosaic shops, telescoping brass tubes from hobby shops selling supplies for model airplanes, boats, cars, etc.

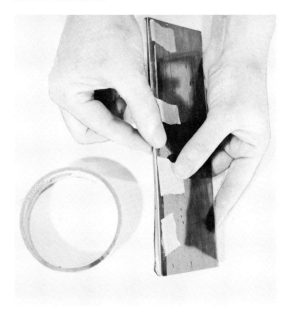

Fig. 411. Spread epoxy along the cut edge of the glass, then fold the foil over it, taping it in place as you go. Smooth the binding with the wooden tool and repeat on other edges. Corners are neater if they are mitred.

Fig. 413. When all sections are bound, remove tape and start assembling the pieces one at a time on a sheet of asbestos. Use small nails to hold the fragments together, and solder several spots along each seam.

Paint flux over binding and supports, then melt away beads of solder over the metal and in crevices between supports and glass. Turn the propane torch to low flame and play it up and down one strip of metal to warm it. Direct heat to a spot of solder until it flows into the seams and creates bright silver droplets and runnels against the copper.

Fig. 412. Let the epoxy harden overnight, then remove tape near the corners. Brush on a coat of flux and solder the seams. The solder can be left rough. It will be smoothed by the torch flame.

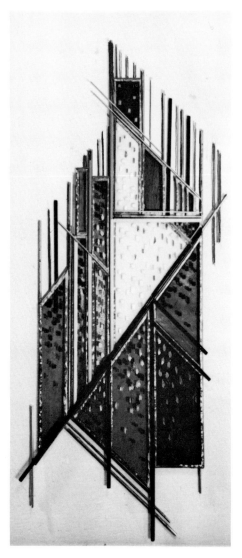

Fig. 414. The basic form of "The Factory" was made of copper-bound glass and several sizes of brass tubing. Short lengths of tubing were soldered to the structure for "chimneys." Opaque glass rods were secured with epoxy for other chimneys and accents. The rods were nipped into tiny segments for the small tesserae. By Mary Lou Stribling.

thin, and a miniature iron is perfectly suitable for this part of the construction. The final soldering step is done with the flame of a propane torch, which will ensure a well-fused unit.

The instructions for binding glass will also apply to binding fragments of metal or fired clay.

You must remember that the torch flame is very hot and should be kept moving along the metal so that the glass will not get overheated and crack. Prolonged burning of the metal will weaken and discolor it.

Continue joining one section to another until the design is finished. Wash away residue of acid, then rub glazing compound into crevices between binding and glass as was described for lead came.

After cleaning, buff metal areas with fine steel wool and antique with a solution of liver of sulphur until the desired patina is obtained.[3]

Additional decorative elements of rods, tubes, or mosaic tesserae can be attached to the basic structure with epoxy.

[3] See Chapter 6.

chapter 25

Sculpture

To most laymen, the word sculpture suggests a figure which has been carved or modeled in some permanent material. But many contemporary sculptures are not figures at all. They are abstract compositions which express some idea or concept of design.

Let us say, then, that sculpture is three-dimensional design which is derived from a tangible *subject,* or an intangible *idea.* It can be fully in the round or be a "relief" projected from a flat base at various levels of prominence.

There are many works, of course, which do not seem to fit anywhere. How would we classify the Watts Towers, for example?[1] Or "Marina" in Chapter 23? They are not two-dimensional compositions, but are they sculpture?

They might, perhaps, be called assemblages or constructions, but, for that matter, so might the whole enormous field of mosaics. It would be as difficult to find the precise line which separates them from sculpture as to find one to determine the exact point at which a ceramic form becomes sculpture instead of pottery.

[1] See Figures 437–440.

WHATEVER HAPPENED TO MICHELANGELO?

Regardless of the possibility that the main branch of sculpture may have put out new shoots which deserve labels of their own, there is no doubt that it has acquired a new look in the past fifty years. It is important to have a little understanding of these changes, for sculpture is sculpture, whether it is mosaicked or not.

Up until the early 1900s, sculptural standards remained pretty close to the ideals established by Michelangelo. These were that sculpture should be monumental in concept, if not in actual size, and be so compactly organized that it could be "rolled down a hill without damage."

Historians disagree as to who deserves the most credit for the upheaval that started at the beginning of the twentieth century. Undoubtedly, many influences and schools of thought contributed to the creative energy that started the rusty wheels of history toward new directions.

Sculpture began to move, and was called "mobiles." Sculpture became airy frameworks of welded metal that contained more space than

Fig. 415. Mosaic relief by Helen Steinau Rich. Abstract fish shapes and marine motifs are cut from stainless steel and plywood, and projected at different elevations from the wall. Obsidian, beach pebbles, gemstones, and slag glass are attached to the plywood forms with black magnesite. *(Collection of Mr. and Mrs. S. L. Ancker.)*

they displaced, or massive organic forms which appeared as much the work of nature as man. Sculpture became "protest" and emerged as defiant structures of tin cans, rusted pipes, and automobile parts, or sullen, angry compositions of torn clay slabs. Sculpture became almost anything that was not two-dimensional.

The nature of the mosaic medium forces us to simplify, even oversimplify, basic sculptural forms.

Up until the very moment the surface is ready to receive the mosaic, we should regard the structure as something which may be changed, or even thrown away. And to begin with at least, it may be best to work with a flexible material which can readily be altered. Clay or papier-mâché permit more freedom than mortar and make it a great deal easier to start over on a piece which has gotten hopelessly beyond control.

The basic structure must be related to the mosaicked surface. We might think of the sculptured form as the skeleton and muscles, with the mosaic providing the skin. Notice the smooth, gently rounded planes in Figure 4 and try to imagine the piece without the decorative pattern. The mosaic is inseparable from the total design, not something added on as an afterthought.

Many problems on large projects can be avoided if scale models are built first in clay or plaster. Color and arrangement of tesserae can be indicated by inks or paints.

For compositions of the type in Figure 415, heavy cardboard shapes can be cut out and tentative arrangements glued together with the layers separated by slices of balsa wood. When a basic design shows possibilities, the surface decoration can be roughed in with dabs of poster paint.

Once you begin the permanent form, keep it progressing evenly all over. Do not overrefine one area before the rest has reached the same stage of development.

Always try to visualize the bulk which will be added by the decorative layer and keep the substructure a little on the lean side.

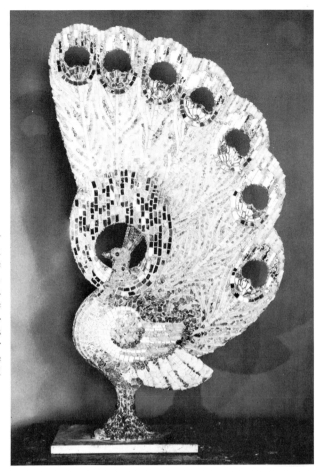

Fig. 416. "White Peacock." One of a pair of five-foot-tall, free-standing garden sculptures by William Justema for the Henry J. Kaiser residence in Honolulu. Plywood and wire mesh are bonded to a steel base and armature to reinforce the structure. The form was modeled in mortar and a variety of decorative materials pressed into the final layer. The feather pattern is made of moonstones and white smalti, and the "eyes" at the tips are gold Venetian glass and mirror.

Fig. 417. A closer view shows abalone shells on the lower breast and legs. Coral, rose, and amethyst quartz are combined with pebbles and smalti in other parts of the figure.

SCULPTURED FORMS

Many natural forms may be used for mosaic. Boulders and weathered rocks sometimes suggest stylized birds or animals or interesting abstract designs. Gnarled roots and driftwood take on new character with mosaic inlays.

Clay, stone, and wood are classic materials for modeling and carving, but there are many other choices, ranging from semipermanent mixtures which are excellent for experimentation, to those which will survive almost any treatment and weather conditions.

Mortar and Magnesite

These materials have already been described briefly in Chapter 4, and we are concerned here only with adapting basic mixes for special sculptural purposes.

Mortar is usually made with 1 part cement and 2 parts fine sand mixed with water to a paste consistency. A higher cement content produces a finer-grained product and may be reserved for the final layer. One part lime putty will improve plasticity and surface quality. Concrete additives will decrease porosity and keep the mix open for a longer period of time.

Figs. 419, 420. The sculpture in Figure 4 by Ray Rice was built of mortar troweled over an armature of steel and hardware cloth. Various aspects of the female figure in motion are sketched on the flat sides of the abstract form. Inside the cave-like aperture, other images appear which are vaguely reminiscent of children's drawings. These details show the strong, flat linear pattern and the textural effects achieved by the arrangements of brilliantly colored Venetian glass and smalti.

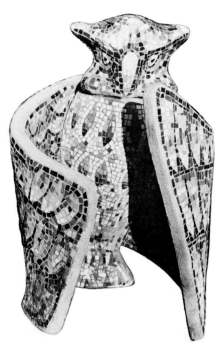

Fig. 418. "The Actor," concrete sculpture by Ray Rice. (Collection of Angelo Margolis.)

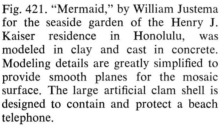

Fig. 421. "Mermaid," by William Justema for the seaside garden of the Henry J. Kaiser residence in Honolulu, was modeled in clay and cast in concrete. Modeling details are greatly simplified to provide smooth planes for the mosaic surface. The large artificial clam shell is designed to contain and protect a beach telephone.

Fig. 422. The coiffure of the mermaid was cast from loops of rope. The mosaic is composed of abalone shells, pearl shells, Venetian glass, and gemstones.

A number of aggregates may be added to either mortar or magnesite to displace some of the volume, thereby creating a lighter, less dense material which is easier to carve. (Remember that magnesite is mixed with a solution of magnesium chloride instead of water.)

Vermiculite, perlite, and powdered asbestos are most popular, and many sculptors like to add a small amount of sawdust. Up to 10 per cent mineral color can be included without significantly weakening the mixture.

To experiment with cement recipes, make up several test batches and let them cure about two weeks. Decrease aggregates if the test seems too crumbly or spongy to meet your needs.

Carving should always be done before the material has completely cured.

Basic Cement Recipes

1. 1 part vermiculite or perlite
   1 part fine river sand
   1 part cement or magnesite

2. 1 part fine sawdust
   1 part fine sand
   1½ parts cement or magnesite

Plaster and Hydrocal

Hydrocal can be mixed and cast as ordinary plaster, but is harder and more durable. (It is used in the ceramic industry for master molds.) We shall stress again one important point: always add plaster to water, not water to plaster.

Blocks of plaster for carving can be formed in a strong cardboard box. All openings must be chinked with plasteline or several layers of masking tape, and the inside surface of the box oiled so that it can easily be peeled from the hardened plaster.

Ceramic grog (either fine or coarse) improves the texture of plaster, and the aggregates suggested for cement mixes may also be used. (A small amount of cement makes plaster more durable.)

Plaster is not recommended for exterior sculpture unless it is protected from weather.

A Basic Plaster Recipe for Carved Forms

  6 parts plaster
  1 part cement
  3 parts grog, sawdust, vermiculite, or
     perlite.

A softer material will be obtained by increasing both the plaster and aggregate proportions.

Papier-mâché

Papier-mâché has been in use for so long that it hardly seems necessary to include directions for making. A pulp made from water-soaked paper toweling or facial tissue can be mixed to a modeling consistency with wheat paste. An alternate method is to soften strips of newspaper in the paste solution and build up forms in layers.

A few drops of oil of cloves will retard spoilage of the wet paste.

Prepared pulp is now on the market which needs only the addition of water. Store leftover batches in the refrigerator in a plastic bag.

Wood Mâché

Wood mâché is made by mixing fine sawdust with diluted white glue. Combine equal proportions of glue with water and moisten the sawdust until it can be shaped with the fingers. It is inclined to be somewhat crumbly, and should be pressed firmly around an armature. Do not add too much bulk at one time or it may collapse.

Wood mâché is quite durable, but should be waterproofed for exterior use.

Starch Putty

Several years ago, Argo Starch Co. worked out a recipe for a plastic material which is very useful for modeling or for making decorative materials where facilities for firing clay are not available. Naturally, it is not as permanent as clay, but will hold up well for interior decorations if the surface is sealed with shellac or spray acrylic.

Combine 2 cups of salt with ⅔ cup of water and stir over low heat three or four minutes. Remove from heat and add 1 cup of cornstarch mixed with ½ cup of cold water. Stir rapidly until mixture is of modeling consistency. It may be thickened further by stirring over low heat about a minute. The putty can be tinted with dyes, mineral pigments, or poster paints, and will keep indefinitely in a plastic bag or aluminum foil. Try it for quick sketches or simple scale models.

ARMATURES

Almost every sculpture which is built of materials which are not to be fired needs an armature of some kind. You can use cores of styrofoam, wadded paper tied tightly with string, or crushed screening bound to metal or wooden supports. Do not make the armature too bulky or it will restrict your design. It should not come closer to the finished surface than ½ to 1 inch in any direction.

To start building upon armatures for plaster or mortar forms, saturate strips of fabric with a fairly thin mixture of the modeling material and wrap them around the core or skeleton. Use several layers and allow them to set before continuing with the plaster or mortar alone.

Some sculptors lighten the weight of large pieces by blocking out the rough structure with wads of excelsior dipped in the modeling material.

If the sculpture becomes dry before it is completed, soak it thoroughly with water so that it will bond with fresh layers.

MOSAICKING THE FORM

Mosaic patterns can be applied to sculpture in any of the ways already suggested for bird baths, planters, etc. To review the two most popular methods:

1. Build the sculpture up to within ⅛ or ¼ inch of the surface (depending on the thickness of the decorative materials), and let it dry. Seal it with shellac, acrylic, or white glue, and attach the tesserae with an adhesive which is

Fig. 423. SIMPLE ARMATURES

1. Balsa wood or Styrofoam makes excellent lightweight cores for simple forms. For garden figures where a base is not desirable, drill a hole in the bottom of the core to match the diameter of a large dowel. It may then be set (without gluing) in a hole in a block of wood to facilitate modeling and mosaicking. When the sculpture is finished, the support may be cut off flush with the figure, or left as a "leg" to position it in the ground.

2. Animal and human figures can be built on skeletons of heavy wire. Bind lighter wire tightly around it as shown to provide an anchor for the modeling materials. Bend the armature to suit your design. It may be free-standing if well balanced, or attached to a base.

3. For compact sculptures, secure a large dowel or metal rod in a block of wood to serve as a central support. Pad it with crushed screening, wadded paper, or excelsior. String or wire can be wrapped around the padding to hold it in place. It should then be covered with strips of fabric saturated with the modeling material.

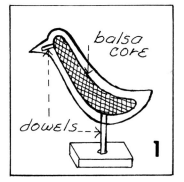 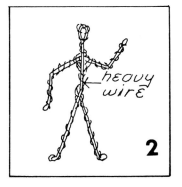 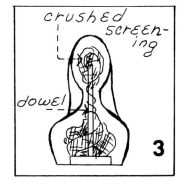

Fig. 424. Solid clay forms should be hollowed out before modeling the final surface. Start at the base and remove clay core as far as can be reached with a wire-end tool, then make long, narrow incisions in adjoining areas and continue. All chambers must be connected or they will accumulate steam and explode. Pack bits of clay along the edges of the incisions until the wall is restored.

"The Bather" is a scale model for a figure to go in a bird bath. Only the hair and the floor of the pool will be mosaicked. Remaining clay surfaces will be textured and left unglazed.

appropriate for the conditions to which it will be exposed. Problems will arise from adhesives which are excessively fluid, since the tesserae may slide out of place on curved or vertical areas. Mastic is an excellent choice.

2. Model the form up to ¼ inch of the final surface. Let it harden without becoming completely dry. Spread fresh mortar or plaster on only a small area at the time, and set the tesserae directly into it.

The second method would be suitable for sculptures made of mortar, magnesite, hydrocal, plaster, or other materials of these kinds. Any base structure, including wood or stone, can be used for the first.

As with other types of mosaics, decorative tesserae for sculpture should be appropriate for its size, form, function, and area of installation. Aside from those most commonly used, sheet cork, metals, and wood veneers lend themselves beautifully to three-dimensional design.

CERAMIC SCULPTURE FOR MOSAICS

Sculptured clay forms which are to be fired must be hollow to permit the escape of steam and gases. There are a number of ways to accomplish this. Simple shapes with fairly large bases can be built upon flexible cores of paper or inflated balloons which are removed before firing. Some sculptors make their forms solid and scoop out the inside while the clay is still plastic. Others build them hollow from coils and slabs of clay.

Basic shells for small sculptures can be thrown on a potter's wheel to specific measurements or built from combinations of cast forms. Plaster molds for casting ceramic objects are available in ceramic supply houses and hobby shops, but they are easy to make from inexpensive glassware and dishes. Instructions may be obtained from books on ceramics listed in the Appendix.

We have selected a group of tumbler, goblet, and bowl molds for the demonstration project. Ordinarily, they would be cast in liquid clay to a thickness of about $\frac{3}{16}$ inch. To make more substantial walls and reduce shrinkage, we shall use moist modeling clay to which 20 to 30 per cent fine grog has been added.

The molds are first sponged liberally with water so that the clay will grip the plaster surface instead of clinging to fingers. If the stems of goblets or compotes are not separate, the holes should be packed with pellets of clay.

CERAMIC SCULPTURES FROM CAST FORMS

Fig. 425. Using your thumb as a scoop, dig out a lump of clay about the size of a quarter. Starting at the bottom of the mold, press it against the wall with a firm rolling motion. Overlap each new addition, and when the inside of the mold is covered smoothly, check the depth of the clay rind by perforating it with a toothpick in a number of places. Add or remove clay as necessary for an even thickness of about ½ inch. Trim the top edge and set aside until it will slip easily from the mold.

Fig. 426. We have decided to make an owl to hang in the garden, and these are the pieces from which we shall build him.

Fig. 427. Before they get too dry, roughen the rims with a modeling tool, then coat liberally with slip.

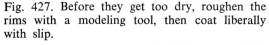

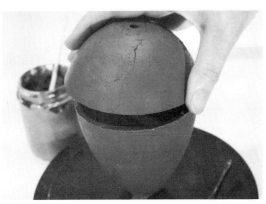

Fig. 428. Join the two pieces together with a firm twist so that a good bond is formed.

Fig. 429. The shallow bowl which will form the top is slightly larger than the deeper shape. Pack a small coil of clay into the crevice and round it off so that the joint is no longer visible.

Fig. 430. Mark the center of the top of the head and pierce with a sharp tool. This will later be used for hanging the sculpture, but also serves as a guide to keep the owl from becoming lopsided. Sketch in the location of eyes, beak, and ear tufts. At this point, he looks more like a sad egg than a wise owl . . .

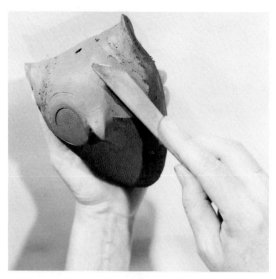

Fig. 431. . . . but we'll add clay here, take it away there, and paddle and pummel him until he has an appropriately fierce, ominous expression. We are going to cut an opening in the bottom and extend the back wall into a short tail. This means he will no longer stand upright and must be supported on a soft bed of towels or foam rubber.

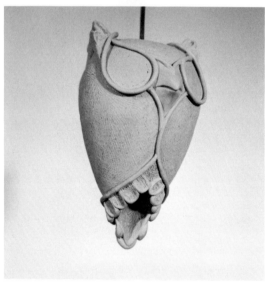

Fig. 432. Parts of the owl will be left plain. Ear tufts, lower edges of wings, and tail have been scalloped and textured. The beak is polished and smooth. Small coils of clay will serve to frame the edges of areas to be mosaicked, and the surface has been scratched for better adhesion of tesserae. The owl has now been bisqued, and is ready to be darkened with walnut stain.

Fig. 433. Since he's only a fun owl and not a nature study, we decorated him in shades of yellow, orange, red, and brown Venetian glass tiles cut into eighths. (The eyes are melted glass nuggets.) Tesserae are attached with mastic and grouted. He is strung on a rawhide thong for a garden watch-bird.

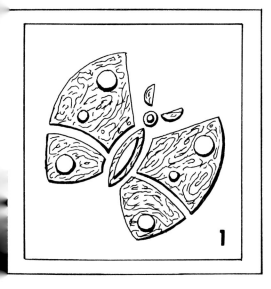

Fig. 434. BAS-RELIEF FORMS

1. Foundations for reliefs of flat, unmodeled planes can be made by attaching sections of ¼-inch plywood or pressed board to a backing of ½-inch to ¾-inch plywood. Cut out the elevated areas with a coping saw or jigsaw, glue them in place, and drive in a few small brads for extra reinforcement. As illustrated, several layers can be used. Finish the edges of the relief with paint, or with tesserae cut into ¼-inch pieces and set against the raised forms.

2. Heavy rope can be glued to a plywood backing to serve as frames for elevated motifs. Small brads tacked lightly along the edges of the rope will keep it from slipping out of place before the glue hardens. Hammer a number of carpet tacks in the "roped-off" sections, leaving the heads slightly raised above the surface. Spread wood putty or plaster over the tacks and level it off to the thickness of the rope. Ropes of different sizes can be used for different elevations. (Always build the lowest plane first.) Coils of plasteline may be substituted for the rope and removed after the relief form has hardened.

BAS-RELIEF FORMS

Reliefs which are modeled in sand and cast in mortar or plaster are described in Chapter 20. Modeled clay slabs can be cast in the same manner.

Two other ways of making relief forms for mosaics are explained in Figure 434.

A mosaic relief does not necessarily consist of elevated planes. It can be formed by raised lines alone, as is illustrated in Figure 441 by Aleksandra Kasuba. Thicker materials used for the linear pattern will create a three-dimensional effect, as will strips of wood, fired clay, or tesserae set on edge so that they are higher than the rest of the mosaic.

Fig. 435. An architectural bas-relief for the San Leandro (California) Medical Center, by Ray Rice. The design is based on elements of the caduceus, the symbol of the medical profession. The relief was built up of mortar on shapes cut from pressed asbestos board. Nails, wire, and metal rods serve to bond the cement to the backing and reinforce the basic structure. The mosaic tesserae were pressed directly into the final layer of colored cement. *(Photo courtesy of Wurster, Bernardi, and Emmons, Architects.)*

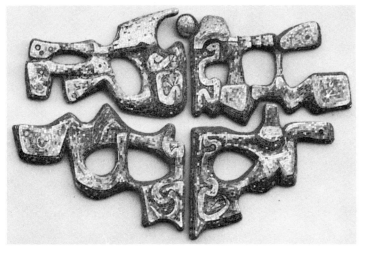

THE WATTS TOWERS

So far, there has been no agreement on a proper art classification for the mosaic towers of Simon Rodia. Perhaps they fall somewhere between architecture and sculpture, incorporating elements of both in such an original manner that they do not fit traditional definitions of either.

Without apparent concern that they serve any purpose whatever beyond that of satisfying some personal, inner need, Rodia built his magnificent structures upon armatures of pipes, old bed frames, and salvaged steel rods, molded them with mortar, and mosaicked them with shells, bottle bottoms, pebbles, broken dishes, and other oddments he found on junk heaps and beaches.

Rodia is a perfect example of the true amateur craftsman, for his work has the quality of uniqueness and perfection which derives only from "love of the doing."

Fig. 436. There is a remarkable kinship between Rodia's towers and the mosaic-encrusted spires of Buddhist temples in Thailand, yet it is doubtful that Rodia even knew of their existence.

THE MOSAIC TOWERS OF SIMON RODIA

Fig. 437. Over a period of thirty-three years, Simon Rodia worked alone to create these mysterious mosaic structures which rise 100 feet above a drab neighborhood in southwestern Los Angeles. From a distance, the spiraling cones of steel and concrete glitter with the color of thousands and thousands of embedded fragments of bottles, crockery, and seashells.

Fig. 438. The sheer physical labor required to engineer and construct the labyrinths and pavilions, the archways and gates, is almost beyond comprehension. Yet Rodia was an uneducated tile setter and worked without designs or plans except as they existed in his mind and imagination.

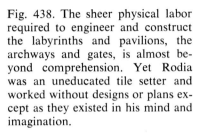

Fig. 439. As one looks up, the towers seem to stretch toward infinity, and one becomes lost among the incredible variety of patterns and structural lacework. This is no random mix. It has been designed with the instinctive precision of a spider building a web. Form within form within form . . .

Fig. 440. . . . and reaching the central supporting shaft of one of the towers, we find his inventiveness has not been exhausted. How many trips to the seashore did it take to collect this staggering quantity of shells and rocks? How many hours did the artist spend patiently sorting through the cast-off debris of a great city in search of colors and textures to weave into his composition? And, more importantly, *why* did he do it? His own answer is simple. "I had in mind to do something big, and I did."

Men now see, as for many centuries they did not, that there are no final rules for either creation or judgment.

—SHELDON CHENEY, *A World History of Art*

chapter 26.

Conclusion

Few of us are content for very long with activities which occupy our hands and leave our minds idle and unproductive. The difference between an art which *creates* and one which *stagnates* is motion. The creative mind is never still. It questions and doubts; it adds and subtracts. Its roots may be planted in the past, but its branches reach restlessly toward the future.

The human being is designed to grow whether he likes it or not. But not all growth is constructive, and not all motion is forward. Today's mosaicist makes many side excursions, some of which simply parallel a well-worn path. Others may lead backward or dwindle into nothingness. But we are moving, and that is significant.

Every generation of artists devises its own battle cry, and ours seems to be "Self-Expression!"—even at the cost of craftsmanship. Although a certain balance between technique and content would seem more ideal, this is a healthy trend, as long as it does not obscure our vision to the point where we accept as art everything that is unintelligible, bizarre, or shocking.

Many new art forms are exciting and have elements of greatness. Many are merely imitative of the great and may in time be recognized as sorry jokes or expressions of pompous contempt. Marvelous discoveries grow out of experimentation, and accidental effects can lead to the development of fresh and unexplored concepts. But mature art is not the result of happenstance. It is the outcome of a perfect meld of imagination, spontaneity, and disciplined control.

The educator's contribution to this control is painfully small, for what can really be taught about mosaics beyond mechanical processes and history? One cannot teach perception or sensitivity or patience. And who would presume to devise a formula for excellence?

We can trace the meandering course of the art of mosaics on the pages of history, and clearly separate the periods of great happenings from those of listless groping. It will take the objectivity of many generations to evaluate the products of our own, but it is evident that progress is being made. It is equally evident that our work has barely begun, and its conclusion remains far out of sight in the unpredictable future.

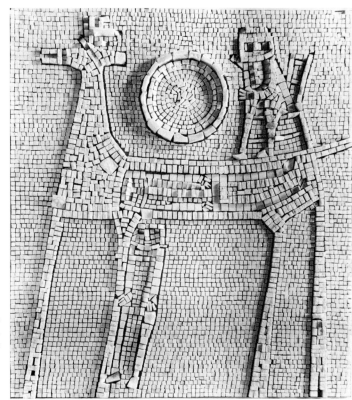

Fig. 441. Bas-relief of split-face white marble tesserae, set on ¾-inch plywood with mastic. By Aleksandra Kasuba.

Fig. 442. Drinking fountain at the University of California at Berkeley, by Ray Rice.

Fig. 443. Left side of ceramic mural for the Strasenburgh Laboratories, showing sources of medicine—flowers, seed pods, plants, mushrooms, etc. By Frans Wildenhain.

Photo Credits

Color Plates

Douglas, Marshall, Polynesian panel
Emerson, Lyman, "Kali"
Hunt, Thomas, "St. John the Baptist"
Justema, William, "Gifts from the Sea"
Planert, Philip J., "Early Thaw"
Ruder, William, "Sunrise"
Stribling, Mary Lou: clock, "Fish," "Moonscape," patio table, pendant, "The Pier," "The Potter"

Black-and-White Plates

Balestrero, Peter, 48, 165, 190
Bevington, Mariette, 164, 350
Bourdon, Edward, 298
Braun, Ernest, 177, 330, 331, 346, 442
Burton, Jim, 313, 327, 370
Campbell Jim, 340, 436
Casebier, Cecil, 341
Cohen, Jimmy, 15
Douglas, Marshall, 51, 181
Du Puy, Edward, 3
Emerson, Lyman, 64
Graff, Howard, 172

Haddox, Bill, 170, 191
Halprin, Lawrence, 324
Harris, Ian, 318, 336, 337, 339
Hartley, John, 294
Hicks, Jack, 30
Hubenig, A. (O.M.I.), 156, 157
Hunt, Thomas, 10, 47
Partridge, Rondal, 320
Planert, Philip J., 183, 323, 325, 332, 333
Rich, Neville, 6, 326
Riek, Karl, 435
Risling, Jay, 321, 416, 417
Ross, 68
Rutledge, Margie, 344
Sloan, James, 77, 315
Snyder, Lewis, 185
Stribling, Mary Lou, 1, 2, 4, 5, 16-23, 27-29, 31-35, 37, 39-46, 49, 50, 52-63, 66, 67, 69, 74-76, 79-129, 133-138, 140, 142-146, 148-154, 158, 160-162, 175, 176, 180, 182, 186-189, 195-223, 225-243, 245, 248-272, 275-293, 295-297, 299-301, 308-310, 312, 319, 328, 329, 334, 343, 345, 348, 349, 351-362, 364, 366-369, 371, 372, 374-400, 402-415, 418-420, 424-433, 437-440
Suen, Raymond, 65
Walden, Herbert, 441
White, Minor, 155, 174, 192-194, 443

Temperature Equivalents of Cones

Slow firing allows heat to soak through ceramic materials, maturing them (as well as cones) a little sooner than a rapid fire. With a heat rise of less than 300° F. per hour, cones may bend from 25° to 50° earlier than the temperatures indicated below. (This is the standard cone temperature chart of the Edward Orton Jr. Ceramic Foundation.)

Cone 022—1121° F.	Cone 05—1904° F.
Cone 021—1139° F.	Cone 04—1940° F.
Cone 020—1202° F.	Cone 03—2039° F.
Cone 019—1220° F.	Cone 02—2057° F.
Cone 018—1328° F.	Cone 01—2093° F.
Cone 017—1418° F.	Cone 1—2120° F.
Cone 016—1463° F.	Cone 2—2129° F.
Cone 015—1481° F.	Cone 3—2138° F.
Cone 014—1526° F.	Cone 4—2174° F.
Cone 013—1580° F.	Cone 5—2201° F.
Cone 012—1607° F.	Cone 6—2246° F.
Cone 011—1643° F.	Cone 7—2282° F.
Cone 010—1661° F.	Cone 8—2300° F.
Cone 09—1706° F.	Cone 9—2345° F.
Cone 08—1742° F.	Cone 10—2381° F.
Cone 07—1814° F.	Cone 11—2417° F.
Cone 06—1859° F.	Cone 12—2435° F.

FRITS AND COLORANTS FOR GLASS EXPERIMENTS

Standard low-temperature frits and glaze colorants can be purchased from ceramic supply houses. Frits numbers 5, 33, 83, and 3419 are among those melting early enough to be fused to window glass at 1425°–1500° F. A few test recipes for transparent colors are given below. It should be understood, however, that requirements for mosaic materials are not always the same as those for coloring decorative glassware. Crazing, for example, is not necessarily a fault for our purposes unless it progresses to the stage of "flaking" or "shivering."

Glaze batches which craze may either be laminated between two sheets of glass, or set glaze side down on a backing so that the surface is protected.

A small amount of tin oxide (2 to 8 per cent) added to the basic recipes will produce semi-translucent glazes that are interesting when combined with translucent materials or with those which are completely opaque.

Low-temperature glazes used on both glass and fully matured bisque will make beautifully related tesserae.

Colorants

Glaze stains are available in many colors. They are not as concentrated as the chemicals listed here, and may be used in larger proportions in the test recipes.

cobalt oxide and cobalt carbonate—blue
iron oxide—brown
chromium oxide—grayish-green
manganese carbonate—mauve and brownish-purple
copper carbonate—turquoise
lead chromate—yellow

Colorants and glaze batches using the same frit can be mixed for intermediate shades.

Experimental Glaze Recipes for Coloring Glass

1. 7–10 parts frit + 1 part lead chromate—medium yellow
2. 7–10 parts frit + 1 part cobalt—dark blue
3. 15 parts frit + 1 part cobalt—medium blue
4. 7–10 parts frit + 1 part copper carbonate—light turquoise
5. 5 parts frit + 1 part copper carbonate—medium turquoise
6. 10 parts frit + 1 part chromium oxide—dark yellow-green
7. 5 parts frit + 1 part chromium oxide—olive green

Combinations of Batches

8. Equal parts of numbers 1 and 4—chartreuse
9. Equal parts of numbers 6 and 2—dark olive
10. Equal parts of numbers 1 and 3—deep leaf-green
11. Equal parts of numbers 3 and 5—greenish-blue
12. Equal parts of numbers 1 and 5—medium chartreuse

Note: Colorants will react differently with lead and alkaline frits.

BIBLIOGRAPHY AND SUGGESTED REFERENCES

BATES, KENNETH F. *Basic Design.* Cleveland and New York: The World Publishing Company, 1960.

BOAS, FRANZ. *Primitive Art.* New York: Dover Publications, Inc., 1955.

CHENEY, SHELDON. *A World History of Art.* New York: The Viking Press, Inc., 1937.

———. *The Story of Modern Art* (rev. ed.). New York: The Viking Press, Inc., 1958.

CHRISTENSEN, ERWIN O. *The Index of American Design.* New York: The Macmillan Company, 1950.

DIAMOND, FREDA. *The Story of Glass.* New York: Harcourt, Brace and Co., Inc., 1953.

DIVINE, J. A. F., and BLACHFORD, GEORGE. *Stained Glass Craft.* Peoria, Ill.: Manual Arts Press, 1940.

FERGUSON, GEORGE. *Signs and Symbols in Christian Art.* Fair Lawn, N.J., and New York: Oxford University Press, 1954.

FORMAN, W. and B. *Exotic Art.* London: Spring Books, n.d.

HOFFMANN, EDITH. *Expressionism*. New York: Crown Publishers, Inc., n.d.

HORNUNG, CLARENCE P. *Handbook of Design and Devices* (2nd rev. ed.). New York: Dover Publications, 1946.

HUYGHE, RENE (ed.). *Larousse Encyclopedia of Byzantine and Medieval Art*. New York: Prometheus Press, 1963.

KENNY, JOHN B. *Ceramic Design*. Philadelphia: Chilton Books, 1963.

KINNEY, KAY. *Glass Craft*. Philadelphia: Chilton Books, 1962.

LANGUI, EMILE. *50 Years of Modern Art*. New York: Frederick A. Praeger, Inc., 1959.

LICHTEN, FRANCES. *The Folk Art of Rural Pennsylvania*. New York: Charles Scribner's Sons, 1963.

LIPMAN, JEAN. *American Folk Art in Wood, Metal and Stone*. New York: Pantheon Books, 1948.

LOCKREY, A. J. *Plastics in the School and Home Workshop* (3d ed.). New York: D. Van Nostrand Co., Inc., 1946.

LYNCH, JOHN. *Metal Sculpture: New Forms, New Techniques*. New York: The Studio Publications, Inc., 1957.

MEILACH, DONA and SEIDEN, DON. *Direct Metal Sculpture*. New York: Crown Publishers, Inc., 1965.

MILES, WALTER. *Designs for Craftsmen*. Garden City: Doubleday & Company, Inc., 1962.

NEWMAN, THELMA R. *Plastics as an Art Form*. Philadelphia: Chilton Books, 1964.

POST, ELLWOOD W. *Saints, Signs, and Symbols*. New York: Morehouse-Barlow Co., Inc., 1962.

ROBB, DAVID M. and GARRISON, J. J. *Art in the Western World* (4th ed.). New York and Evanston: Harper & Row, Publishers, 1963.

SCHRIJVER, ELKA. *Glass and Crystal* (Volumes I and II). New York: Universe Books, Inc., 1964–1965.

SOWERS, ROBERT. *The Lost Art*. New York: George Wittenborn, Inc., 1954.

WETZLER, ROBERT and HUNTINGTON, HELEN. *Seasons and Symbols*. Minneapolis: Augsburg Publishing House, 1962.

GLOSSARY

Abstract Design: A design using nonrepresentational or unnaturalistic motifs.

Acetate Overlay: A thin sheet of clear or frosted acetate used for preparing illustrations for reproduction. Also useful as a separator between plastic castings and a working surface.

Acrylics: Glasslike thermoplastic resins which may be cast into molds, used in solution for coating of materials, or as an adhesive. For the mosaicist, most useful in block or sheet form.

Anneal: To temper, or harden by reducing heat gradually.

Applied Decoration: Surface ornamentation of a form.

Armature: A framework or support for a structure or sculpture.

Bisque: Unglazed clay which has been fired to a state of permanent hardness.

Body Stains: Colorants used to tint clay bodies.

Calcine: To reduce to powder by heat.

Came: Channeled strips of lead used to bind together sections of stained glass. (Sometimes spelled *calm*.)

Casein-based Adhesives: Water-resistant glues formulated with milk derivatives and alkaline solutions. (Often called white glues.)

Cast: To form objects by pouring a solidifying material into a mold.

Catalyst: An agent (or condition) which will accelerate the normal progress of a chemical reaction. An additive for synthetic resins to initiate polymerization.

Ceramic: Relating to the art of making objects from clay or other silicate compounds.

Coefficient of Thermal Contraction and Expansion: The ratio by which a substance changes its dimensions upon increase or decrease of temperature. A determining factor in the suitability for fusion of two or more substances.

Cold Joint: A term for a soldered metal seam on which the solder is melted but not actually fused.

Collage: A design made of assorted flat materials (such as paper, fabric, dried leaves, etc.) pasted onto a backing.

Color Intensity: The degree of purity or brilliance of a color.

Color Value: The relationship of a color to lightness or darkness.

Craze: Random cracks in fired glaze or glass.

Cullet: Crushed glass.

Cure: The process of hardening plastic materials into a durable substance.

Dalles: Thick, textured slabs of glass.

Design: A composition, scheme, or arrangement. A plan for organizing separate materials into a unified pattern.

Earthenware: Objects made of low-fire clay.

Engobe: Tinted slip used for obtaining an all-over coat of color on a clay form.

Epoxy: A thermosetting resin of great strength and flexibility used for adhesives and embedding.

Expressionism: A name given to a type of art expression where reality is modified by the artists' emotional reaction.

Faceted Glass: Thick slabs of glass which are boldly textured by breaking small fragments from the face with a hammer.

Fibrous Glass Mat: A Fiberglas inclusion to strengthen panels or windows made of liquid resin.

Flashed Glass: Clear glass with a surface coating of tinted glass which gives it the appearance of being colored throughout.

Fresco: A wall decoration made by painting on wet plaster.

Fuse: To unite or melt together by heat.

Geometric: Applied to a type of design which reduces shapes to basic geometric elements —lines, triangles, circles, rectangles, etc.

Glass Blanks: Undecorated shapes cut from glass.

Glass Glaze: Low-temperature glazes used to flash glass.

Glaze: A thin skin of glass used to decorate or waterproof clay or glass.

Glaze Stains: Prepared colorants for glazes.

Grog: Ground bisque which is added to moist clay for texture or to decrease shrinkage.

Grout: A mixture of cement and fine sand or marble dust used to fill the crevices between mosaic tesserae.

Hue: Color.

Inhibitor: An agent (or condition) which will slow down or stop a normal chemical reaction.

Kiln Wash: China clay and flint which is mixed

with water to·the consistency of white-wash and applied to the bottom of the kiln and tops of shelves so that glaze drippings can easily be removed.

Laminate: To bond layers of materials into a solid unit.

Lapidary: The art of polishing and cutting precious (and semiprecious) stones.

Leather Hard: A stage of drying clay at which it has lost plasticity, but is not yet hard and brittle.

Liver of Sulphur: Used in solution for antiquing copper, silver, and lead materials.

Magnesite: Oxychloride cement used as a setting bed for interior and exterior mosaics.

Magnesium Chloride: Crystals, dissolved in water to make a solution which is used as a wetting agent for magnesite.

Malleable: Pliable; plastic; easily shaped.

Marmi: Small hand-cut cubes of marble.

Mastic: A rubber-based adhesive used for setting mosaic tesserae.

Maturing Temperature: The temperature at which clay materials reach the ideal state of viscosity.

Medium (pl. media): The material used for an art expression.

Mineral Pigments: Concentrated dyes used to color such materials as clay and cement.

Mold: A form for duplicating a shape.

Mosaic: An art form distinguished by its fragmentation; a decorative arrangement of separate fragments into an organized expression.

Mosaic Canes: Decorative materials produced by fusing together a bundle of glass threads and drawing them out into long rods. Slices of miniature mosaic canes are sometimes used for copper enameling and are called pattern chips.

Mylar: A foundation sheet which can be peeled away from hardened plastic forms.

Naturalistic: Imitative of nature; in art, an expression which is concerned primarily with the physical appearance of a subject.

Nichrome: Trademark for an alloy which is resistant to deterioration by heat. Used for elements in kilns and household appliances.

Opaque: The quality of a material which impedes the transmission of light.

Overglazes: Materials which are applied on top of fired glazes and set by firing again to a lower temperature. The category includes china paints, lusters, and fused metallic platings.

Oxidation: Surface coloring or deterioration caused by exposure to oxygen in the air or to chemical substances which produce the same effect.

Patina: A colored film produced by natural aging or artificial treatment.

Pattern: A guide for construction; a surface decoration; an arrangement of decorative motifs.

Plasteline: A permanently plastic material made of clay, oils, and waxes. Used for sculptured sketches or models from which molds are made. (Also called "plasticene.")

Plastic: Flexible; capable of being shaped, cast, or manipulated. The popular name for synthetic resins.

Polyester Resins: A group of thermosetting resins which may be cast into molds or used for laminated sheets.

Polymerization: The chemical reaction by which liquid plastics are changed to a hard, solid substance.

Porcelain: A fine-grained, vitreous, high-fire clay body having the quality of translucence when fired to maturity.

Pressed Glass Tiles: Transparent and opaque glass squares which have been formed in waffle-like molds. They are usually pasted face down on 12-inch-square sheets of paper which contain 225 tiles.

Pyrometer: An instrument which records the interior temperature of kilns.

Pyrometric Cones: Elongated pyramids of minerals formulated to melt at specific temperatures; used for determining the interior temperature of kilns.

Realistic: Applied to art expressions which attempt to portray the physical aspects of a subject.

Refraction: Diffusion or bending of light rays as they are transmitted through a transparent material.

Reverse Method: Mosaics made by gluing tesserae upside down onto a paper backing, then embedding them face up in mortar or mastic. Used to produce a level surface, or for certain textural effects.

Silicate: A material derived from silicon dioxide.

Slip: Liquid clay.

Smalti: Small opaque glass squares which have been hand-chipped from larger glass "pancakes." (Also called "Byzantine tiles" or "enamels.")

Sodium Silicate: A deflocculant which can be added to slip to make it more fluid. Usually used in 10 per cent solution in proportions of about 1 tablespoon per gallon of slip. (Also called "water glass.")

Stoneware: A dense, high-fire clay body characterized by a rugged quality and ability to withstand fluctuating temperatures. Especially suitable for cooking utensils and boldly modeled forms.

Stylization: An interpretation of naturalistic forms which simplifies, exaggerates, or distorts certain aspects without complete separation from reality.

Symbolism: A sign or badge which represents something—usually invisible—other than itself.

Synthetics: Man-made products derived from chemical combinations rather than natural processes.

Tessera (pl. tesserae): Popularly used to designate all the small decorative fragments from which mosaics are constructed. (Derived from a Latin word meaning "cube" or "little square.")

Thermoplastic: Applied to substances which may be repeatedly softened by heat, becoming rigid again after cooling.

Thermosetting: Applied to substances which become permanently hard after exposure to heat.

Traditional Design: Motifs and styles which

are handed down from one generation to another.

Translucent: Pertaining to a material which permits the diffused transmission of light.

Transparent: Permitting an unobscured transmission of light.

Tumbler: A machine used for polishing pebbles, gemstones, and glass by revolving them in grit and water.

Undercut: A shape which angles or curves inward to form a ledge or protrusion which will lock a cast form inside a mold.

Underglazes: Colors which are applied to raw or bisqued clay and finished with clear glaze.

Vent: An opening to permit escape of gases or fumes. A kiln is vented by propping the lid or door open about an inch for the first part of the firing cycle.

Vitrify: To become hard, impervious, waterproof, and glasslike.

Wedging: Pounding and kneading moist clay to remove air bubbles and distribute colorants or grog evenly.

SUPPLY SOURCES

Ceramic Supplies

American Art Clay Company
Indianapolis 24, Ind.

B. F. Drakenfeld & Co., Inc.
45 Park Place
New York, N.Y.

Ceramichrome, Inc.
15215 S. Broadway
Gardena, Calif.

Duncan's Ceramic Products, Inc.
5673 E. Shields Ave.
Fresno, Calif.

Ettl Studios, Inc.
Studio 31, Ettl Art Center
Glenville, Conn.

Standard Ceramic Supply Co.
Box 4435
Pittsburgh, Pa.

General Craft Supplies and Accessories

Craftools, Inc.
Wood-Ridge, N.J.

Creative Merchandisers
285 Jacoby St.
San Rafael, Calif.

J. L. Hammett Co.
290 Main St.
Cambridge, Mass.

Sax Brothers, Inc.
1101 N. 3rd St.
Milwaukee, Wis.

Thompson C. Thompson Co.
Dept. CH, 1539 Deerfield Rd.
Highland Park, Ill.

Glass Colors (Fired) and General Supplies for Glass Craft

Kay Kinney Contoured Glass
725 Broadway
Laguna Beach, Calif.

Glass Colors (Unfired)

Stained Glass Products
Box 756
Cleveland, Ohio

Kilns

Denver Fire Clay Co.
3033 Blake St.
Denver, Colo.

J. J. Cress Company, Inc.
323 W. Maple Ave.
Monrovia, Calif.

L & L Mfg. Co.
Chester 10, Pa.

Paragon Industries, Inc.
P.O. Box 10133
Dallas, Tex.

Skutt and Son
Box 202 C
Olympia, Wash.

Metallic Overglazes

Ceramic Research Corp.
Box 8562
Los Angeles 8, Calif.

Hanovia Chemical and Mfg. Co.
East Newark, N.J.

Mosaic Materials

Creative Merchandisers, Inc.
285 Jacoby St.
San Rafael, Calif.

Leo Popper and Sons
Dept. W, 143–7 Franklin St.
New York, N.Y.

The Mosaic Arts Co.
Pittsburgh 13, Pa.

Mosaic Workshop
8426 Melrose Ave.
Los Angeles 69, Calif.

Plastics

The Castolite Company
Woodstock, Ill.

Natcol Laboratories
Redlands, Calif.

Taylor and Art Plastics, Inc.
Oakland, Calif.

Stained Glass

Allcraft Tool and Supply Co., Inc.
15 West 45th St.
New York, N.Y.

Glass-Art
Box 2010
Santa Fe, N.M.

Kokomo Art Glass Supply
110 Arundel Ave.
Kokomo, Indiana

Leo Popper and Sons
Dept. W, 143–7 Franklin St.
New York, N.Y.

The Mosaic Shop
3522 Blvd. of the Allies
Pittsburgh 13, Pa.

Index